Degas

Degas

by IAN DUNLOP

GALLEY PRESS
A Division of W. H. Smith Publishers Inc.
112 Madison Avenue
New York City 10016

To Rory

Published by Galley Press
A Division of W. H. Smith Publishers Inc.
112 Madison Avenue
New York, New York 10016

Manufactured in Hong Kong
Printed and bound by Mandarin Offset Ltd

This book was designed and produced by
John Calmann and Cooper Ltd, London

1 2 3 4 5 6 7 8 9 10
Library of Congress Catalog Card Number 82–81447
ISBN 0–8317–21758

Contents

List of illustrations

Preface

DEGAS BELIEVED THERE WAS little or no purpose in writing about paintings. 'Beauty is a mystery,' he used to maintain; writers attempting to explain works of art and bring them to the attention of a wider public were attempting the impossible. 'Among people who understand,' Degas once said to George Moore, 'words are not necessary. You say humph, he, ha, and everything has been said.'

Despite his cautionary remarks, an extensive literature has formed round his work and his personality. During his lifetime he was the subject of essays and criticisms by such writers as Edmond Duranty, Emile Zola, Edmond de Goncourt, Joris-Karl Huysmans, and George Moore; and following his death several friends and admirers recorded their memoirs of him, the best being those by two painters, Jacques-Emile Blanche and Walter Sickert, and two writers, the historian Daniel Halévy and the poet Paul Valéry. Since the Second World War art historians have provided several valuable studies of his style and catalogues of his work, including the four-volume *catalogue raisonné* of his paintings and pastels by P. A. Lemoisne in 1946, a catalogue of his sculpture by John Rewald, of his prints and monotypes by Jean Adhémar and Françoise Cachin, and a recent catalogue by Professor Theodore Reff of the thirty-eight Degas notebooks in the Bibliothèque Nationale and other collections. The subtlety, sensitivity and underlying intelligence of Degas's art seems to exert a particular fascination for scholars and over the last twenty-five years a number of specialist studies have appeared, including books on his ballet pictures by Lillian Browse, on his racing pictures by Ronald Pickvance, on his portraits by Jean Sutherland Boggs, on his technique by Denis Rouart, on his pastels by Douglas Cooper and Alfred Werner respectively, on his sculpture by Charles Millard, and on his monotypes by Eugenia Janis; a collection of essays by Reff on his relationship to the writers of his time and other specific topics has also appeared in one volume, *Degas: The Artist's Mind*.

The more Degas's art is studied in detail, however, the more complex it appears to be and the more difficult to analyse. There is a mysterious and fugitive beauty to many of his pictures which is apt to disappear under the scholarly microscope. Recent studies have tended to treat only fragments of him and the whole man, that complex multi-faceted character admired by Paul Valéry, has been lost from view. Indeed, the area which has been more or less neglected in recent years is the artist's life. There is no full-scale biography of Degas in English, and in French the fullest accounts remain that given by Lemoisne in the first volume of his *catalogue raisonné* (which, because it was published in a limited edition, is not readily available) and Pierre Cabanne's study published in 1957. Since then new information has come to light: the notebooks, which have a great deal to say about Degas's training and early enthusiasms, some additional unpublished letters, which were not included in the original Marcel Guérin edition of the letters first published in 1931, and useful new facts about his family in Naples and New Orleans published by Riccardo Raimondi, Boggs, Rewald, and J. B. Byrnes. The researches of Ronald Pickvance into his early ballet pictures and Aaron Scharf into his use of photography have yielded valuable insights into Degas's working methods. Much of this information, however, lies scattered in old exhibition catalogues and in back numbers of the *Gazette des Beaux-Arts*, the *Burlington Magazine* and the *Art Bulletin*.

The aim of this book is to bring together in one volume the results of recent researches, to tell the story of Degas's life, to take a fresh look at his personality, and to put his art into the context of his time and his friendships. An intriguing and complex character emerges who is almost as difficult to pin down and analyse as his art. He was a mass of contradictions: brusque and intolerant one day and kind the next, a recluse who enjoyed dining out with a few close friends and liked to travel, a man who often expressed a dislike for writers – 'the terrible literary gentry' was his term for them – but who was well-read, a lively letter-writer and an accomplished sonneteer. Although he earned a reputation as a misogynist and liked to maintain that he had a cold heart, he placed great value on friendship and enjoyed many close relationships with women as well as with men. As an artist he retained a lasting respect for tradition and for the Old Masters but he was among the first of the moderns, possessing the most original mind among all the painters of the Impressionist circle. His art retains its freshness and can still provide unexpected facets however often it is reproduced and exhibited.

My debt to the researches of the many scholars and art historians who have written about Degas can never fully be expressed, but where possible I have tried to acknowledge their work either in the text or in notes. Museums in Europe and America have been most helpful in providing the illustrations for this book, but I would like to pay tribute to the tireless efforts of Madeleine van der Hecht as picture researcher, the assistance of my colleagues at Sotheby Parke Bernet, and the help of the Acquavella Gallery, Reid and Lefevre, and Thomas Gibson Fine Art in securing material for some of the colour plates. I would also like to thank Sarah Riddell and Elisabeth Ingles for their work on the text, Elwyn Blacker for designing the book, the staff of John Calmann and Cooper, and John Calmann himself, without whose enthusiasm and commitment to this project the book might never have been realized.

1. Degas about 1910. Photograph attributed to Sacha Guitry

Chapter 1

Early years 1834 to 1865

IN HIS INVERNESS CAPE and bowler hat, thrusting out his stick to feel his way, Edgar Degas, the 'terrible Monsieur Degas', could be seen in the streets of Paris at the beginning of this century, walking quickly, and always alone. About 1914, when Degas was eighty, Sacha Guitry in a still from his film *Ceux de Chez Nous* caught him on one of his walks (plate 1). It is a shot reminiscent of one of Degas's own paintings: the passers-by have been cropped at the edges, and it shows an old man with a heavy beard, still erect despite his age, weight shifted to his heels, toes pointed out, walking like Charlie Chaplin.

Guitry, who had filmed Renoir without encountering any difficulty, had expected to be able to film Degas in his apartment, but he failed to take into account Degas's horror of publicity, his fierce sense of privacy, his desire, as he put it, 'to be famous and unknown', and when Degas refused his request, Guitry was forced to lie in wait for the aged artist on the street outside. 'A few minutes later', the dealer Ambroise Vollard recalled, 'a crowd gathered, and there was much commotion; Guitry was "shooting" Degas.'[1] Despite the fact that he saw only a few close friends, his refusal to seek or accept public recognition for his work, his determination to avoid any contact with 'the terrible literary gentry', writers and critics, Degas became a celebrated figure in his own lifetime. His art was admired and prized by a few discerning critics and collectors from the moment it was first exhibited, and his incisive *mots* were famous. The uniqueness of his art and his character, his uncompromising stance, attracted the attention of two gifted young writers, the historian Daniel Halévy and the poet Paul Valéry; long before his death they had begun to make notes, either written or mental, of his conversation and opinions, recognizing that they were privileged to be listening to one of the giants of a heroic period in French painting, one whom many believed to be the greatest painter in France in the second half of the nineteenth century. If Degas had been aware of their activities, he would not have approved. When George Moore attempted to meet Degas again in 1891, having published a eulogy of him, the artist refused and, according to Daniel Halévy, went off into a wild rage against anything resembling a journalist. 'Those people trap you in your bed, strip off your shirt, corner you in the street, and when you complain, they say: "you belong to the public".'[2] To protect himself against intruders, even admiring ones, Degas developed a brusque exterior, which became even more pronounced with age.

Ernest Rouart, who knew Degas as well as anyone, since his father had been a schoolfriend of Degas, pointed out: 'If he seemed surly or inhospitable to visitors who chanced to disturb him while at work, the reason was that his work was sacred to him and he meant to safeguard it at any price.' But, says Rouart, 'this seemingly bearish man was capable on occasions of mellowing to the point of showing affection . . . For friendship was a cult with him, and he had so lofty a conception of it that he could not allow anything to pass which, to his way of thinking, might do harm to that noble sentiment.'[3] Indeed, all who came to know Degas well, the Halévys, the two Rouart brothers, Paul Valéry and painters like Jacques-Emile Blanche and Walter Sickert glimpsed another side to Degas, a man who could be kind, a man of great sensitivity. One has only to read the letter written in 1890 to his old colleague from his student days in Italy, Evariste de Valernes, who reproached him for his harshness and lack of self-confidence, to see the gentle side to Degas's character. 'I was, or I seemed to be, hard with everyone,' Degas wrote, 'through a sort of passion for brutality, which came from my uncertainty and my bad humour. I felt myself so badly made, so badly equipped, so weak, whereas it seemed to me that my calculations on art were so right. I brooded against the whole world and against myself. I ask your pardon sincerely if, beneath the pretext of this damned art, I have wounded your very intelligent and fine mind, perhaps even your heart.'[4]

This uncertainty, not immediately apparent to those who came to know him as an old man, had always been part of his character. 'How doubt and uncertainty tire me', he wrote in his journal when he was in his twenties.[5] The early self-portraits, for example, the one with paint-brushes in the Louvre (plate 14) and the etching done in Rome (plate 5),

2. *Degas and de Valernes*, c.1864-5. Oil on canvas, 45⅜ × 35½ in (117 × 90 cm). Paris, Louvre

son of a banker meant something, for as Stendhal observed: 'The bankers are the nobility of the bourgeois class.' (The Degas in fact spelt their name in the aristocratic form 'De Gas'; but Edgar seems to have decided that this was pretentious and after 1860 he signed his work in one word, 'Degas'.) By 1834 the bourgeoisie was sufficiently well established and secure in its fortunes to be turning its attention to art and other cultural activities, art being viewed by some as a substitute for the spiritual values eroded or destroyed by the materialism of the age.[8] The sons of the prominent members of the bourgeoisie were beginning to enter the arts and ignoring the opportunities of commerce and the professions. Among Degas's near contemporaries were Edouard Manet (born 1832), the son of a rich lawyer, and Paul Cézanne (born 1839), the son of a manufacturer and banker in Aix-en-Provence; and just thirteen years earlier (1821) Gustave Flaubert was born, the son of a surgeon and doctor.

Degas's father Auguste, born in Naples in 1807, was the son of a successful adventurer and banker, and he

3. Study for portrait of René-Hilaire (Ilarios) de Gas, c.1856. Pencil (Notebook 4). Paris, Bibliothèque Nationale

reveal a serious, intelligent, and deeply committed person, without reserves of self-confidence. They also show a man who early on was destined to walk a lonely path, who felt it necessary to keep a certain distance from the world, who valued the friendship of his fellow men, but who was reluctant to fall, and may even have been incapable of falling, in love with a woman. The journals of his early years confirm this impression: one entry reads, 'I must steep myself in solitude.'[6] The loneliness of Degas's last years, an isolation intensified by his blindness, was present from the very beginning. As Valéry observed: 'Degas always felt himself to be solitary, and so he was, in all senses of solitude; solitary in character, solitary in his natural and exceptional principles and judgements; solitary above all in his art, that is, what he expected of himself.'[7]

Degas was born in Paris on 19 July 1834; his father was a banker, who was in turn the son of a banker, and his mother was the daughter of a successful businessman from New Orleans. He was born into the 'purple' of the bourgeoisie, at a time when this class had amassed great fortunes and was at the beginning of its domination of the cultural, political and social life of many Western countries. To be the

4. *René-Hilaire (Ilario) de Gas*, 1857. Oil on canvas, $21\frac{5}{8} \times 16\frac{1}{8}$ in (55×41 cm). Paris, Louvre (Jeu de Paume)

too was more inclined towards the arts and music than to business. When he died in 1874, the affairs of the small family bank which he ran in Paris were found to be in a disastrous state and Degas was nearly ruined in his efforts to meet the bank's debts and save the family name. Auguste, according to Daniel Halévy, was a 'gentle man, witty and above all devoted to music and painting'.[9] He knew many of the leading collectors of the day, including Henri Valpinçon, a patron of Ingres, Prince Nicolas Soutzo, a Greek collector and an amateur engraver, and Eudoxe Marcille, a grain merchant and amateur painter, who was an enthusiastic collector of eighteenth-century French painting at a time when it was not in fashion and owned thirty Chardins, forty Bouchers and twenty-four Fragonards, all crammed higgledy-piggledy into his house in Paris. The young Degas used to accompany his father on visits to these collectors and it was in their houses that his interest in art was first aroused.[10]

Auguste, however, owed his position in life to his father, René-Hilaire De Gas (plate 4). It was this man who founded the family fortune and ruled over the family up to his death in 1858. Born in 1770 in Orléans, he was a trader on the grain exchange in Paris when the Revolution broke out in 1789. Four years later, word having reached him that his life was in danger, he fled to Naples. According to Paul Valéry, he had been put on a list of suspects because he was a fiancé of one of the 'young virgins of Verdun', several of whom had paid with their lives for the welcome that they gave in 1792 to the invading Prussian army sent to restore the French monarchy.[11]

In Naples he made rapid progress both financially and socially: within two years of his arrival he was given the task of making an inventory of the Neapolitan debts, and he subsequently married in 1804 a young girl from Genoa of a noble family, the Freppas. Grandfather Degas, known in Naples as 'Ilario', flourished, building up a large fortune, the size of which can be gauged by the imposing palazzo of over a hundred rooms which he bought in the city, his country villa and the large dowries of 20,000 ducats he gave to each daughter.[12] Degas's portrait of Ilario (plate 4) shows a man of strong character and determination. But he had a softer side. When Degas was born, his wife went to Paris to see her grandson and Ilario plagued her with questions: 'You will give me the pleasure of embracing Celestine [Degas's mother] and the little *marmot* Edgar. Write to me about them I beg you. How is the little fellow? Has he teeth? Does he walk a little? After all he is one year old. Is he healthy? Write to me in detail; it will give me pleasure.'[13]

Ilario kept a close watch on his family. Three sons remained bachelors while he was alive, living in the palazzo with him. His daughters were married to respectable but minor Italian nobles. In the case of Laura, the most attractive and the aunt to whom Degas felt the closest, a husband was found not without difficulty. One rejected suitor complained that the family attitude was 'more devoted to the business aspects than to those of the heart'. In the end Laura was married to Baron Bellelli, but the marriage was not a happy one. The Bellelli household, however, became the subject of Degas's first great painting (plate 37).

From Ilario Degas probably inherited his own sense of determination, pride and perhaps his

5. *Self-portrait*, 1857, etching. $9\frac{1}{4} \times 5\frac{1}{2}$ in (23 × 14 cm). New York, Metropolitan Museum of Art (Bequest of Mrs H. O. Havemeyer, 1929)

longevity (Ilario lived to be eighty-six, Degas to be eighty-three). From his Italian grandmother he inherited his excitable Italian nature and the Neapolitan tendency to gesticulate when talking. Valéry concluded that this habit had its origins in the Neapolitan tradition of mime where 'There is never a word without a gesture, a story without acting, no individual without his store of parts to play, always available and always convincing.'[14]

Degas's grandparents on his mother's side were from New Orleans and the French West Indies. Germain Musson was of French descent and was born in Port-au-Prince, Santo Domingo. He moved to New Orleans in 1810 and married Doña Maria Celeste Rillieux, daughter of one of the prominent families in Louisiana (which had been under Spanish control up to 1803). His wife died in 1819, leaving him with five small children whom he took to France to be educated and married off. One daughter married the Duc de Rochefort and the other, Celestine, married Auguste Degas in 1832 at the young age of sixteen. It seems that the Degas family did not approve of the match. Perhaps her dowry was considered inadequate, or perhaps they thought she was too young to make a wife. Ilario probably distrusted Germain Musson as a rival adventurer. The latter was a man of initiative and independence, because soon after the marriage of his daughter Celestine he left France, despite his family's entreaties, and went to Mexico to look after a silver-mine in which he had an interest. There in 1853 he was killed when his coach overturned.

Celestine Musson, Degas's mother, is a shadowy figure. Her life was spent in domestic duties and was dominated by a series of births – seven in fourteen years. Five children survived: Edgar, born 1834, Achille, born 1838, Thérèse, born 1840, Marguerite, born 1842, and René, born 1845. Celestine felt her life lacked the amusements that a young married woman in Paris might reasonably expect, 'My youth is passing without a single ball,' she complained to her in-laws. 'Auguste is becoming more and more disgusted with the world and refuses to listen to my prayers.'[15] The relationship between husband and wife does not appear to have been a close one. Degas told Valéry of a typical scene: his mother, annoyed by something his father said, would 'drum her fingers irritably on the edge of the table, with an "Auguste! Auguste!" His father would sit tight, and then, the meal over, sidle through the door, fling a cloak around his shoulders and glide noiselessly downstairs.'[16]

Daniel Halévy, whose parents had known Degas from their schooldays, maintained that Degas's childhood was not happy. He was probably right. Degas's portraits and drawings of his younger brothers and sisters (plates 6 and 7) and his own self-portrait executed when he was twenty (plate 14) seem to confirm this impression. Those faces look so sad, so serious. The portrait of René (plate 7), in particular, painted when he was ten, dressed in his schoolboy smock and his books and ink-bottle at his side, reveals a model well-behaved Victorian child, but one without a sense of *joie de vivre*.

Degas's mother died in 1847 when he was thirteen and we do not know for sure what effect this event had on him. Perhaps it made him withdrawn and unsure of himself, perhaps his later mistrust of women stemmed from being deprived of his mother at a sensitive age. At the time it brought him closer to his sisters (he became particularly attached to Marguerite and was upset by her eventual departure to Argentina) and also to his father, who came to occupy a central role in his life as counsellor and guide.

(ii)

When his mother died, Degas was already a pupil at the Lycée Louis-le-Grand which he had entered in 1845. The school was one of the oldest and largest in Paris. It was formerly the Jesuit College of Clermont and was founded in 1560 on a site on the rue Saint-Jacques opposite the Sorbonne. Molière, Voltaire, Robespierre had studied there. Many of his greatest friends were pupils at this lycée, including Paul

6. *Marguerite de Gas*, c.1854. Pencil, $11\frac{5}{8} \times 9\frac{1}{2}$ in (29.7 × 24 cm). Stuttgart, Staatsgalerie

Valpincon, son of Henri Valpinçon, the Rouart brothers and the Halévys. If nothing else, the lycée established the social milieu in which he subsequently moved. In terms of education the lycée provided a strictly classical grounding in Latin, Greek, philosophy and literature with very little instruction in science or mathematics. Valéry was astonished by 'the complete absence of the simplest notions of the most elementary practicality in a man so intelligent – what is more – *classically educated*. In some ways he had no more sense than an old woman.'[17]

We do not know if he enjoyed his schooldays; if he was like the majority of pupils he probably did not. The lycées of that period were run like a cross between a monastery and a barrack. The atmosphere was unhealthy and unhygienic, and highly competitive. Again as Valéry remarked: 'Neither cleanliness, nor the smallest notion of hygiene, nor deportment, nor even the pronunciation of our language, had any place in the programme of that incredible system, conceived as it was to exclude carefully everything to do with the body, the senses, the sky, the arts, or

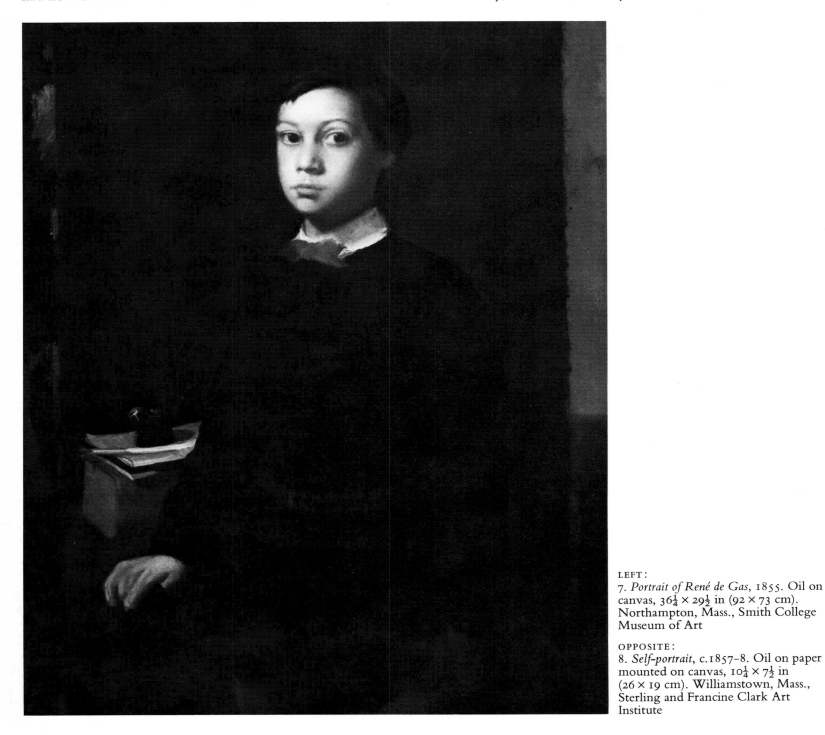

LEFT:
7. *Portrait of René de Gas*, 1855. Oil on canvas, $36\frac{1}{4} \times 29\frac{1}{2}$ in (92 × 73 cm). Northampton, Mass., Smith College Museum of Art

OPPOSITE:
8. *Self-portrait*, c.1857–8. Oil on paper mounted on canvas, $10\frac{1}{4} \times 7\frac{1}{2}$ in (26 × 19 cm). Williamstown, Mass., Sterling and Francine Clark Art Institute

social life.'[18] The system did, however, foster a respect for intelligence and Degas, who was cerebral by nature, no doubt learnt to place the mind over the body while a pupil at the lycée. As a student he did reasonably well. His grades are recorded in P. A. Lemoisne's great work,[19] and when he took his baccalauréat in 1852 he received for Latin Verse eighth place, History seventh place, Drawing first place and 'Excellence' first place.

Having taken his baccalauréat, Degas was anxious to study art and to continue his drawing, for which, to judge by the early portraits of his sisters and brothers, he already showed a great aptitude. In 1853 his name appears as one of the students allowed to copy from the engravings held at the Cabinet d'Estampes of the Bibliothèque Nationale. Among the products of this period was a copy on tracing paper of Marcantonio Raimondi's engraving of Raphael's lost *Judgement of Paris* (plate 9). By coincidence the same figures were copied by Manet and used as a model for his *Déjeuner sur l'Herbe*. Auguste, however, wanted his son to have an alternative career and insisted that he study law. Degas dutifully complied, but after a year he abandoned his legal studies. There was a family row and, according to the painter's niece, Mme Fèvre[20] (who is not always to be relied on), he was forced to leave home for a draughty attic. After a short while Auguste relented. He was impressed by his son's devotion to his calling and, on the advice of Henri Valpinçon, placed his son in the care of an artist who today is known only as one of the most obscure followers of Ingres, Louis Lamothe.

Lamothe was a man of exceptional timidity whose life and career were spent under the shadow of his famous teacher. He only took in a few pupils at a time, unlike some other teachers of the day who crammed their teaching studios with pupils. Degas was, therefore, spared the inconveniences and distractions suffered by so many art students of the period, who only had a brief glimpse of the master and whose concentration was continually interrupted by noisy arguments, horrific practical jokes and initiation ceremonies. Thus, early in his development, Degas acquired a taste for working in solitude and became largely self-taught. Unlike Manet, who spent five years in the studio of Thomas Couture, Degas was in Lamothe's studio for just over a year.

Degas was also spared the rigours of the academic system with its prizes and examinations. He spent only a few months at the Ecole des Beaux-Arts, the principal academic art school in Paris, to which Lamothe had introduced him in 1855. He retained a lasting dislike for the Ecole, probably because he disapproved of the competitive atmosphere it fostered, the jealousies which developed there and its stifling effect on imagination. However, Degas

9. Various studies of figures after Italian Renaissance engravings by Marcantonio Raimondi, c.1853–56. Pen and wash on *papier calque* (tracing-paper), $12\frac{1}{4}$ × 6 in (31.7 × 15.2 cm). Cambridge, Mass., Courtesy of the Fogg Art Museum, Harvard University (anonymous gift in memory of W. G. Russell Allen)

Italian painting between 1450 and 1550, and Reff notes that among the artists he copied more than five times were Benozzo Gozzoli, Signorelli, Mantegna, Perugino, Leonardo, Raphael and Michelangelo. These would have been the masters recommended by Ingres, but contrary to the accepted practice he seldom copied the complete work. His eye was apt to be caught by a movement of a figure or group away from the centre of the composition. He developed a taste for the eloquent fragment, the unobserved detail, a taste which became a characteristic of his mature style. An example of this tendency can be seen in his copy of Navasi Lal's *Portrait of Shuja-ud-Daulau with his sons* (plates 10 and 11).

Jean Sutherland Boggs has observed[23] that his early copies of portraits by Franciabigio and Bronzino show

10. NAVASI LAL, *Portrait of Shuja-ud-Daulau with his nine sons and a courtier.* Gouache, $18 \times 15\frac{1}{2}$ in (46.4 × 39.5 cm). Paris, Louvre

11. Partial copy of Navasi Lal's *Portrait of Shuja-ud-Daulau with his sons* (notebook 18). Paris, BN

OVERLEAF, LEFT:
12. *Achille de Gas in the uniform of a cadet*, c.1855. Oil on canvas, $25\frac{3}{8} \times 20\frac{1}{8}$ in (64 × 51 cm). Washington, DC, National Gallery of Art (Chester Dale Collection)

OVERLEAF, RIGHT:
13. *Portrait of Giulia Bellelli*, 1859–60. Oil sketch on paper, 14×10 in (36 × 25 cm). Washington, Dumbarton Oaks Collection

was quite content to follow the teaching methods laid down by Ingres and his followers, where the emphasis lay heavily on drawing and copying, first copies of engravings of classical sculpture, then plaster casts and finally the live model. Unlike Manet and the Impressionists, he did not find the curriculum tedious and dispiriting. He drew and painted innumerable copies, filling notebook after notebook with his jottings and sketches.

Just how thorough were his preparations can be seen by examining the notebooks which have recently been published by Theodore Reff.[21] Degas's copies after the Old Masters and classical sculpture cover a wide range. As Reff has pointed out[22], in a notebook in use in 1859–64 there are drawings after John Flaxman, Delacroix, Constantin Guys, Signorelli, Titian, Rogier van der Weyden, an Assyrian relief and a Mogul miniature. If his copies are seen as a whole, it becomes apparent that Degas's main interest lay in

a taste for the disturbed and the effeminate, and there is a suggestion of both these tendencies in his self-portrait of 1855 (plate 14). The young man portrayed in this picture appears slightly defensive, uncertain of himself, withdrawn and a little aloof. The note-books in use at this time contain several revealing passages: 'It seems today if one wants to work at art seriously and make a small niche for oneself which is original, or, if one wants at least to retain one's innocence, one must steep oneself in solitude. There are far too many distractions [cancans]. One might say that pictures are produced like stock market prices by the excitement of people greedy for gain. . . . But all this commerce corrupts the soul and destroys one's judgement.'24 In the same notebook there follows the mysterious question: 'The heart is an instrument which rusts if it is not put to work. Can one be an artist without heart?' Then, almost as a reply, a few pages later there are five lines of writing which Reff observes have been scratched out and are barely legible beyond the following phrases: 'I cannot say how much I love this girl since she . . . Monday April 7. I cannot refuse to . . . to say it is shameful . . . a girl without defence. I would do it the least possible.'25 In the centre of the page there is a faint drawing of a girl.

What can be concluded from these cryptic remarks? Did he briefly fall in love? Did he 'take advantage' of a young girl, perhaps a model? Clearly the experience frightened him. He evidently became very sensitive on the subject and even became embarrassed at the thought of mentioning the incident in his own note-books (though it may have been another hand which did the erasing). If we combine this rare glimpse into Degas's interest in the opposite sex with a study of his self-portrait of 1855, we see a young man who was intensely shy, vulnerable, nervous, easily wounded, with few friends apart from those whom he met through his father, deeply serious, with a high moral commitment to art and prone to feelings of guilt. His contact with the outside world was limited. Apart from a trip to Lyons and to Montpellier, he knew little of the world outside Paris. In the refined and disciplined world of Lamothe's studio his horizons had been set on those fixed by Ingres and his followers. But at twenty-one, his short period of tutelage over, he was free to discover a world of art which was in the midst of great changes. The year 1855, indeed, marks a point, to use the art historian Joseph Sloane's phrase, when French painting 'lay between past and present'.26

OPPOSITE:
14. *Self-portrait*, c.1855. Oil on canvas, 32 × 25 in (81 × 64 cm). Paris, Louvre

15. Photograph of Ingres in his old age

OVERLEAF, LEFT:
16. *Young Spartan girls provoking the boys*, c.1860. Oil on canvas, 43 × 60¾ in (109 × 154.5 cm). London, National Gallery

OVERLEAF, RIGHT:
17. *Jephthah's daughter*, 1859–60. Oil on canvas, 77 × 117½ in (183 × 296 cm). Northampton, Mass., Smith College Museum of Art

(iii)

French painting in the first half of the nineteenth century was dominated by Ingres and Delacroix. It is natural to think of them as opposites: the one an upholder of line and of Classicism, the other a defender of colour and Romanticism. But as Sloane has pointed out,27 despite their stylistic differences, despite the battles they helped to create between their followers, both regarded themselves as belonging to a great tradition in art stretching back through the eighteenth century to Raphael and the Italian masters of the high Renaissance, and both believed that 'the future of "great" art in France could not lie outside tradition'.28 Both also believed in the painting of historical subjects which ennoble and uplift the spectator, and in the study of the human figure. In 1855, when Degas was twenty-one, he had the opportunity to study their work in depth in two special one-man shows organized within the context of the International Exhibition, which had been instituted by Napoleon III in imitation of the Great Exhibition of 1851 in London as a way of celebrating French industry and culture.

These two great artists were then at the zenith of their reputations, but not of their powers: they were both frail – Ingres was seventy-five and Delacroix fifty-six. If the great tradition was to be kept alive, it was soon going to be necessary to find a successor, or successors. Although there were a large number of able figure painters, none seemed to have the mark of originality or of greatness which Ingres and Delacroix clearly demonstrated. Ingres's pupil Hippolyte Flandrin had his supporters; so too did followers of Delacroix, like Théodore Chassériau, and the Orientalists, Alexandre Decamps, Eugène Fromentin and others. Successes at the regular Salon exhibitions[29] included Paul Baudry, Alexandre Cabanel and William Bouguereau; the neo-Greeks, Jean-Léon Gérôme and Thomas Couture, and the immensely successful battle painter Jean-Louis Meissonier. None seemed marked for true greatness. The perplexity felt by the critics was summed up in an article in 1853 by the writer and critic Théophile Gautier, who drew attention to the uneasiness felt by many observers of the French artistic scene. He wrote: 'Today art has at its disposal only dead ideas and formulas which no longer correspond to its needs. From this [comes] this uneasiness, this vagueness, this diffusion, this facility for passing from one extreme to another, this eclecticism, and this cosmopolitanism, this travelling in all possible worlds which leads from the Byzantine to the Daguerreotype, from a far-fetched mannerism to a deliberate brutality. It is well known that something must be done, but what?'[30]

The despair felt by Gautier was largely due to the fact that he was looking in the wrong direction. His eyes were still on the great tradition. But the most original talents were to be found elsewhere – in landscape painting, in Realism and in caricature, or, to be more specific, the work of Corot and the Barbizon school, Jean-François Millet, Gustave Courbet and Honoré Daumier.

By background and training Degas was drawn to Ingres (plate 15), whose work he had seen at the house of family friends, like the Valpinçons, and whose influence was paramount in Lamothe's studio. But the attraction to Ingres was not just artistic: Degas respected him as a man of commanding authority, of deep moral commitment to art, of complete inflexibility in the face of change. They held many views in common, even at this stage in Degas's life. The notebook quoted earlier in which Degas expressed his fear of commercial pressures on art is reflected in Ingres's low opinion of the Salon: 'The Salon stifles and corrupts the feeling for the great, the beautiful. Artists are driven to exhibit there by the attraction of profit, the desire to get themselves noticed at any price, by the supposed good fortune of an eccentric subject that is capable of producing an effect and leading to an advantageous sale.'[31] Degas's often quoted remark to the Irish writer George Moore, that his art was the product of study of the Old Masters, is matched by Ingres's question: 'Is there anything new? Everything has been done, everything has been found. Our task is not to invent, but to continue, and we have enough to do in using, after the example of the masters, these innumerable types which nature constantly offers us, in interpreting them with all our heart's sincerity, in ennobling them by that pure firm style without which no work is beautiful.'[32]

To begin with Ingres's influence was mainly apparent in Degas's drawing, in the use of a sharp hard pencil to produce drawings with a clear line but little shading. Later Ingres came to influence Degas as a personality; Degas's brusqueness, patrician attitude and reputation as a curmudgeon almost seem modelled on the older man. Even Ingres's liking for short crisp aphorisms is reflected in Degas's fierce *mots*. 'It is curious,' Degas once observed, 'that there is Delacroix, an admirable artist, whose little pamphlets are so dull. You cannot, on the other hand, quote a remark of Ingres that is not a masterpiece.' Then, standing to attention, he would reel off some of Ingres's dictums:

'*Shadow is not an addition to the contour but makes it.*'
'*A reflection on the shadows of the contour is unworthy of the majesty of art.*'
'*One must master the inner structure in order to express the planes.*'
'*Muscles I know; they are my friends. But I have forgotten their names.*'
'*You must follow the modelling like a fly walking on a sheet of paper.*'[33]

Degas's admiration for 'Monsieur Ingres' was lifelong. Over the years he built up a sizeable collection of the master's works, twenty paintings and ninety drawings. At the Ingres exhibition of 1911 Degas, who was then almost blind, came to pay homage to the paintings he had admired for so long. He stood close to the pictures, touching them, running his hands over their immaculately finished surfaces.

In about 1855 Degas actually met his hero. At the International Exhibition mentioned earlier Ingres was given the honour of having a special one-man show in a pavilion to himself. He selected his exhibition with care and turned to Henri Valpinçon for the loan of his *Le Bain Turc*. Valpinçon refused because he was frightened that fire might break out in the exhibition buildings. When the young Degas heard this, he was furious. 'You cannot refuse Monsieur Ingres a request like that,' he remonstrated.[34] Valpinçon relented and offered to take Degas with him to see Ingres and tell him of his change of mind.

In later life Degas loved to tell the story of this meeting. He embellished and polished it to the point where it is hard to know where reality ends and raconteur's licence begins. But it was among the jewels of his repertoire. There are various versions, but the one told to the writer Moreau-Nélaton has a tragi-comic flavour:

'We climbed the stairs to his studio, rang the bell and the master appeared. My old friend excused himself for his rudeness, then having introduced me, he explained that it was because of me that he had reversed his decision to lend the painting in question. We chatted for a short time and then took our leave. But as he was showing us out, the old man slipped, I don't know how, and there he was laid out full length on the floor. I hurried towards him but his head was all bloody and he could say nothing. He had lost consciousness and only came to slowly and with difficulty. Perhaps a sudden attack of dizziness caused the fall. I left M. Valpinçon with him and ran to the rue de Lille to tell Mme Ingres. I did my best to explain what had happened and brought her back with me. When we reached the threshold of his studio we found M. Ingres, supported by M. Valpinçon and the concierge, getting into his guest's carriage to return home. We restored him to the hands of his wife and our adventure ended.'[35]

In other versions Ingres's fainting spells are omitted and the great man merely gave the young artist some good advice: 'Draw lines . . . many lines, after

nature, and from memory.[36] Degas had another favourite story about Ingres:

'I saw M. Ingres a short time afterwards. He organized one day a small exhibition in his studio in the manner of the Old Masters. I did not know him, but I went with a friend who did, and who was able to get him talking. He had there among other things, three paintings . . . first a picture of Homer supported by I don't know what companion, but the master explained the subject. My friend congratulated him on his perceptive translation of antiquity. The compliments were accepted with the master remaining unmoved. Other compliments, apropos the portrait of Mme Moitessier . . . proved to be no less acceptable, you understand. Then, spotting a circular version of "Le Bain Turc", my companion let out a cry, "Ah! now that is something different." "But", replied M. Ingres, "I have several paint brushes!"'

Degas repeated the phrase three or four times, laughing to himself: ' "I have several paint brushes!" Isn't it delightful?'[37]

Ingres was the contour which Degas drew around himself as a young artist, a line of protection against the outside world. But within that line other influences were at work. Early in his life he developed a taste for Romantic literature. He read Gautier, Vigny, Sand and Musset and his notebooks reveal a liking for Romantic subjects, such as, for example, the departure of Mary Queen of Scots from France. He also appreciated that Romantic painter *par excellence*, Delacroix, and later acquired a fine collection of his paintings and drawings. He never met Delacroix, but he once caught a glimpse of him rounding a corner with his collar turned up. 'Every time I pass that place I see Delacroix again, pressed for time and hurrying,' he told Moreau-Nélaton.[38]

At what point Delacroix entered his artistic consciousness cannot be identified precisely, but he certainly saw the Delacroix one-man show at the International Exhibition of 1855. Although he did not make any copies after Delacroix at that time, he soon wrote to his father expressing his enthusiasm for the great colourist. Auguste was concerned and felt it necessary to sound a warning note:

'You know that I am far from sharing your opinion of Delacroix – this painter has given himself up to the flash of his inspiration and, unfortunately, neglected the art of drawing, that keystone on which everything depends – he's completely lost his way. As for Ingres, his stature has risen through his drawing; all the same he has stayed well below the level of the great Italian masters, and when you look at him objectively, disregarding of whom his pictures are and when and where they were done, you remain convinced of his relative inferiority.'[39]

But despite these warnings Degas became more

and more attracted to Delacroix, particularly to the great Romantic's use of colour, and this influence can be seen in several paintings executed between 1860 and 1865 and in several entries made in his notebook during this period. The bright colours of *The Woman with Chrysanthemums* (plate 59), begun around 1859 and finished in 1865, owe much to Delacroix's still lifes of flowers, and *Jephthah's Daughter* (plate 17) shows the results of Degas's study of Delacroix, both in the colouring and the swirling composition.[40]

Degas was not the only 'Ingre-ist' to fall under the spell of his great rival. Chassériau, for example, had begun as a pupil of Ingres but had come to believe that 'He will remain as a memory and a repetition of certain periods in the art of the past, having created nothing for the future.'[41] While Chassériau went on wholeheartedly to embrace the style and subject-matter of Delacroix, to the point when some even accused him of plagiarism, Degas retained a respect for both masters and his work never become subordinate to either. Thus he continued to admire Ingres's line while adopting Delacroix's colour. In many ways his art can be interpreted as an attempt to resolve the debate on the stylistic differences between Ingres and Delacroix, the contrast between line and colour. His painting shows both Classical restraint and a Romantic sensibility. And it is the tension between these two forces which gives Degas's art its unique character.

There was a third person of influence, however, whom he must have noticed before his departure to Italy in 1856 – Gustave Courbet. Ever since the Salon of 1851, in which he had exhibited his paintings of the *Stone Breakers* and the *Burial at Ornans*, Courbet had been a figure of controversy, inflaming the passions of partisans and foes alike. His technical accomplishments were respected even by academics, but his subjects were criticized and, in particular, the people he painted were considered ugly. But he had some ardent supporters – Baudelaire for a time, the critic Jules Castagnary, Edmond Duranty and the great socialist thinker Pierre-Joseph Proudhon, whose posthumous publication *Du Principe de l'Art et de sa Destination Sociale* Degas read and appreciated.[42]

As personalities Courbet and Degas were complete opposites: Courbet, brash, robust and bucolic; Degas shy, slender and patrician. But Courbet's ideas and aims were not easily disregarded and they may even have forced Degas to think of alternative solutions. Thus the portrait of the Bellelli family (plate 37) is in many ways a 'Realist' painting, but a picture of a higher social world than that depicted by Courbet; Degas's *Self-Portrait Saluting* (plate 20) is, as many writers have pointed out, a bourgeois answer to

21. *The Duchessa Morbilli*, c.1857. Pencil and watercolour, $13\frac{3}{4} \times 7\frac{1}{2}$ in (35 × 19 cm). New York, Collection of Mr and Mrs Eugene V. Thaw

22. *Adelini Morbilli*,
c.1857. Pencil and
watercolour, $11\frac{3}{8} \times$
$8\frac{1}{2}$ in (29 × 21 cm).
New York,
Collection of Mr
and Mrs Nathan
L. Halpern

Degas

Courbet's *Bonjour M. Courbet*, and the *Woman with Chrysanthemums* (plate 59) a more sensitive, less vulgar rendition of Courbet's *Woman Arranging Flowers*. Before leaving for Italy, Degas had probably had a chance to examine many of Courbet's most controversial works in the special exhibition Courbet staged in 1855 in a temporary structure, when he was excluded from the official exhibition. It would be fascinating to know for certain if Degas was among the visitors.

(iv)

Degas left for Italy in June 1856. It was probably his first visit to the birthplace of his father and the adopted country of his grandfather. Italy was the natural goal for young artists from all over Europe, the accepted finishing school. Degas was fortunate in having independent means and was therefore spared the rigours of having to win the Prix de Rome[43] to study there. He took full advantage of his situation. 'It was the most extraordinary period of my life,' he later recalled. Just how many drawings he made over the

26. *The engraver Joseph Tourny*, 1857. Etching, $9 \times 5\frac{5}{8}$ in (22.8 × 14.3 cm). Paris, BN

next three years can be seen in ten notebooks he filled with sketches, copies and notes. It was a period of intense study, of moments of indecision – 'Oh, how doubt and uncertainty tire me,' he wrote on one occasion – and flashes of inspiration. He spent most of his time in three cities: in Naples, where most of his Italian relations lived; in Rome, where young French artists clustered around the French Academy; and in Florence, where his aunt Laura Bellelli lived with her husband and daughters.

In Naples, when he was not copying the paintings and statuary in the museum, he spent his time making portraits of his relatives. These works, the drawings of his aunt and uncle (plates 21 and 22) and the restrained portrait of his grandfather (plate 4), show the influence of Ingres at its strongest. The colours of the surrounding countryside, however, attracted his attention and he made one of his rare incursions into landscape painting, first drawing the fortress near his grandfather's villa at Capodimonte and then painting

OPPOSITE, ABOVE: 23. *On the race-course*, c.1860–62. Oil on canvas, 17 × $25\frac{3}{4}$ in (43 × 65.5 cm). Basel, Kunstmuseum (Gift of Martha and Robert von Hirsch)

OPPOSITE, BELOW: 24. *Carriage in front of a country inn*, 1859–64 (Notebook 18).

25. *Self-portrait*, 1863. Oil on card, 21 × 15 in (53 × 39 cm). Possible study for Degas' *Self-portrait saluting*. New York, Collection of John Hay Whitney

the small *Italian Landscape seen through a Window.*

Naples made a lasting impression on him. Its songs and colours lodged themselves in his memory and in later life he would often hum a Neapolitan air. Degas returned there on many occasions, his last visit being in 1907, and at his death he still owned a one-fifth interest in the family palazzo. In Paris his Neapolitan cousins were frequent visitors and kept him in touch with family affairs.

In Rome Degas met colleagues from his days as a pupil of Lamothe, artists like Jules-Elie Delaunay, who in 1856 won the Grand Prix de Rome, and became one of the most successful of the younger history painters of the Second Empire. Joseph Tourny, a painter and engraver who won the Prix de Rome for engraving in 1847, was then in Rome (plate 26), as was Léon Bonnat, one of the most acclaimed portraitists of the Second Empire and the Third Republic. These young artists were drawn to Rome by the presence of the French Academy at the Villa Medici, then run by the easy-going Victor Schnetz; some had scholarships to study there, others like Degas, who had private means, were able to use it as a place of study. Of all the acquaintances made in Rome the most important for the young painter's art and for the broadening of his style over the next five years or so was Gustave Moreau.

Moreau was eight years older than Degas, intelligent, well-read and passionately fond of music, having, according to Georges Bizet who became a friend in Rome, 'a charming tenor voice'. Moreau had received a solid grounding at the Ecole des Beaux-Arts and had subsequently fallen under the spell of Delacroix and Chassériau. It was their colour which appealed to him rather than their subject-matter, and it became his ambition to continue to paint historical subjects, drawing his inspiration from Greek myths and demi-gods, at the same time using the exotic rich warm colour of the Romantics. Degas attempted a similar marriage between colour and line in his art a few years later and in this he was undoubtedly helped by Moreau's example.

Moreau was something of a late developer, being thirty-one when he left France in 1857 to continue his artistic studies in Italy. Because he was older than most of his French colleagues in Rome, he was in a position to play a somewhat avuncular role in the lives of his young artist friends. When Moreau told his father about a new friendship, almost certainly with the young Degas, his father assumed that he would be the mentor in this new relationship: 'About your young companion, *guided by you, of course.* Does he have an intelligent grasp of what he sees? Will he be a painter? Though knowing very little about him,

27. *The angel St John*, 1857. Pencil and watercolour, $17\frac{1}{2} \times 11\frac{1}{2}$ in (44.5 × 29 cm). Wuppertal, Von der Heydt Museum

we are interested enough in him to learn with pleasure that you may make a friend and a pupil of him, one who will always understand your ideas and who, if need be, could give you some good work.'[44] Degas's father too seems to have understood his son's need for an older and wiser artist colleague. When Degas later informed him that he wanted to prolong his stay in Florence rather than return to Paris, Auguste replied: 'The presence of M. Moreau in Florence will keep you there still longer, that I can well understand.'[45]

Moreau seems to have charmed all who met and befriended him in Rome. Léon Bonnat later recalled,

'We were all crazy about Moreau,' and Georges Bizet, who was in Rome having won a Prix de Rome for musical composition, wrote when the painter left Rome for Florence in 1858: 'I want to thank you for your good friendship and the good times we have had together. My greatest desire is to see you again next year. Do let us get to know each other better and to see each other more often.'[46]

A particularly warm bond developed between Degas and Moreau, first in Rome where they were to be found drawing the same male figure at the French Academy, and later in Florence where they made sketches of the same frescoes (not necessarily at the same time) and had long philosophical discussions on art and life. Being a colourist, Moreau was particularly drawn to the study of the Venetian artists, Titian

28. *Italian beggar-woman*, 1857. Oil on canvas, 39 × 29½ in (100 × 75 cm). Birmingham, Museum and Art Gallery

being his favourite; and it was undoubtedly through Moreau's example that Degas began to copy two Giorgiones and a Veronese in Florence after Moreau's departure for Venice in mid-August. Degas's father approved of his son's new interest in colour and wrote to him on 30 November 1858 to say: 'I am very glad that you are studying Giorgione a good deal. Your colouring, accurate though it is, needs to be warmed up a bit. But beware of gingerbread. That is the pitfall of all those who ostensibly wish to get warm tones which they do not see or do not know how to see in copying the Venetian masters and then in trying to reproduce them after nature.'[47]

Moreau did more than encourage Degas's interest in the Venetians and colour in general; he also seems to have stimulated Degas to read Pascal, as Pierre-Louis Mathieu has noted in his recent monograph on Moreau,[48] and he also helped Degas as a moral guide. Both artists regarded their art as a high moral calling, one which required years of study and also pain and loneliness. In February 1858 Moreau wrote to his parents: 'I think that a long education is required, a whole difficult initiation. Therefore I do not reckon on the triumphs and successes that satisfy one's vanity.'[49] In September of the same year Degas wrote to Moreau expressing similar thoughts:

'*Great patience is needed on the hard road I've undertaken. I had encouragement from you; but, as though I had not, I'm beginning to despair a bit, as I have before. I remember the conversation we had in Florence on the unhappiness which is the lot of those devoted to art. There was less exaggeration than I thought in what you said. This unhappiness has hardly any compensation really. It increases with age and experience, and youth no longer consoles you with a few more hopes and illusions. Whatever affection you have for your family, whatever passion for art, there is a void which even that can't fill. You understand me, I think, although I don't express it well.*'[50]

Throughout his life Degas was prone to fits of gloom and self-doubt, but as a young artist in his twenties he was particularly vulnerable. Moreau provided the right kind of moral and artistic support and mutual friends of both seem to have realized that only Moreau was capable of lifting his friend's spirits. There is a revealing letter from the painter Antoine Königswarter in the archives of the Musée Gustave Moreau in Paris, which shows the impression that the young Degas made and the role Moreau played in his life. 'He is a really charming young man', wrote Königswarter of Degas, 'with a naïveté and a freshness of feeling which it is a pleasure to meet in this matter-of-fact world of ours. The poor chap seems to be a good deal out of spirits at the moment. He too is beginning to come up against material

29. *Portrait of Gustave Moreau*,
c.1868. Oil on canvas, $15\frac{1}{2} \times 10\frac{1}{2}$ in (40 × 27 cm). Paris,
Musée Gustave Moreau

30. GUSTAVE
MOREAU, *Portrait of
Edgar Degas*, 1859.
Pencil, 6 × 3½ in
(13.3 × 9 cm). Paris,
Musée Gustave
Moreau

taken a few months earlier. It was one of those journeys which the French sometimes call a *vaga-bondage*, in that the traveller follows no preconceived plan but can stop at places of interest as the whim dictates. In the nineteenth, as in the previous century, Italy cast a magical charm on Northern visitors and an Italian journey often seemed to unlock their creative forces, inducing young painters and poets to dream and wonder. The Italian journeys of Byron and Goethe are two famous examples; less well known is Degas's journey. It is surprising that his account has not received more attention since it is an import-ant document and offers a rare glimpse into his youthful mind, at a moment in his life when every-thing lay before him, when he could be candid about his feelings and thoughts and before the gruff, bitter and withdrawn man of later years took over.

His enthusiasm and sense of excitement can be felt from his first entry: standing on a high plateau, a great sweep of landscape lay before him – yellow fields of

31. *Sketch of funeral procession*, Italy, 1858–60 (Notebook 13). Paris, BN

worries, and on that account he is, if not discouraged, at least downcast. He has been a bit spoiled by the warm and really exceptional affection which his parents lavish upon him. I rely much on you [Moreau] to raise his spirits.'[51]

As has been pointed out,[52] Degas outgrew Moreau and in later years he produced one of his most celebrated *mots* on the subject of Moreau's art, 'He taught us that the gods wore watch chains.'[53] Degas also disliked the museum which Moreau created for himself. 'How truly sinister,' he remarked as he emerged. 'It might be a family vault . . . All these pictures crammed together look to me like a Thes-aurus – a *gradus ad Parnassum*.'[54] But his portrait of Moreau (plate 29) remains in the museum as well as the delicate pencil drawing of Degas by Moreau (plate 30), and these items stand as reminders of their early friendship.

In July 1858 Degas set off on a journey from Rome to Florence, one which Moreau had himself undercut wheat and in the distance mountains bathed in evening grey. 'The Italy of one's dreams', he wrote. It is interesting to note his attitude to landscape as the journey unfolded. At first it gave him nothing but pleasure; a little later he wrote: 'To travel alone one must cross a country where there is life or plenty of art. I quickly become bored contemplating just nature.'[55] Fortunately there were plenty of paintings and sculpture to see and copy: the town of Viterbo, which reminded him of Avignon, the Signorelli frescoes in the S. Brizio chapel of Orvieto Cathedral, whose swirls and arabesques threw him into raptures and made such a contrast with the calm and dignity of the Fra Angelicos just above them. Then came the discovery of the Giottos at Assisi in which he saw a depth of expression and a sense of drama which quite astonished him. He was so overcome that he preferred to commit them to memory rather than attempt a quick sketch.

Throughout his travels he observed the importance of religion in the life of the people, and although he declared he was not religious according to the accepted practices of his day, he was frequently moved to tears by the sights and sounds he witnessed: an organ playing during a high mass, or the sight of peasants running and singing out the names of their patron saints before the grille of the high altar. In Assisi he was quite overwhelmed by the religious atmosphere of the town, and by his conversations with a French priest. 'Ah! these people here know the meaning of life,' he wrote. 'They never renounce it. It's as if the Sower is one of their family. I wish I could be one of them. I would like to become someone with the conviction to paint works which have the value of sermons. At least, even if I do not become a painter of religious scenes, I would like to feel as they feel here.'[56]

As he left Assisi, Degas began to understand the implications of his vocation, the solitude into which he would be thrown, the possible celibacy of his later years. His notebooks show him wavering between being 'single, and without children', leading a monk-like life in a monastery, and being married. The sight of a happily married English couple made him dream of finding a companion for himself: 'Could I find a good wife, simple, tranquil, someone who will understand my mental follies and with whom I could spend a modest life working, isn't that a beautiful dream?' And again: 'But I want to return to the hubbub [*mouvement*] of Paris. Who knows what will happen? I will always be a decent fellow [*honnête homme*]. I hope I can rely on my memory because the little I have written does not begin to express all my thoughts. . . .'[57]

(v)

Degas reached Florence in August 1858. One of his reasons for going there was to see his aunt Laura Bellelli, but when he arrived he found she had been called away to Naples to look after Grandfather Degas, who was ill and who died on 31 August. Laura's husband the Baron (a title given to his father by Napoleon's general Murat) was in exile from Naples because of his revolutionary activities (he was caught up in the *risorgimento,* the movement for the unification of Italy); he invited Degas to stay with him and wait for his aunt's return. The young artist set to work copying in the Uffizi, and among the portraits which caught his attention were two heads of women by Bronzino and Pontormo. His father was at first pleased to find his son was studying at the fountain-head of the Italian Renaissance and in his letters to Degas he liked to remind him that they 'are the only true guides; when one is full of them . . . one ought to arrive at a result'.[58]

As the weeks went by, Degas began to feel more and more at home in Florence and a visit which was intended to be for perhaps a few weeks became

32. Study for *The Bellelli Family* (Notebook 12). Paris, BN

33. Study for *The Bellelli Family* (Notebook 12). Paris, BN

extended to nine months, despite repeated and almost frantic attempts by Auguste to persuade his son to return. The letters from father to son, of which extracts have been published by Lemoisne,[59] offer a fascinating insight into their relationship and into the genesis of Degas's first great composition *The Bellelli Family* (plate 37). Unfortunately, Edgar's letters to his father have not survived and we can only guess at the excuses and reasons he gave for remaining in Florence. It would appear that, perhaps to keep his father happy, Degas forwarded a package with drawings and sketches. Auguste was delighted with his progress:

'*I was very pleased and I can tell you, you have taken a tremendous step forward in art; your drawing is strong, the tone of your colour is right. You've got rid of the flabby, trivial Flandrinian or Lamothian drawing and that dreary grey colour... You've no need to torment yourself any more, my dear Edgar. You're on the right track. Calm down and, by working peacefully but steadily and not weakening, follow this path you've opened up. It's up to you, nobody else. Work calmly and stick to this path, I tell you, and you can be quite certain that you'll succeed in doing great things. You have a wonderful destiny ahead of you, don't lose heart, don't get into a turmoil.*'[60]

In November Degas began to make plans to do a portrait of his aunt with her daughters. At first he was hesitant. Portraiture bored him, he told his father, but Auguste would have none of this:

'*You mention the boredom you feel at doing portraits; you'll really have to overcome this eventually because portraiture will be the finest jewel in your crown. The question of cash, in this world, is so serious, so pressing, so crushing even, that only idiots can lose sight of it or scorn it. It's not a question of having to come down to that level, but you need to be able to put up with the irritations that go with it. To believe that, in this world, you can always indulge your own whims and take no account of the necessities of existence is a foolishness that you pay dearly for, I've told you again and again.*'[61]

Auguste became concerned when Degas wrote to inform him that he had begun a portrait of his aunt in oils. He knew enough about painting technique to know the project would mean prolonging even further his stay in Florence, and on 25 November he wrote:

'*If you have begun the portrait of your aunt, I can understand that you would wish to finish it. But you haven't even roughed it out, and an outline must dry for some time before you can come back and add something, otherwise you make a mess of it. If you want this to be something good and lasting it is impossible, unfortunately, for you to do it in a* month, and the more rushed you are the more your impatience will make you do it and redo it and thus waste time. It seems to me therefore that you'll have to limit yourself to doing a drawing, rather than start off on a canvas . . . And then hurry up and fold your gear and pack your bags and get back here.'[62]

By the end of the year Auguste was reconciled to his son's plans and was astute enough to realize that he would need more than two months if he was going to make progress with his work:

'You start so large a picture on 29 December and then think you'll be finished by 29 February. That's extremely doubtful. If I can give you a piece of advice, it's to do it calmly and patiently, as otherwise you would run the risk of not finishing it at all and giving your uncle Bellelli good cause for complaint. Since you wanted to undertake this picture you have to do it and do it well . . . Your imagination gets far, far too excited and then, when you fetch up against harsh and intractable reality, you come down to earth with a bump. Spend more time perfecting your methods without launching into dreams which, by continuously misleading and discouraging you, ceaselessly deflect you from your goal.'[63]

Degas was ready to return home at the end of March. On 2 April he stopped in Genoa where he was much impressed by the Van Dyck portrait of Paolina Adorno, Marchesa Brignole-Sale (plate 34). He made a quick sketch in his notebook and wrote, 'One couldn't represent a woman better, a more supple, refined hand. You are really struck. Perhaps there is more than a natural talent on Van Dyck's part. She is as straight and slight as a bird. Her head shows breeding and life in its grace and refinement.'[64]

And to Moreau he wrote:

'Genoa, beautiful proud city! Oh, the fine Van Dycks! – go to the Palazzo Brignole, if you come through Genoa on your way back, and have a good look at the single portrait of the Countess Brignole, then a lady of the family with her daughter, a Veronese, and a portrait of a Venetian lady, all in light tones. No one has ever rendered the grace and refinement of woman, the elegance and nobility of man, nor the distinction of both, the way Van Dyck has. I feel that very often he would reflect on his subject and would penetrate its essence as a poet would.'[65]

Moreau approved and replied:

'It is a great pleasure for me to see your wholehearted admiration for Van Dyck, whom I one day made light of (by your account). If so, I was wrong, or rather if I did it must have been by way of a joke. Like you, my friend, I am well aware of the great master and great painter in the works signed with that name, and I am only apt to pick a quarrel in moments when my passionate love for ideal beauty and works of a certain deeply noble order makes me leap on my high horse and my high emotion.'[66]

The Van Dyck portrait became one of the starting points for his treatment of his aunt Laura in the Bellelli painting. Once back in Paris, Degas installed himself in a studio found for him by his father in the rue Madame. There he set up a large canvas, measuring over six feet by seven, and began his portrait of the family using the sketches, drawings and oil studies that he had brought with him from Italy as guides. The canvas was probably finished by the end of 1861 (plate 37). Today it stands in the Jeu de Paume in Paris, not far from two large group portraits painted by Henri Fantin-Latour a few years later. By comparison with the other Impressionist paintings in the same museum this portrait has almost

34. ANTHONY VAN DYCK, *Paola Adorno, Marchesa Brignole-Sale*. Genoa, Galleria di Palazzo Rosso

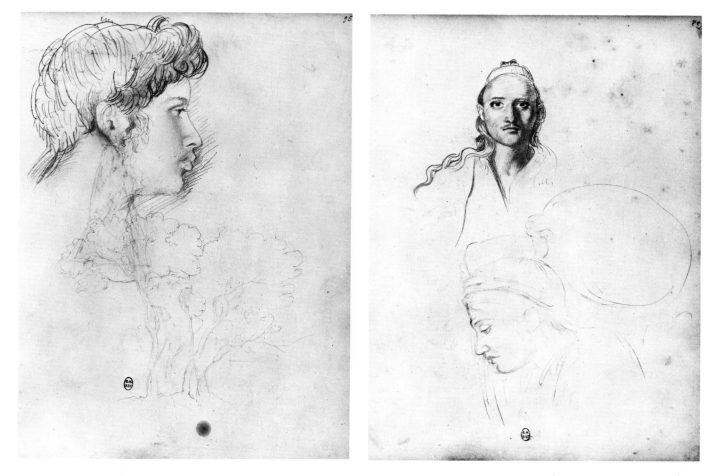

LEFT:
35. *Head of a youth*
(Notebook 18).
Paris, BN

RIGHT:
36. Partial copy of a
lithograph by L.
Dupré (Notebook
18). Paris, BN

a cold academic air. Its audacity may not be at first apparent, and the sombre colouring and severe expressions of the sitters are not immediately appealing, but recent studies by Reff and Boggs have uncovered layers of meaning within this painting. It is helpful, for example, to know that the framed drawing on the back wall has been identified by Reff as a portrait of his grandfather.[67] Thus, in a sense, the painting commemorates the death of the head of the Degas family and explains why the women in the picture are wearing mourning. It is also helpful to know that the Baroness's full black dress hides the fact that she is pregnant, and, as Boggs has pointed out,[68] the picture shows Degas's awareness of individuals existing in a cycle of time; the womb, the infant, the child, the adult and finally death are all represented in this painting.

More obviously the picture is a portrait of a marriage, in which the strains between husband and wife have been given a visual definition. The Baron, it appears, was a man of uneven temper who found the strain caused by his exile from Naples almost unbearable. 'You cannot have any idea what it is like to live with a family for several long years in furnished rooms,' he once complained.[69] The Degas

family was naturally concerned at the state of the marriage and Achille, Degas's uncle, wrote on one occasion: 'The domestic life of the family in Florence is a source of unhappiness for us. As I predicted, one of them is very much at fault and our sister a little, too. Incompatibility of personality and background and, as a result, a lack of affection and leniency enlarges like a magnifying glass the individuals' natural faults.'[70]

Degas was particularly fond of his aunt Laura, who was once the belle of the family and who retained until her death the love of a man she was not allowed to marry. Her sad face appealed to the painter. Without recourse to dramatic effects, Degas managed to capture the psychology of his sitters and their feelings towards each other. They are caught in a nineteenth-century dilemma in which divorce is not possible and the marriage is barely tolerable. Laura stares into space, her expression is impenetrable, her hand rests gently on the table to her side and her right arm is placed protectively round the shoulder of her daughter Giovanna. The Baron is isolated from his family, and the tensions and frustrations from which he suffered are captured in his somewhat awkward and unheroic pose as he sits hunched in his chair with

37. *The Bellelli Family*, 1858–62. Oil on canvas, 79 × 99½ in (200 × 253 cm). Paris, Louvre

his back to the onlooker. One daughter, Giulia, the more independent one (plate 13), almost returns his gaze. Her pose is equally unconventional, though very lifelike, as she sits on her chair with one leg tucked under her skirt. The subject was not unfamiliar to mid-century painters, but was treated much more liberally: if one compares an English work of the period – for example, Augustus Egg's painting of married troubles in *Past and Present, No. 1* (1858) (plate 38) – one finds the same attention to detail, but the narrative element is more pronounced, and the scene is overtly dramatized. The wife lies prostrate with remorse on the floor, the father sits back in his chair in a stupor and the card-house, which the two daughters are building, is on the point of collapse. Degas's eye for character and dramatic tension was much more subtle and it is astonishing to think he was only twenty-five when he began this work.

Was there any precedent for this portrait? Or, to put the question another way, what was a young French artist, a follower of Ingres, one steeped in Italian painting of the Renaissance, doing, painting the kind of subject the Dutch masters of the seventeenth century might have chosen? It has been suggested that one model might have been Ingres's many drawings of family groups like the Gatteaux family or the Forestier family. But it is not certain whether Degas would have had an opportunity to see drawings like these; if he had, it is the differences between Ingres's approach and his own which are striking. In an Ingres drawing the sitters all look towards the artist who is studying them; in Degas's painting only Giovanna could be said to be aware of the artist's presence in the room. In an Ingres the background is only suggested in a summary fashion; but here the room is rendered with great attention to detail. Carpets, wallpaper, furniture, small details like the bassinet and bag for holding wools, books and newspaper, are included to help define the character of the family, its interests and social status.

The influence of Ingres does not, therefore, provide an explanation of the structure and scope of this painting. Indeed, it is hard to think of any painting which Degas might have used as a point of departure. Only in literature can one find a parallel, notably Flaubert's portrait of bourgeois life in the provinces, *Madame Bovary*, published in 1857. (Interestingly, the Goncourt brothers thought that the noblest and strongest parts of the book were 'much closer to painting than to literature'.) But it is possible to read too much into these parallels and coincidences. Degas's painting remains on its own, an independent work of art which stands as a harbinger of things to come.

Portraiture, however, was not enough to satisfy an artist with Degas's ambition. He still had to face the greater test of producing a work based on an incident to be found in the Classics or in the Bible. From 1859 to 1865 he became preoccupied with large-scale historical pictures. The surprising thing is that he was not better at them. He had all the necessary skills: he was intelligent, well versed in the Classics, full of ideas. He worked diligently, producing a host of preliminary drawings, oil sketches and studies of

details. He worked and reworked his pictures but somehow he was never satisfied with the results. His father kept a watchful eye on his progress: 'Our Raphael works all the time,' he wrote in 1863, 'but he has produced nothing finished although the years are passing.'[71] Perhaps he tried too hard. Perhaps all the work he put into these paintings obscured the original inspiration, which was always a danger if the Academic approach was followed too closely.

In the general reaction against Academicism and history painting which accompanied the rise to popularity of Manet and the Impressionists, Degas's history paintings have tended to be looked down on by art historians and critics writing earlier this century. It is true that they have their faults: *The Misfortunes of the City of Orléans* (plate 46), for instance, lacks dramatic tension, and *Jephthah's Daughter* (plate 17), although full of movement and colour, hardly tells the story which inspired it. But these paintings are more original than their outward appearance might suggest and they mark a break with the conventions of the day. The Classics, for example, were considered to be the proper inspirational source for a history painting, but *Semiramis Constructing a Town* (plate 45) was not inspired by a classical writer but an opera. The Bible was another accepted source, but Degas's painting of *Jephthah's*

38. AUGUSTUS EGG, *Past and Present No. 1*, 1858. Oil on canvas, 25 × 30 in (63.5 × 76 cm). London, Tate Gallery

Daughter is based not on the version given in the Book of Judges, but on a text by the Romantic poet Alfred de Vigny. The Middle Ages and the Renaissance could provide the artist with subjects (even the Classicist Ingres had found inspiration in these epochs, although Academic theory on the whole cautioned against this trend); Degas's *The Misfortunes of the City of Orléans* is set in the Middle Ages, but he used this theme as a parable for the misfortunes suffered by his relatives in New Orleans as a result of its capture in 1862 by the Union troops in the American Civil War.

Of his history paintings the two most successful are *Jephthah's Daughter* and *The Young Spartans* (plate 16). The first is resonant with colour and movement and shows the influence of Delacroix on Degas in the early 1860s, and the second is a delightful classical composition in pale green colours and light earth tones. Degas was particularly proud of *The Young Spartans* and it occupied a prominent position in his house on the rue Victor-Massé, where it was seen and admired by many of his visitors.[72] It too marked a break with tradition because the figures of the Spartan boys and girls have not been idealized; instead, they appear to have been modelled, as many

writers have noticed, on children whom he might have found playing in the streets of Naples or Paris. Early in his career Degas seems to have been drawn to pre-adolescent boyish figures, a preference which was to reappear in his studies of the *rats*, or young dancers, members of the corps de ballet. The Academician Jean-Léon Gérôme, who liked to fill his paintings of harems with shapely curvaceous figures in the tradition of Ingres, once criticized Degas's ungainly figures. 'I suppose it [the picture] isn't Turkish enough for you,' was Degas's answer.[73]

By the mid-1860s Degas began to tire of his labours as a history painter and he turned again to portraiture, a field which he had never completely abandoned and one in which he had already demonstrated his ability. His father rightly discerned that it would become one of the brightest jewels of his crown. Events within his family circle provided the excuse for two paintings of this period. His sister Thérèse was given a special dispensation to marry her cousin Edmondo Morbilli. Degas painted them in two versions (plate 42) soon after their marriage and his portraits convey a much more tender side of married life than the Bellelli picture of five years earlier. In

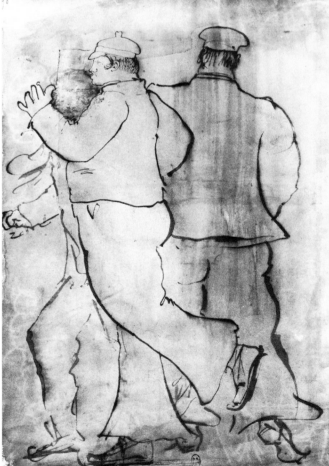

LEFT:
39. *A lady and gentleman in evening dress*, brown ink (Notebook 18). Paris, BN

RIGHT:
40. *Three sailors*, brown ink with wash (Notebook 18). Paris, BN

41. Study for the *Portrait of Mme Julie Burtin*, 1863. Pencil with touches of white chalk, $14\frac{1}{2} \times 10\frac{3}{4}$ in (36×27 cm). Cambridge, Mass., Courtesy of the Fogg Art Museum, Harvard University (Bequest of Meta and Paul J. Sachs)

46

OPPOSITE:
42. *Edmondo and Teresa Morbilli*, 1867. Oil on canvas, 46¼ × 35½ in (116 × 89 cm). Boston, Mass., Courtesy of the Museum of Fine Arts (Gift of Robert Treat Paine II)

43. *Portrait of Thérèse de Gas, Duchessa di Morbilli*, 1863. Oil on canvas, 35 × 23½ in (89 × 77 cm). Paris, Louvre (Jeu de Paume)

45. Study for
*Semiramis
constructing a town,*
1861. Pastel, 15¾ ×
26 in (40 × 67 cm).
Paris, Louvre
(Cabinet des
Dessins)

1863 the arrival in France of his New Orleans cousins, escaping from the terrors of the occupation of their home town, not only prompted *The Misfortunes of the City of Orléans* but also a charming and sad portrait of his aunt Odile Musson and her two daughters, Désirée and Estelle, pictured at Bourg-en-Bresse in January 1865 (plate 44).

Estelle, in particular, caught the attention and the sympathy of both Degas and his youngest brother René. She was a young widow whose husband had been killed in battle in October 1862, only a few months after their marriage, leaving her pregnant. 'One cannot look at her without thinking of her misfortune,' wrote Degas.[74] René, however, subsequently fell in love with her, and in 1869 he was given papal dispensation to marry her. It is perhaps a measure of the confines of the Degas family circle that two of the five surviving children of Auguste and Celestine married their first cousins.

In about 1865 Degas finished *Self-Portrait Saluting* (plate 20). He was thirty, and the picture shows a more confident and debonair individual than the one depicted ten years earlier. He greets the world, hat and glove in hand, with a flourish and a proud stare. Photographs taken of Degas at this time indicate that ·he has exaggerated his robustness, giving himself a fuller face and a more assured appearance than he in fact had. This is a man at a turning point in his life, about to leave the family circle and enter the world at large.

OPPOSITE:
44. *Mme Michel Musson with her two daughters,* 6 January 1865. Pencil with brown and grey wash, 14 × 10¼ in (35.5 × 26 cm). Chicago, Art Institute (Gift of Tiffany and Margaret Blake)

Chapter 2

1865 to 1870

In 1865 Degas exhibited for the first time at the Salon. He chose for his début *The Misfortunes of the City of Orléans* (plate 46), but it was listed in the catalogue with a less specific title, *Scenes of War in the Middle Ages*. As a work on paper it was included in the drawing section and among the 3,559 items on view that year few visitors gave it a second glance.[1] Their attention lay elsewhere, with the new paintings by the Salon favourites, Paul Baudry, William Bouguereau, Alexandre Cabanel and Jean-Louis Meissonier and with a new work by Edouard Manet, *Olympia*.

The Salon of 1865 gives in many ways a representative view of the changes of taste which had taken place under the Second Empire and reveals the great range of art with which visitors were confronted. The jury that year had been more liberal-minded than in previous years: not only did Manet have both his works accepted, but younger painters like Monet and Renoir were also included in the exhibition. The number of works in all mediums had been growing with each year and the variety of subjects and styles displayed side by side was enormous and confusing. As might be expected, the preponderance of the paintings took their subjects either from the Bible or the Classics, but there were paintings drawn from other epochs, the Middle Ages and the Renaissance proving to be increasingly popular with artists and the public. There were also battle pictures and scenes of military life; pictures of harems and desert encampments; portraits, landscapes, still lifes, animal pictures, pictures of rural life, peasants returning from fields and so on. The high ideals of the Academics, the 'greatness' demanded by Ingres and Delacroix, had not been maintained; instead the court of Napoleon III, the critics and the visitors to the Salon had settled for an art which was eclectic rather than exalted, bourgeois rather than aristocratic, domestic rather than exclusively public. Clive Bell's observation that official painting during the Second Empire, 'perhaps for the first time on record, certainly for the first time since Roman days, had nothing to do with art',[2] in a way misses the point. Most of the paintings on view at the Salon of 1865 were about 'art'. They revealed a self-conscious 'artiness' produced by the

academic system and encouraged by the rich and extravagant bourgeois public. The paintings which broke new ground, like Manet's *Olympia*, were decried, as the writer Emile Zola noticed,[3] because Manet's patches of colour and swathes of paint did not look like 'art', i.e. old 'art'. This was the great age of stylistic imitation: furniture was based on eighteenth-century models and buildings were put up in the 'Gothic' or 'Romanesque' style. Painting too was expected to look like the art of the past.

The administration seems to have been aware that the artists exhibiting at the Salon had lowered their sights to appeal to the bourgeois public. A warning note was sounded as it had been in previous years. At the prize-giving ceremony held in the Salon Carré at the Louvre on 14 August, standing on a platform facing Veronese's *Marriage Feast at Cana*, Marshal Vaillant, minister of the emperor's household and of fine arts, rose to his feet to address the assembled dignitaries. Having congratulated the artists for continuing the ancient and glorious tradition of the French School, and having drawn attention to the great number of works deserving a medal, he went on to say:

'Last year, I asked you to direct your studies to the great forms of art. Allow me to insist on this idea. I would like to hope that the taste for beauty which animates you will draw you up to higher regions, and will not allow second-class works, which are still being produced in too large a quantity, to hold back the development of so many talents capable of more serious effort. I well know that it is often difficult to resist public taste; but, after as happy a campaign as the one you have just undertaken, it is a good moment to point out to you the dangers that art runs, if you do not hold out against this urge towards easy compositions that the public encourages and applauds today, only to repudiate them tomorrow.'[4]

The main prize that year went to Cabanel for his portrait of Emperor Napoleon III, in civilian dress as opposed to the usual military uniform, which gave him an aristocratic air and which also managed to convey the stability and prosperity of his regime. It was admired by the imperial family who preferred it to the colder but more penetrating portrait by Hippolyte Flandrin exhibited two years earlier. A medal went to another portrait of Napoleon III, a work in enamel on copper by Claudius Popelin, which showed the emperor in the guise of a victorious Roman, a tribute to the forthcoming publication in three volumes by the emperor of his study of Julius Caesar.

Among the other prize-winners it is interesting to find the name of Degas's old friend Gustave Moreau, who exhibited that year a painting dedicated to the memory of Théodore Chassériau and one of his grand metaphysical creations, *Jason*. Bonnat and Delaunay, both friends from Rome, were among the exhibitors and his teacher Louis Lamothe was represented by a work called *The Origin of Drawing* (subtitled *A Young Greek traces the Outline of his Love's Shadow on a Wall*). James Tissot, a former pupil of Lamothe and another old friend, sent in a painting set in the sixteenth century, which, like Degas's contribution, also showed an abduction. Tissot had fallen under the influence of the Antwerp painter Henrik Leys and his work reveals the attention he devoted to historical accuracy, to the clothes and accoutrements of the period.

James Whistler, who was a friend of Tissot since 1856 when both artists had copied Ingres's *Angélique* in the Louvre, exhibited a remarkable painting which pointed to a growing interest among French and English artists in Japanese art and artifacts, *The Princess from the Land of Porcelain*. It showed a young girl swathed in a kimono standing on a Chinese carpet in front of an oriental screen holding a fan. The exotic East was also the subject of an elaborate painting exhibited by Jean-Léon Gérôme on which he had laboured for three years, a painstaking record of the reception of the Siamese ambassadors by the emperor and his wife at Fontainebleau in 1861. Degas's future collaborators in the first Impressionist exhibition – Renoir, Monet and Berthe Morisot – were, as mentioned earlier, included in the exhibition and their landscapes and Berthe Morisot's still life were favourably received. Courbet, too, escaped the hostility with which his work had been greeted in the previous decade. He was represented by a landscape, *Entrance to the Valley of the Puits-Noir at Dusk*, and a portrait of his old defender Pierre-Joseph Proudhon. Courbet's work was beginning to be accepted both by the public, who liked his landscapes and animal pictures, and also by the administration. That year the painter Comte de Nieuwekerke selected a landscape from his studio for the emperor's collection and the following year the great critic and Realist champion Théophile Thoré pronounced his famous epitaph: 'Well, my dear friend, your business is done, accomplished, ended. Your brave days are over. Here you are accepted, medalled, decorated, glorified, embalmed.'[5]

46. *The misfortunes of the city of Orleans*, 1865. Oil on paper with canvas, $32\frac{1}{2} \times 45$ in (83 × 115 cm). Paris, Louvre

The artist who had replaced Courbet as a controversial figure and who now became a target for the critics and a rallying point for the rebels was Manet. The process had been under way for five years. At the Salon of 1861 his *Spanish Guitar Player* had attracted the attention of Théophile Gautier, and also a group of younger artists including Alphonse Legros, Fantin-Latour and the engraver Félix Bracquemond, all later acquaintances of Degas, who went as a deputation to call on Manet and congratulate him on his success. In their wake came Baudelaire who recognized Manet's originality and who welcomed his interest in subjects found in modern life. Later still came Emile Zola, who found in him an artist of temperament, a painter of great skill and a man of charm and distinction.[6]

At the Salon des Refusés[7] of 1863 Manet had become known to a wider public as a result of the controversy stirred up by the inclusion of his ambitious painting *Déjeuner sur l'Herbe*. The painting seemed to many to be an elaborate art joke. It was attacked both on the grounds of its subject, which was considered immoral, and for the way it was painted in broad simplified colours. *Olympia* seemed to confirm these tendencies. Not only was the public shocked to see a goddess in the form of a courtesan, a naked lady on a bed, they were also horrified by the way in which she had been painted. They disliked the look of her white body silhouetted against the dark background. Even a progressive critic like Jules Castagnary, a supporter of the Realist school, thought *Olympia* looked like a figure on a playing card – a Queen of Tarts, he might have said. It would have been interesting to have heard Degas's comments. He would have recognized the element of parody and plagiarism in *Olympia*. Later he used to say that Manet was 'the most mannered painter in the world, never making a brush stroke without first thinking of the masters',[8] and in 1882, when Manet exhibited the *Bar at the Folies Bergère*, he used Castagnary's attack, calling it a 'playing-card with no depth'. But Degas had a deep respect for Manet's talent: Valéry says that he 'admired and envied the assurance of Manet, whose hand and eye were certainty itself, who could infallibly find in his model the wherewithal to convey all force and completely realize his aim'.[9] It was an approach totally different from his own: he had toiled over his Salon entry, drawing and redrawing the figures in his composition.

Despite the disappointing lack of attention given to his picture, Degas took part in the next five Salons. He no longer sent in history paintings but portraits, a steeplechase scene and a picture based on a ballet of the period. On the whole he was not at home in the Salon. His art was too personal and subtle to be seen to advantage in that crowded and competitive atmosphere and his work was repeatedly hung in inappropriate positions and in the wrong company. One portrait was placed so high that the critic Ernest Chesneau said he was unable to judge its merits. Degas became dissatisfied with the Salon not because he had difficulty in having his work accepted (which, with one or two exceptions, was not the case), but because he disliked the way the exhibition was hung. In April 1870 he addressed a letter to the *Paris Journal* making some specific recommendations:

'It seems to me that the organization of the salon requires several alterations. . . .

1. Hang pictures in no more than two rows and leave a space between them of at least 8 to 12 inches, otherwise neighbouring pictures detract from one another.

2. Take over a few rooms of drawings to accommodate the prunings from rule 1.

3. Stand large and small screens about, as the English did for the Universal Exhibition, and hang on them the displaced drawings; distribute them around the two large rooms known as dumps, or elsewhere. You have seen how effective this very simple method is – the drawings would be brought back from the wilderness and mixed with the paintings, as they deserve to be.

I even think that, by pushing the seats further back in the ordinary rooms, there would be room on these screens for a certain number of paintings. Leighton, who has at least the same standing in England as Cabanel has here, had a painting hung on a screen and it didn't seem at all demeaning.

4. Every exhibitor will have the right to withdraw his work after a few days; for nothing should force him to leave on view something which makes him blush and lets him down. And then it's not part of a trophy. Symmetry has nothing to do with an exhibition. If one picture goes you just have to move the remaining ones nearer each other. I believe it's a fair rule to allow these few days, and that after this nothing further should be allowed to be taken away.

5. With only two rows of pictures the following should happen: the exhibitor can specify on his label which of the two rows he wants to be hung in. The dado, that horrible dado, source of all our disagreements, will no longer be a favour or a risk he is forced to take. It will be chosen for one or gladly passed up for another: one painting is made to be seen up high, another to be viewed lower down.

It's well known that the average height of pictures which really need to be above the dado is perhaps three or four feet or less, including frame. When trying for the second row, the exhibitor will therefore simply ask to be placed 7 or 8 feet from the floor.

6. The large marbles, the weight and handling of which are a great business, can stay on the floor, but I beg you to scatter them around at random. As for the medallions, busts, small groups and so on, you should put these high up on shelves or on screens. If the normal space isn't sufficient, open up some other rooms. You surely would not be refused.

I could go on.

There's been a rumour that you're going to divide the paintings into three categories: the first to be hung on the dado, the second above, and the third even higher. It's just a bad joke, isn't it?'[10]

His letter went unnoticed, and after 1870 he gave up sending his work to the Salon.

During his years as an exhibitor, that is from 1865 to 1870, Degas's art underwent a transformation. The process originated partly within himself, and from his long training and inner need to find an original vision, and partly from outside as a result of new friendships, new ideas in circulation and new techniques such as photography. There is no single answer to the question why Degas gave up history painting to become a Realist, only a series of clues.

(ii)

Influence is perhaps too strong a word, example might be more appropriate: in either case Manet must be cited as one of the principal factors behind Degas's transformation. They met in about 1862. The story goes that Degas was copying the *Infanta Margarita* by Velásquez in the Louvre, and Manet, who was a devotee of Spanish painting – he was once nicknamed Don Manet y Courbetos y Zurbarán de las Batignolas – complimented him on his work and the friendship began. The story is corroborated by the etching based on the Velásquez which Degas made at the time and by Manet's somewhat disparaging remark, 'When I was painting modern life, Degas was still painting Semiramis'[11] (plates 48 and 49).

Two years older than Degas and more worldly, Manet was in a position to introduce him to his wide circle of friends and followers and to café life. Manet had great charm and style and Degas was one among many to fall under his spell. It is perhaps significant that in the mid-1860s Degas made numerous portraits and studies of his friend (plates 50, 55 and 81) in different poses, showing Manet at home sprawled on a sofa listening to his wife at the piano, or at the races, but there have survived no portraits of Degas by Manet. In discussions at the Café Guerbois where Manet and his friends used to meet, it was Manet who, according to the critic and supporter Théodore Duret, was 'the dominating figure; with his animation, his flashing wit, his sound judgements on matters of art, he gave the tone to the discussions.'[12] Degas, who was hot-tempered, refrained from entering into these public discussions and preferred to confine himself to a few well-chosen words, an ability which soon earned him a fearsome reputation.

48. Sketch after Velásquez's *Infanta Margarita* in the Louvre, 1861–2. Etching, 5¼ × 4¼ in (13.2 × 10.8 cm). Paris, BN

Intellectually Degas was Manet's equal; but he did not have Manet's technical fluency and inspirational approach to painting. One of Manet's often repeated sayings was: 'The only true way is to paint straight off what you see. If you've caught it, all right. If not, then try again. All the rest is humbug.'[13] On the other hand, one of Degas's most quoted sayings states the opposite: 'No art was ever less spontaneous than mine. What I do is the result of reflection and study of the great masters; of inspiration, spontaneity, temperament I know nothing.'[14]

Although Manet was an instinctive painter and Degas was methodical and intellectual in his approach, they both believed that the importance of a painting lies not in the subject but in the artist's vision. They both claimed that perception was more important than observation and they both argued that the artist should train his memory. Manet's advice was: 'Cultivate your memory, for nature will never give you anything more than references. This is like a guard rail which keeps you from falling into banality . . . It is necessary always to remain master and to do that which amuses.'[15] Degas advised the painter Georges Jeanniot also to work from memory rather than nature so that 'you reproduce only what has

struck you, that is, the essential; in that way your memories and your imagination are liberated from the tyranny that nature holds over them.'[16]

What drew the two together was not so much artistic agreement as a common social background. Renoir observed to the dealer Ambroise Vollard, 'They were on good terms. Beneath Manet's "boulevard" manners, Degas found a man of good education and of good middle-class principles like his own. But as with all great friendships, theirs was not without frequent quarrels and reconciliations.'[17]

A famous incident occurred over a portrait Degas made of Manet and his wife (now in a collection in Japan). For some reason or other Manet disliked the depiction of his wife (it may have made her look too fat) and he sliced off the right-hand third of the canvas leaving just his wife's back. When Degas came to collect his portrait after one of their many quarrels, he was horrified: 'I had a fearful shock when I saw it like that at his house,' he told Vollard. 'I picked it up and walked off without even saying good-bye. When I reached home I took down the little still life he had given me, and sent it back to him with a note saying, "Sir, I am sending back your *Plums*".'[18] As a footnote to this story and as a testament to Degas's underlying respect for Manet it is worth noting that he later regretted his action: 'The trouble is that he soon sold the *Plums*. It was a beautiful little canvas . . .', and when Manet died he admitted, 'He was greater than we thought.'[19]

Between two great painters there was bound to be

49. EDOUARD MANET, sketch after Velásquez's *Infanta Margarita* in the Louvre. Etching. London, courtesy of Sotheby Parke Bernet

50. *Edouard Manet*, watercolour. Formerly collection Rouart

that they frequented, and they both painted the writers who were their main supporters, Manet painting Zola in 1868 and Degas Duranty in 1879. But perhaps nothing emphasizes more clearly the differences between them than the fact that Manet throughout his career painted the most delicious still lifes, while Degas, with the exception of one minor oil done in his student days, never painted one. The reason lies partly in the fact that Manet was interested in 'pure' painting and Degas, a draughtsman by training, was more concerned about 'pure' art, and partly in the more prosaic fact that Manet was a bon viveur while Degas had a delicate stomach. Valéry writes that meals with Degas were an ordeal: 'Degas had a dread of intestinal obstruction or inflammation. There was a faultless insipidity in the all-too-innocent veal and the macaroni cooked in plain water, served, very slowly, by old Zoe [Degas's maid].'[20]

A similar difference can be seen in their attitudes to dress. They both wore conventional bourgeois black, and were not to be seen on the streets without their silk top hats, gloves and canes but, unlike Degas, Manet took great pains about his dress. He was a true *flâneur* and lived up to Baudelaire's idea of a modern hero, the dandy who combines coolness and self-sufficiency with a sense of superiority. Degas, who was timid and shy, cool-hearted but given to periods of explosive rage, was 'influenced' by Manet who introduced him to a different and more sophisticated world. In the end, however, it is their similarities rather than their differences which are worth re-membering. They were both snobs, both were proud, both were stylists and neither was interested in conventional morality. They painted their subjects without social or religious implications; both seem to say 'this is life, this is my painting, take it or leave it'.

Degas seems to have attracted artists who were dandies and high livers, men of style and wit. Most of those who became his friends in the 1860s fit that description – James Tissot, Alfred Stevens and the irrepressible James Whistler. Although there is no label by which to describe them, they and their friends, Alphonse Legros, Fantin-Latour and others, all broke free from historical and academic subjects to paint modern life. All in a broad sense of the term were Realists, but Realists of the *beau-monde*. Some were already highly successful socially and financially: Stevens earned large sums from his paintings and lived in great style in a house in the rue des Martyrs surrounded by eighteenth-century furniture, tapestries, oriental carpets and a Chinese boudoir, and Tissot was sufficiently well-established in Parisian social life to be commissioned to paint a select

an element of rivalry, but they never developed a working relationship as happened between Monet and Renoir at Argenteuil in 1872 or between Van Gogh and Gauguin at Arles in 1889. They were drawn, however, to the same subjects. Thus, they both painted racing scenes, but from different points of view and at different times, Degas starting in 1862 and concentrating on moments of quiet just before the start of the race, Manet in studies about 1864 showing the horses at full gallop coming down the home stretch. They both found subjects in the cafés

52. JAMES TISSOT,
Portrait of Degas,
Paris, BN (Cabinet
des Estampes)

OPPOSITE:
51. *James Tissot*,
1868. Oil on canvas,
59½ × 44 in (151 ×
112 cm). New York,
Metropolitan
Museum (Rogers
Fund, 1939)

gentlemen's club, Le Cercle de la rue Royale, which featured Charles Haas, the model for Proust's dandy hero Swann.

Tissot was also a pupil of Lamothe and his friendship with Degas went back to their student days. Their affection for each other can be seen in a letter Tissot sent to Degas from Venice between 1860 and 1862:

'And then I couldn't stay any longer, without letting you know better than I could in person how grateful I am to you and how touched I was by the kindly friendship you showed me during the last few days when I was ill, as well as for the farewell you bade me – that touched me particularly, and I congratulate myself more than ever on knowing someone like you – enough of these sentiments.'[21]

During his days of what he called his *vagabondage* in Italy Tissot, like Moreau, was greatly impressed by the Carpaccios in Venice:

'I am deep in the Carpaccios and can't get out of them. What a heart this painter had – the way he portrays that life of St Ursula is most touching – you should see the nobility of the fiancé's farewell, who is aware that he is on a mission of marriage – the audience at the presentation of the ambassadors, the departure, the return . . . it's admirable – I won't talk to you about other painters, you can more or less see them in Paris.'[22]

Later, on his return to Paris he first painted historical genre pictures and then in the mid-1860s he gave up historical subjects for painting women of Paris and London going about their daily lives. Like Whistler, he used to dress his models in the oriental costumes which began to appear on the market in Paris in the early 1860s. When Rossetti visited Paris

in 1864 he went to La Porte Chinoise, a shop specializing in Far Eastern wares, and found that Tissot had already snapped up the Japanese kimonos.

Degas was aware of his friend's interests and the portrait of him painted in 1866–68 (plate 51) is, as Reff has pointed out,[23] a pot-pourri of references to Tissot's taste and paintings. It is also a masterly portrayal of an intriguing character who, like Manet, was something of a dandy and is seen in a studio poised nonchalantly on a chair, his top hat and silk-lined cloak thrown on a table behind him, with an expression which is worldly, almost world-weary. Tissot's head is set off against and contrasted to a portrait of Frederick the Wise attributed to Cranach, a reference to Tissot's interest in the German primitives, which Degas shared. Above him is a painting with Japanese figures inspired by Japanese prints, an allusion to both painters' Far Eastern enthusiasms. Two other pictures in the studio seem to refer to the picnic paintings of Manet and Monet, a subject which Tissot had also painted in the mid-1860s. The third work, Reff suggests,[24] is a reference to both artists' interest in Venetian art, more particularly Degas's enthusiasm for the Venetian colourists, which he was then studying and copying.

Tissot never developed into the spontaneous artist his *Déjeuner sur l'Herbe* suggested. But in his way he became a master of detail, careful observation, mood, colours and tones. Degas respected his powers of observation and on at least one occasion sought his advice.[25] Tissot saw Degas's *Interior* while it was still in progress and left his comments on the back of an envelope which is now in the Bibliothèque Nationale. Degas wanted him to join him in forming a salon of Realists, but Tissot refused. After 1874 their ways parted and Degas was upset to learn that Tissot had sold one of his (Degas's) paintings. But at this period there was a close rapport between them and Degas found in him a man of the world and an artist with whom he could discuss the Italian and German primitives, Japanese art and such mundane matters as how to find buyers for his work and a dealer in London to represent him. Tissot, like Degas, was only interested in people, showing little concern for landscape painting, and, like Degas, never seems to have painted a still life.

It is a pity that Degas did not paint Whistler. It would be interesting to see what references he would have made to Whistler's passion for blue and white china, for Japanese art, for Vermeer and Velásquez. Whistler also had the advantage of a magnificent appearance, but Degas seems to have found his pretensions in this area rather ridiculous. William Rothenstein recalled that Degas was the only man of whom Whistler was a little afraid. ' "Whistler, you behave as though you have no talent," Degas had said once to him; and again when Whistler, chin high, monocle in his eye, frock-coated, top-hatted, and carrying a tall cane, walked triumphantly into a restaurant where Degas was sitting: "Whistler, you have forgotten your muff." Again, about Whistler's flat-brimmed hat, which Whistler fancied, Degas said: "Yes, it suits you very well; but *that* won't get us back Alsace and Lorraine!" '[26]

Whistler's movements between London and Paris make it difficult to pin down the moment when their friendship developed. They could have met either through Manet or through Tissot, who were both friends of Whistler. It seems likely, however, that in the 1860s they knew each other more by reputation and by their paintings than through personal contact.

Degas no doubt saw Whistler's *Woman in White* at the Salon des Refusés in 1863 and he must also have noticed *The Princess from the Land of Porcelain* at the Salon of 1865. He made a pencil sketch of Whistler's *Symphony in White No. 3*, which is dated 1865-67. But it would be more fascinating to know for sure whether he was aware of Whistler's earlier domestic scenes, like the painting based on a Vermeer, *At the Piano* (plate 53) of 1858, and the *Music Room* of 1860. Degas's later statement that when they were both beginning they were on the same path, 'the road from Holland',[27] implies some knowledge of Whistler's early forays into Realism; or it could mean that they both independently and early in their careers began to take an interest in Dutch seventeenth-century art.

In the 1850s and early 1860s the Dutch genre

OPPOSITE:
54. *The collector of prints*, 1866. Oil on canvas, 21 × 15¾ in (52 × 39 cm). New York, Metropolitan Museum (Bequest of Mrs H. O. Havemeyer, 1929)

53. JAMES WHISTLER, *At the piano*, c.1859. Oil on canvas. Cincinnati, Taft Museum (Louise Taft Semple Bequest)

Degas

55. Study for a
portrait of Edouard
Manet, c.1864.
Black chalk and
estompe, 13 × 9 in
(33 × 23 cm). New
York, Metropolitan
Museum (Rogers
Fund, 1918)

56. THEODORE
FANTIN-LATOUR,
sketch for *A studio
in the Batignolles
quarter*, 1870. Conté
crayon on paper,
11½ × 15½ in (28.9 ×
38.8 cm). New
York, Metropolitan
Museum (Gift of
Mrs Helena M.
Loewel, in memory
of her brother,
Charles W.
Kraushaar, 1919)

painters were studied with increased enthusiasm by French critics and painters – these artists including landscape painters of the Barbizon school and painters of rural life, like Millet and Courbet, and also society painters, like Stevens and Tissot. Théophile Thoré, who was one of the outstanding critics of the 1850s and an early champion of Courbet, had done much to revive interest in the Dutch school and was largely responsible for the rediscovery of Vermeer; he was also an early admirer of Stevens, whose paintings seemed to him to hark back to the *petits maîtres* of the seventeenth century, Gabriel Metsu and Gerard Terborch.

Degas knew Stevens; he was a godfather to Stevens's first daughter and he had the opportunity of seeing him with Manet and meeting him at the Café Guerbois which Stevens sometimes attended. Affable and amusing, Stevens had a wide circle of friends among writers and painters. One moment he could be found in the company of the socialist Courbet (who painted his portrait), the next he could be seen in the drawing-room of the Princesse Mathilde, the Vicomtesse de Pourtales and the Princesse Metternich, who lent him their dresses for his models. Stevens's speciality was the portrayal of women and their costumes in sumptuous settings. Jacques-Emile Blanche, who knew both Degas and Stevens,

maintains that Degas admired the Belgian artist's technical virtuosity and was not afraid to learn from him. Stevens's influence, however, seems to have been confined to matters of detail, to the placing of figures in a room, to the gentle even light with which his domestic scenes are rendered. Degas did not share his sense of feminine charm nor did he show any interest in the magnificent and extravagant *haute couture* in which Stevens delighted, Degas being more concerned at this time with character than appearance.

Fantin-Latour was another artist who took 'the road from Holland' in the 1860s. He was one of the first French painters to become a friend of Whistler and he and Legros formed Whistler's original society of three.[28] He was also among the deputation which called on Manet after his success at the Salon of 1861 and throughout the 1860s he remained within Manet's circle. His admiration was made manifest in the portrait of Manet surrounded by his colleagues, *A Studio in the Batignolles Quarter* (1870). Two earlier sketches for this painting show a shadowy figure of a man in a top hat which was presumably meant to represent Degas (plate 56). But Degas was dropped from the finished work, perhaps indicating a quarrel between Manet and Degas or some kind of falling-out between Fantin-Latour and Degas. All these artists were drawn to the representation of contemporary life, which was no longer a matter of controversy. Stevens was once urged to apply his talents to higher things (his devotion to women was considered *risqué*), but he waved aside the prospects of a gold medal at the Salon, 'Keep your medals,' he replied. 'As for me I'll keep my genre.'[29]

Outside France paintings of contemporary life had been accepted a decade earlier. John Everett Millais, for instance, and the pre-Raphaelites had found their subjects not only in medieval romances but in the Victorian middle-class world in which they lived. Degas could have heard about their work from Tissot and Whistler, and he was able to see it for himself at the International Exhibition in Paris of 1867, where Millais's *Eve of St Agnes* or *Lady in Green* was much admired. Degas formed a high opinion of Millais's talents and asked Tissot to bring them together.[30]

In Germany Adolphe von Menzel had been painting naturalistic landscapes and domestic interior scenes from the mid-1840s. His work began to be known in Paris in the 1860s and Degas and his friend Duranty both became enthusiastic admirers of the German artist (although at what date it is hard to say). In 1883, when Menzel had an exhibition at Goupil's gallery in Paris, Degas forced Pissarro and Mary Cassatt to come to the exhibition to look at a painting called *A Supper Ball* which he particularly admired. Afterwards Degas dashed off a copy from memory. Pissarro was much more impressed by Degas's copy than by the original which he thought was a 'dirty-looking dark picture, executed with care, it is true, but totally lacking in art and delicacy.'[31]

Given his friendships with Manet, Tissot and Stevens, and the general interest in France in the domestic art of the Dutch masters as well as a growing awareness in France of Realist painting in neighbouring countries, it was inevitable that Degas should find himself caught up in a general wave of interest in contemporary subjects. This wave did not affect painters alone. It also carried along the great novelists of the Second Empire, Flaubert, the Goncourt brothers, Zola and Daudet – which leads to the complex question: to what extent did their novels, many of which were published in the 1860s, influence Degas's viewpoint?[32]

(iii)

In conversation with Daniel Halévy Degas maintained that the painter was superior to the writer: 'In a single brush-stroke we can say more than a writer in a whole volume.'[33] But by the time Halévy began to keep a record of Degas, the old friendships which he had enjoyed with writers during the 1860s and 1870s had withered: animosities had taken the place of alliances and the competitiveness which writers and painters now felt for each other coloured Degas's view. Nevertheless, Degas was still prepared to admit to one visitor that the Goncourts' novel *Manette Salomon*, published in 1867, was a direct source for his interest in contemporary subject-matter. In one of the famous passages from this novel the artist protagonist Coriolis makes a claim that all ages carry within themselves a beauty of some kind:

'The feeling, the intuition for the contemporary, for the scene that rubs shoulders with you, for the present in which you sense the trembling of your emotions and something of yourself – everything is there for the artist. The nineteenth century not produce a painter! – but that is inconceivable – A century that has endured so much, the great century of scientific restlessness and anxiety for the truth – There must be found a line that would precisely render life, embrace from close at hand the individual, the particular, a living human, inward line in which there would be something of a modelling by Houdon, a preliminary pastel sketch by Latour, a stroke by Gavarni – A drawing truer than all drawing – a drawing – more human.'[34]

Although the Goncourts did not know Degas at this point, it is uncanny how this cry for a living human 'line', for a drawing truer than all drawing, seems to refer directly to Degas. And it is perhaps not surprising that when Edmond de Goncourt called on Degas in his studio in February 1874, he came to the conclusion that he was 'among all the artists I have met so far, the one who has best been able, in representing modern life, to catch the spirit of that life'.[35]

To a large extent the Goncourts must be given the credit for extending the range of subject-matter available for the novelist in France. In the preface to their novel *Germinie Lacerteux* (1864) they asked 'whether what one calls the "lower classes" have no right to the novel, whether the society, below society, the common people have the right to remain under the weight of literary interdict and of the scorn of writers who have, up to now, kept silence on the heart and spirit it might have'. In drawing attention to the possibility of finding subjects among the poor urban classes, the Goncourt brothers looked for a stylist like themselves, a dispassionate observer. They were not looking for a moralist or proselytizer. And this attitude does seem to have struck a responsive chord in Degas.

Goncourt liked to claim that Degas's choice of laundresses as a subject was derived from *Manette Salomon*, but, as Reff has shown,[36] this is not substantiated by the book itself; but the Goncourts' belief that their novels had influenced Zola's choice of subject has greater substance. Zola's first great success as a novelist was *Thérèse Raquin* (1867). It was a thriller set in the world of poor shopkeepers and impoverished clerks. Despite the squalor of the setting, the tale has a stark and compelling beauty, and one memorable scene became, as Reff again has noted,[37] the chief inspiration for one of Degas's greatest paintings of this decade, *The Interior* (plate 66). In the defence of his novel Zola explained his intentions: 'I had only one desire; given a highly-sexed man and an unsatisfied woman, to uncover the animal side of them and see that alone, then throw them together in a violent drama and note down with scrupulous care the sensations and actions of these creatures. I simply applied to two living bodies the analytical method the surgeons apply to corpses.'[38]

The mention of 'the analytical method of the surgeons' leads to the common interest in scientific method shared by the Goncourts, Zola, Flaubert and, in turn, Degas. For both writers and painters the scientist or surgeon was somebody to be emulated. Zola had studied the work of one of the most brilliant scientific minds of the day, Claude Bernard, whose *Introduction to the Study of Experimental Medicine* was published in 1865; and Zola liked to believe that his novels were a form of sociological experiment, conducted with the objectivity of a scientist.[39]

Degas had a similar respect for scientific method and was a keen student of the half-science, half-art, physiognomy, the belief that character can be deduced from the features of the face and body. In his student days he had followed the standard practice of copying *têtes d'expression*, schematized heads in which emotions such as rage, pain and laughter are rendered by means of exaggerated facial expression. He also read the work of the Swiss poet and theologian Johann-Kaspar Lavater, whose *Physiognomic Fragments* appeared in 1775–78, and he presumably read Edmond Duranty's article of 1867 on physiognomy[40] which maintained that Lavater's theories were no longer relevant to modern sensibility. In an 1868 notebook Degas stated the problem as he saw it: 'Make of the *tête d'expression* (in academic parlance) a study of modern feelings. It is Lavater, but a Lavater more relative, as it were, with accessory symbols at times.'[41]

The belief that a man's character resides in his face and his physique was shared by Realist writers, like Zola, who went to great pains to describe the physical appearance of their characters. Zola even began his defence of Manet with a careful description of his appearance.[42] This attitude to description, the scientific surgical approach, was something Degas and the novelists of the 1860s both reached independently

and simultaneously, and it formed part of the cultural atmosphere of the time. Flaubert's rather earlier *Madame Bovary* (1857) is perhaps the work which best exemplifies, and marks one of the high-points, in the objective analytical method.[43] The critic Charles-Augustin Sainte-Beuve likened the author to a man of science who remains a completely impersonal observer: 'Son and brother of distinguished doctors, M. Gustave Flaubert holds the pen as others do the scalpel.'[44]

There is no record of Flaubert and Degas having met and there is no definite indication that they knew each other's work, although Degas's niece maintained that her uncle read and reread Flaubert's novels.[45] (It would certainly seem unlikely that he did not know them.) But the parallels between them are remarkable and are worth stating because they indicate how two artists born into bourgeois society in the first half of the nineteenth century developed a common approach to subject-matter and style. Both placed the pursuit of art above the comfort of their lives and both became in time unrelieved pessimists.

Flaubert, like Degas, was born when the Romantic movement was in its final flowering. From early on he decided to devote his life to art, although he was forced for a brief period to study law. But life outside art had no appeal for him. 'I was born with little faith in happiness,' he wrote. 'When I was young, I had a complete presentiment of life. It was like a nauseous smell of cooking escaping from a vent. You don't need to eat it to know that it will make you sick.'[46] Flaubert felt himself destined for unhappiness and seems to have deliberately fallen in love with a lady who was unattainable and remote. Marriage, anyway, was out of the question because it would have interfered with his art, which was writing. Where sex was concerned, he preferred to look for it in the context of the brothel. His voyage to Egypt, like Degas's trip to New Orleans, cured him of any curiosity about foreign places and convinced him that the artist must find his subjects within his own experience and imagination. To his writing he devoted an attention which was fanatical: he toiled at his work, spending weeks looking for the right phrase, becoming a puritanical stylist and an indefatigable researcher. Although an affectionate son, he despised the bourgeois world from which he came, hating its conventions and materialism. He developed a pessimistic attitude to politics and believed democracy to be a hopeless illusion. His answer to the disillusionment he felt was to seek not happiness but detachment. He also found satisfaction in the observation of human futility, and the romantic urge, which had led him as a young man to seek fulfilment as an artist, was transformed in his later years into a belief in the objectivity of scientific realism.

Early in his life Degas too seems to have abandoned the search for domestic happiness and found solace in becoming a detached observer of the human scene. There is a strong 'voyeuristic' streak in both Degas and Flaubert, and also in the writings of the Goncourt brothers. At times they enjoyed the company of their fellow men, going to dinner-parties, sitting in cafés and restaurants, or visiting brothels, but these were excursions; their real life lay in their studios or at their desks. Again it seems to be the case that Degas and the writers of the 1860s seem to have reached a similar point of view, not because there was any direct causal link between one art form and the other, but because they had similar personalities and came from similar social backgrounds.

(iv)

There were two developments in the cultural life of Paris in the 1860s which did have a direct effect on Degas's art and his Realist paintings of the late 1860s and the 1870s: the discovery of Japanese prints and artifacts at the beginning of the decade and the growth of photography, particularly outdoor snapshot photography. At times it is hard to say whether Degas's compositions – his use of acute angles, looming foregrounds and abrupt cropping-effects at the edges – have their origin in one or the other medium.[47]

The interest in Japanese art taken by French artists in the nineteenth century is a favourite topic for thesis writers and the same facts tend to be repeated: Bracquemond's discovery of a Japanese print in a packing case, the opening of the shop called La Porte

57. Madame Camus with a fan, 1870. Oil on canvas, 28¾ × 36 in (73 × 92 cm). Washington, DC, National Gallery of Art (Chester Dale Collection)

58. Study for portrait of Mme Hertel (*A woman with chrysanthemums*), 1865. Pencil, 14 × 9 in (35.7 × 23.3 cm). Cambridge, Mass., Courtesy of the Fogg Art Museum, Harvard University (Bequest of Meta and Paul J. Sachs)

OVERLEAF:
59. *A woman with chrysanthemums* (*Mme Hertel*), 1865. Oil on canvas, 29 × 36½ in (74 × 92 cm). New York, Metropolitan Museum (Bequest of Mrs H. O. Havemeyer, 1929)

What attracted Degas, however, to Japanese art was not its exotic quality but the print-maker's use of line and contour. Here was a draughtsman's art to which a pupil of Ingres could respond and which could be adapted to his own use. At the same time he was struck by the Japanese sense of perspective, the use of silhouetted objects or people in the foreground which partly obscure the landscape or scene in the distance. It corresponds to the way we see things in real life. In the theatre, for example, our view of the stage can be partially obstructed by a column, the front end of the box, the spectators' heads in front, or even the musicians' instruments in the orchestra pit, particularly the distinctive scroll of a double bass. Degas began to make use of these compositional devices towards the end of the 1860s and with even

60. DISDERI, *Carte-de-visite* photograph of the Prince and Princesse de Metternich, c.1860

61. *Princesse Pauline de Metternich*, c.1861. Oil on canvas, 16 × 11½ in (40.5 × 29 cm). London, National Gallery

62. Sketch for portrait of Yves Gobillard (Berthe Morisot's sister), 1869. Pencil

Chinoise, the use of Japanese costumes by Whistler, Tissot and Monet to dress up their models, followed by a later period when French artists assimilated Japanese compositions into the fabric of their work.[48] The event which seems to mark the start of this craze was the arrival of the Japanese ambassadors in Paris in 1862 to ratify a trade treaty first made in 1855. Their appearance in Paris in full ceremonial costume, armed with swords (photographed by Nadar), caused a sensation, and within a year quantities of Japanese goods began to appear on the market. In 1863 the Goncourts bought a Japanese album of erotica and wrote enthusiastically about their discovery, praising: 'the violence of the lines, the unexpected conjunctions, the arrangements of the accessories, the caprice in the poses and the objects, the picturesqueness, and, so to speak, the landscape of the genital parts. Looking at them, I think of Greek art, boredom in perfection, an art that will never free itself from the crime of being "academic".'[49]

greater effect in his theatrical subjects and ballet paintings of the 1870s.

Photography became a commercial business in France in the 1850s. By then technical developments were sufficiently well advanced to allow the photographer to market his wares and his talents. One of the main areas of commerce was in portraiture and Eugène Disderi is credited with the idea of pasting photographs on to visiting cards (plate 60). It was one of these cartes-de-visite which Degas used as the basis of his portrait of Princesse Metternich (plate 61). He may have also used one for his painting *A Woman with Chrysanthemums* (plate 59) and, as Aaron Scharf has pointed out,[50] he probably based his *Self-Portrait Saluting* (plate 20) on another.

Studio portraiture was a clumsy and time-consuming process. The sitter had to hold his position for long periods and the result in many cases was a frozen stiff expression. But by 1858 it became possible to take photographs with an exposure of 1/50th of a second and in the 1860s snapshot photography, mainly of city views, began to appear on the market. These views often caught people in full motion and sometimes the photographer was not able to fit everything in, so that people and objects were cut or 'cropped' by the edge of the photographic plate. Degas was attracted by this effect, and made use of it in his paintings, noticeably in those with outdoor subjects, like the *Carriage at the Races* (plate 84) of 1870 and the picture of Vicomte Lepic with his daughters at the place de la Concorde (plate 155) of 1875.

OVERLEAF, LEFT:
63. *Sulking (The banker)*, 1875-6. Oil on canvas, 12¾ × 18¼ in (32 × 46 cm). New York, Metropolitan Museum (Bequest of Mrs H. O. Havemeyer, 1929)

OVERLEAF, RIGHT:
64. *The orchestra of the Opéra*, 1868-9. Oil on canvas, 21 × 13¾ in (53 × 45 cm). Paris, Louvre

Degas

(v)

A Woman with Chrysanthemums (plate 59), which is signed and dated 1865 over an earlier date which seems to read 1858, is generally regarded as a work which marks a turning point in Degas's development.[51] It is an enchanting and unusual work: indeed part of its charm lies in the asymmetrical composition of the picture which has the woman on the far right of the canvas, the centre being dominated by a magnificent arrangement of chrysanthemums, painted in hot fiery colours reminiscent of some of Delacroix's flower pieces. It has been suggested that Van Dyck's *Self-Portrait with Sunflower* may have prompted this composition. Degas had been an admirer of Van Dyck since his visit to Genoa and it is possible that he studied engravings of this work after his return to Paris. It has also been suggested that Courbet's painting of a girl arranging flowers, *The Trellis* (1863), may have served as a model. But Degas's picture differs from both these works and from most other paintings of women arranging flowers (which was a favourite motif for nineteenth-century artists) in that his woman ignores the flowers on the table beside her and stares with a dream-like expression into a space beyond the picture frame. The gesture of her hand to her chin is also a familiar device and was used by Ingres; but while other artists used the gesture to accentuate the delicate curves of their sitters' chins, to elicit their charm and grace, Degas's woman uses it to conceal her beauty – she seems hesitant and reluctant to compete with the beauty of the flowers next to her.

A Woman with Chrysanthemums is also significant in that it marks the beginning of a series of portraits and studies of women whom Degas met beyond his immediate family circle, and as such it indicates his growing awareness of life and subjects outside his home and his studio. For this he had Manet to thank: it was at his house that he met many of the sitters of the 1860s – Yves Gobillard (plate 62), who was the eldest of the three Morisot daughters and sister of the painter Berthe Morisot, Mme Lisle, Mme Loubens, Mme Camus, the wife of a physician and herself a talented pianist, and Mlle Dubourg who was a painter and who later married Fantin-Latour. Although many of his subjects project charm and vivacity, none could be called a beauty. Degas did not have Manet's eye for female attractions nor did he share Tissot's and Stevens's interest in the magnificent costumes of the Second Empire. The clothes worn by his sitters are mainly those a woman would wear in the street, out shopping or on day-time visits. They are often treated in a summary fashion

and the detail is confined to the head and deportment.

With women Degas proved to be impossibly gauche. Manet observed to Berthe Morisot that Degas was 'incapable of loving a woman, even of telling her so'. Berthe once had the uncomfortable experience of sitting next to the painter who began by paying her compliments but ended by preaching a sermon on the theme that women are the desolation of the just man.[52] Still, she respected him and was a little put out to notice him on another evening at Manet's paying attention to Mme Lisle and Mme Loubens: 'I must admit that I was a little annoyed when a man whom I consider to be very intelligent deserted me to pay compliments to two silly women.'[53]

In his notebooks of this period Degas drafted a lighthearted poem which expressed his amorous thoughts better than he could in real life:

> *Vive, sensible, un peu coquette*
> *Suivons la gloire et les plaisirs*
> *C'est à la fois la violette*
> *La rose amante du zéphyr*
> *Elle s'emporte, elle s'apaise*
> *Elle pleure et sourit tour à tour*
> *En même temps elle est française*
> *Et constante dans son amour.*[54]★

But a few pages later he quotes a passage from one of the seventeenth-century writer Charles de St-Evremont's ethical observations: 'Happy the soul which could entirely give up certain passions, and would only promise itself others. It would be without fear, sadness, hate or jealousy, it would desire without fervour, hope without anxiety, and enjoy life without rapture.'[55]

Degas seems to have been frightened of women, and possibly of sex too. Like Flaubert, he perhaps felt that an involvement with a woman would interfere with his work. In many respects his attitude to marriage was typical of the time. Men brought up in the bourgeois tradition tended to regard women either as mothers, inviolate goddesses, the upholders of morality and religion, or as whores; you had children with the one and sex with the other. This was the great age of the courtesan, and Zola's Comte Muffat in *Nana*, who finds little satisfaction with his wife and falls for the charm of the courtesan, is just one illustration from fiction. Women as portrayed in Degas's paintings also fall into two categories: they are either relations or the wives and daughters of friends, or they are working-class girls who iron, tend shop, dance or work in a brothel – in other

★*Lively, sensitive, a little flirtatious, Let's follow glory and pleasure. She's the violet, She's the rose caressed by the breeze, She flares up, she calms down, She smiles and weeps in turn And still she is a Frenchwoman And constant in her love.*

OPPOSITE:
65. *La répétition de chant* (*The rehearsal*), c.1873. Oil on canvas, $31\frac{3}{4} \times 25\frac{1}{2}$ in (81 × 65 cm). Washington, DC, Dumbarton Oaks Collection

OVERLEAF:
66. *Interior* (*The rape*), 1868–9. Oil on canvas, $31\frac{1}{2} \times 45\frac{3}{4}$ in (81 × 116 cm). Philadelphia, Henry P. McIlhenny Collection

73

67. *Degas's father listening to Pagans,* c.1869. Oil on canvas, 21¼ × 15¼ in (54 × 39 cm). Paris, Louvre

words, objects to be treated objectively as an artist might paint a landscape or still life. They are not objects of desire.

On rare occasions, mainly when he was away from home, Degas toyed with the idea of marriage, but he was probably put off by the responsibilities of a bourgeois marriage – children, nurses, servants and the household. Marriage, if it was to be arranged correctly, also entailed financial independence which, while his father was alive, he was probably not in a position to enjoy and which, after his father's death, proved impossible. The bachelor status among artists and writers, and among the bourgeoisie as a whole, was more common than it is today – Delacroix never married, for example – and it would be wrong to assume just from Degas's cultivation of misogyny that he disliked women or that he was a secret homosexual.[56] Degas was often asked why he never married and, as expected, he had the perfect reply: 'I, marry? Oh, I could never bring myself to do it. I would have been in mortal misery all my life for fear my wife might say, "That's a pretty little thing," after I had finished a picture.'[57]

One of the main attractions of an evening at the Manets', which was also true in most bourgeois families of the time, was music. No respectable home was complete without its large cumbersome piano, and no lady was considered educated unless she could display some musical gift. Mme Manet, however, was more than just a talented pianist, she was an excellent musician and her salon attracted many of the leading musicians of the day. According to his biographer Antonin Proust,[58] Manet himself was bored by music; he was too restless and lacked concentration. Their different attitudes to music were nicely caught by Degas in the portrait which Manet cut up (see p. 54); the surviving fragment in which Manet straddles a sofa shows how successful Degas was in capturing his energetic personality. So convincing a portrait was it that George Moore later wrote: 'Those who knew Manet well cannot look without pain upon this picture; it is something more than a likeness; it is as if you saw the man's ghost.'[59]

Degas was probably more responsive to music than Manet, but his taste was limited to the Romantics and on the whole he preferred the work of the French and Italian composers. He did not respond, as a number of his contemporaries did, to the growing popularity of Wagner. While Fantin-Latour and Renoir were inspired by the first performance of *Tannhäuser* at the Opéra on 13 March 1861 to paint their tributes to Wagner and his opera, Degas found his inspiration in the music of Délibes who supplied

part of the music for the ballet by Saint-Léon, *La Source* (first performed in November 1866), and by Meyerbeer's first French opera, *Robert le Diable* (first performed in 1831). On the whole Degas liked to avoid listening to the serious German composers. When a pianist suggested playing a Beethoven sonata one evening Degas gently dissuaded her: 'When I hear a theme of Beethoven's,' he observed, 'I feel as though I was walking alone in a forest filled with all my troubles. Play something else.'[60]

Degas enjoyed the company and friendship of musicians. Lorenzo Pagans, a Spanish tenor and guitarist (who made his debut in Paris in the opera *Sémiramide* which had also inspired Degas's history painting [plate 45]), was a family friend who often performed at Degas's house and also at the Manets'. Marie Dihau, a pianist and concert singer, whose portrait Degas painted around 1869, and her brother Désiré Dihau, a bassoonist at the Opéra, were both close friends. A reference to Marie in Degas's letters hints at a romantic attachment between them, but nothing definite can be stated. As a concert singer, she frequently travelled between Paris and her home town, Lille, and Degas once depicted her with a travelling bag sitting in Mère Lefebvre's restaurant in the rue de la Tour d'Auvergne, a favourite meeting-spot for Opéra musicians. It was there that Degas came to know other members of the orchestra, and these friendships inspired him to paint a group portrait (plate 64), with Désiré Dihau at the centre of a complex composition formed by the sharp angular lines of the instruments sandwiched between the front and back of the orchestra pit. Above the heads of the musicians a ballet is in progress but the spectator is only allowed to see a glimpse of the dancers as the top edge of the canvas cuts them off at their shoulders.

The composition may owe something to Daumier who in a caricature of 1852 drew a picture of the orchestra during the performance of a tragedy.[61] But there is no element of caricature in Degas's treatment of the musicians, who are depicted with uncanny accuracy, concentrating on their music and their playing. Degas even manages to suggest the physical effort involved as Dihau puffs out his cheeks to blow into the mouthpiece of his bassoon.

Perhaps the finest of his paintings inspired by music in his portrait of Pagans playing to Degas's father (plate 67), which, like that of Dihau, is dated around 1869. This work is in the tradition of Vermeer and Watteau in that it manages to capture the spellbinding power of music on player and listener alike. The figure of Pagans, with his robust Latin looks and energetic character, might be compared to Watteau's picture of the guitarist Mezzetino,[62] but the overall

OVERLEAF, LEFT:
68. *Young woman in street costume*, 1872. Brush drawing and wash on coloured paper, 12¾ × 9¾ in (32.2 × 24.9 cm). Cambridge, Mass., Courtesy of the Fogg Art Museum, Harvard University (Bequest of Meta and Paul J. Sachs)

OVERLEAF, RIGHT:
69. *Jeantaud, Linet and Lainé*, March 1871. Oil on canvas, 14½ × 17¾ in (37 × 45 cm). Paris, Louvre

70. *The cellist Pillet*, 1868-9. Oil on canvas, 19 × 23¾ in (48 × 60 cm). Paris, Louvre

composition, the balance suggested between player and listener is reminiscent of Vermeer's picture *The Concert*. The bond formed by the music is given a visual definition in Degas's picture by its structure, which, like the painting of the orchestra, is also based on a triangle, formed in this case by the line of the guitar and the two heads.

The character of the two sitters is conveyed both by means of facial expression - Pagans concentrated, forceful; Auguste Degas pensive, remote - and also by the positions of their bodies. Pagans leans forward energetically, Auguste conveys his age in the way he supports his weight, resting his arms on his knees with his hands clasped together. The treatment of the figures fulfils the instruction he gave himself in a notebook in use from 1868. 'Make portraits of people in familiar and typical attitudes and especially give the same choice of expression to the face that one gives to the body.'⁶³

Related to Degas's enjoyment of music was his awareness and appreciation of the ballet. From the age of twenty he had held a season ticket at the Opéra, then located in what was intended as a temporary building called the Salle de la rue Peletier. In 1858 an attack was made on the emperor and his wife as their carriage drew up before it and it was decided a new opera house should be built. A competition was staged which was won by Charles Garnier, and in 1862 the cornerstone was laid for his huge building which was eventually completed by the end of 1874.

Degas was too young to see the great stars of the French Romantic ballet. Marie Taglioni, famous for her role in *Les Sylphides*, retired in 1847 and Fanny Elssler, her great rival, retired four years later. The dancers he came to know and to paint in the 1860s were relatively minor figures, such as the dancer-turned-actress Mme Gaujelin. He did, however, see Eugénie Fiocre (plate 71) at one of the high points of her career, dancing the role of Nouredda in *La Source*, a performance much admired by the critic Paul de Saint Victor and by Théophile Gautier.

Degas's painting of Mlle Fiocre hardly gives any indication that a ballet is in progress or that the scene depicted is actually taking place on a stage. *La Source* was an elaborate Persian extravaganza and it was staged with great realism, both the pool in which Nouredda dips her feet and the horse beside her being real. The scene Degas chose to paint was from the first act at a relatively still moment after the end of Nouredda's *pas de la Guzla*, which Gautier thought was the prettiest dance in the ballet, when she has kicked off her shoes, cools her feet in the pond and sinks deep into thought, contemplating her future. Degas's choice of this scene was partly motivated by the fact that at this point he had not mastered the ability to convey movement, and partly because he was attracted to moments of inner conflict either before or after periods of dramatic action. This predilection is particularly noticeable in two genre

paintings of the late 1860s, which both give the impression that a scene from a stage drama is taking place – the painting sometimes called *Le Viol*, but more appropriately entitled *Interior* (plate 66), and a painting which is sometimes called *Sulking* and at other times *The Banker* (plate 63).

Interior was largely inspired by Zola's *Thérèse Raquin*, which was published in serial form late in 1867. Thérèse, married to a sickly and under-sexed son of a shopkeeper, finds sexual fulfilment with her husband's best friend, Laurent. Eventually the two lovers conspire to murder the husband and they manage to achieve the perfect murder. After a decent interval they marry, but guilt and mutual fear has killed their passion and on their wedding night they cannot bear to look at, let alone touch, each other.

71. *Mlle Fiocre in the ballet of 'La Source'*, 1867–8. Oil on canvas, 51 × 57¼ in (133 × 144 cm). New York, Brooklyn Museum (Gift of James H. Post, John T. Underwood and A. Augustus Healy)

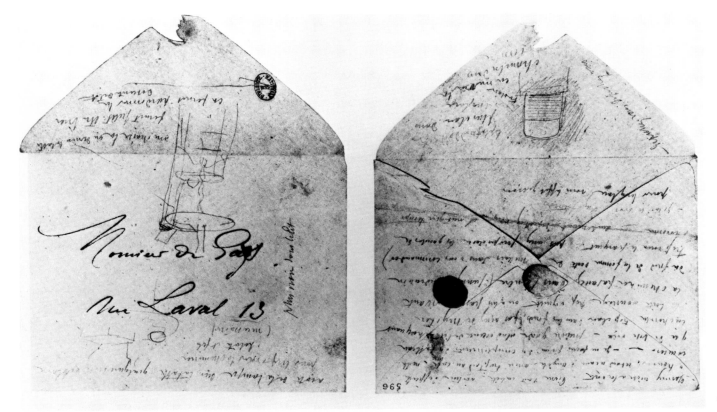

Their passion turns to hatred and they are driven to a joint suicide before the eyes of the murdered husband's mother. It was a gothic horror story given a contemporary urban setting in one of the poorer quarters of Paris and its dramatic scenes lent themselves to a stage production. Degas's picture does indeed give the impression of a tableau from a stage drama. The characters are lit from below as if by footlights, but in fact the source of the light is the lamp on the table and the glowing fire in the grate. Degas was very interested in lighting effects and made an entry in a notebook at that period: 'Study nocturnal effects a great deal, lamps, candles, etc. The smartest thing is not always to reveal the source of light, but the effect of light. This area of art can become very important today. Is it possible not to realize that?'[64]

In selecting his subject from Zola's book, Degas ignored the outwardly dramatic moments – the first scenes of passion between Thérèse and Laurent, the murder, the sight of the drowned husband in a public morgue and the suicides – for the moment of intense inner conflict when Thérèse and Laurent confront each other on the wedding night, alone for the first time since the murder, and standing in the very room in which their affair had started. It is possible that Laurent's impotence on this occasion may have struck a responsive chord in Degas, but the scene would also have appealed to him because of the very difficulty in capturing the characters' inner conflicts. As an exercise in the visual portrayal of emotion, it is an achievement of the highest order. The painting glows with ominous sultry feelings and it can be appreciated on its own without foreknowledge of Zola's work.

In preparing for this painting Degas as usual made numerous pencil studies and oil sketches, but it is interesting to learn that he was not afraid, at this stage in his life, to seek the advice of his contemporaries. Reff points out[65] that a letter in the Bibliothèque Nationale, almost certainly from Tissot, gave Degas some useful hints:

'I shall compliment you on the picture only in person. Be careful of the rug beside the bed, shocking. The room too light in the background, not enough mystery. The sewing-box too conspicuous, or instead not vivid enough. The fireplace not enough in shadow (think of the vagueness of the background in the "Green Woman" by Millais without subjecting yourself). Too red the floor. Not proprietary enough the man's legs. The ceiling should be lighter in a mirror. Very light, while throwing the room into shadow. Beside the lamp on the table, something white to thrust the fireplace back, a ball of thread (necessary). Darker under the bed. A chair there or behind the table would perhaps be good. It would make the rug beside the bed acceptable.'[66]

Degas appears to have followed some of Tissot's advice. The lid of the box on the centre table is indeed painted a bright pink.

Smaller in scale and probably of a later date, *Sulking* (plate 63) also seems to be based on a work of fiction or a stage drama. The picture is an enigmatic and puzzling work and to date no literary or other source has been found which can provide the identity of the couple or what is taking place between them. Originally it was thought to have been a scene of affectionate intimacy; since then it has been variously suggested that it is a scene between a husband and wife in a business office, that the man is a bookmaker, that he is a banker, that he is angry with his wife, and even that it is a scene between a father and daughter.[67] More recently Reff has observed[68] that it is an exercise in facial and bodily expression and he notes that the man whose head is turned away in apparent anger resembles Degas's friend and fellow student of physiognomy, Edmond Duranty. Until a source can be identified for certain Reff's explanation will have to suffice. Within the context of Degas's work, however, it marks his continuing concern for expressing the tensions which can exist between man and woman, a subject first tackled in his portrait of the Bellelli family and treated again in *Interior*.

(vi)

On the wall behind the couple in *Interior* can be seen an English sporting print, a work based on Frederick Herring's *Steeplechase Cracks* (plate 73), a reference to a general interest in France at that time in English racing scenes and also to Degas's own particular

awareness of it on a visit to Normandy in 1862. Staying with his schoolfriend Paul Valpinçon at his family's château at Ménil-Hubert near Ornes, he was struck by the Englishness of the landscape. Looking down the avenue of trees which led up to the château, he noted in his journal: 'Absolutely similar to the ones in those English prints of hunting and racing scenes.'[69] He was reading Henry Fielding during his stay at Ménil-Hubert and this, combined with his study of English sporting prints, coloured his view. In the breeding and racing of thoroughbreds, the English were then in advance of the French. As Ronald Pickvance has noted,[70] the French Derby was started in 1836, some fifty years after the English version, the French jockey club was founded in 1833, eighty-three years after the English original, Longchamp was not opened until 1857 and it was not until 1863 that the Société des Steeplechases de France was formed. Although racing was attacked before the Revolution for 'bringing confusion to fortunes and making the workers desert their workshops',[71] subsequent regimes encouraged racing and supported the development of breeding establishments, largely because it seemed to be of national and military importance. Louis-Philippe established the French stud-book in 1833, and Napoleon III took an active interest in the regulations governing the sport, handing over responsibility in 1866 to the three principal societies which supervised flat-racing, steeplechasing and trotting respectively. What, however, made it a popular sport was the establishment of a betting system which later formed the basis of the

73. J. F. HERRING, *Steeplechase Cracks*, 1847. Colour engraving. Paris, BN

Degas's knowledge of horses and riders came from his study of art. In Florence he had made sketches of the horse (plate 74) ridden by Charles V in the equestrian portrait in the Uffizi, and on his return to Paris his notebooks contain numerous copies after Théodore Géricault. Later Meissonier provided him with some useful models. But his chief source was the English sporting prints by Herring, Henry Alken and others who enjoyed a vogue in Paris in the 1860s, not only because of the increasing popularity of the sport but also because of a general fashion for things English encouraged by Napoleon III. Degas was not the only artist to turn to English models for his racing pictures: when Manet was commissioned to paint a racing scene, he relied on an English sporting print, confessing to Berthe Morisot, 'Not being in the habit of painting horses, I copied mine from those who know best how to do them.'[73]

The demand for racing pictures in France in the 1860s was considerable and attracted several artists, including John Lewis Brown and a painter with the improbable name of Georges Washington, who

74. Partial copy of Van Dyck's *Equestrian portrait of Charles V* in the Uffizi, Florence (Notebook 12). Paris, BN

75. Sketch of the head and forequarters of a horse (Notebook 16). Paris, BN

Paris Mutuels, and the publication of a newspaper devoted to racing, the *Journal des Courses*.[72]

Degas was not particularly interested in racing as such. He went with his friends the Valpinçons because it was part of their country life; they took him to see the stud at Haras-du-pin, which was one of the foremost breeding establishments of the day. Back in Paris he also accompanied Manet to the races (plate 81) because racing was one of the pastimes enjoyed by men-about-town. The races themselves (who won what and in what time) held little appeal for him; most of his paintings concentrate on the preliminaries, the moments when the horses and the riders first come on to the track, and shortly afterwards when they jockey for position before coming under starter's orders. What attracted Degas to racing was the opportunity of depicting the age-old artistic subject of horses and riders in a contemporary setting. It was similar to his use of the ballet as a means for expressing a lifelong interest in the human figure.

76. Sketch of landscape at Haras-du-Pin (Notebook 18). Paris, BN

77. Sketch of landscape (Notebook 18). Paris, BN

exhibited a picture of a steeplechase at the Salon of 1865. It may have been this work which prompted Degas to send a steeplechase scene (plate 79) to the Salon of 1866. He prepared for it with his usual thoroughness, making sketches of horses leaping over fences and persuading his brother Achille to model for the part of the wounded jockey lying on the ground. The composition for the large canvas (it measures six by five feet) was taken from an English print, but with differences. Whereas English sporting artists tended to depict a broad scene with many animals and figures in an expansive landscape, Degas concentrated on a close-up, showing only three horses and riders and treating the landscape in a sketchy and imprecise manner. It is not a completely successful work and Degas himself seems to have been dissatisfied with it. But it marked a beginning; it, and the small canvases of about 1862, stand as a prologue to the great racing pictures of the next two decades.

Another world which Degas began to explore at the same time was the world of the café. Again Manet, who enjoyed café life, may have encouraged him in this. In the early 1860s it was Manet's usual practice, once the day's painting was over, to go to the Café Tortini and the Café de Bade, classy establishments in the centre of Paris. But towards the end of the decade he switched his allegiance to a café near his studio in the Batignolles quarter, in the avenue de Clichy (then grande rue des Batignolles), the Café Guerbois. The first artists to discover this café were Frédéric Bazille, Fantin-Latour and Antoine Guillemet. The latter brought Zola there in February 1866; Edmond Duranty, novelist and critic, went regularly on Fridays; and the photographer Félix Nadar was another patron.

The café was decorated in the typical style of the day, with gilded mirrors, marble-top tables and hat stands. The waiters wore white aprons and black waistcoats, and at the back there was a billiard room. The discussions which took place there were lively. Monet described the scene in an interview with *Le Temps* in 1900:

'It wasn't until 1869 that I saw Manet again, but we became close friends at once, as soon as we met. He invited me to come and see him each evening in a café in the Batignolles district where he and his friends met when the day's work in the studio was over. There I met Fantin-Latour and Cézanne, Degas, who had just returned from a trip to Italy, the art critic Duranty, Emile Zola who was then making his début in literature, and several others as well. I myself brought along Sisley, Bazille and Renoir.'

78. *Plough horse*, 1860. Pencil, 5¾ × 7¾ in (14.6 × 19.7 cm). Switzerland, Private Collection

OPPOSITE:
79. *Steeplechase – The fallen jockey*, exhibited in the Salon of 1866, retouched by the artist at a later date. Oil on canvas, 70¾ × 59¾ in (180 × 152 cm). Washington, DC, Collection Mr and Mrs Paul Mellon

80. *Woman at the races*, 1869–72.
Oil on canvas, 13¾ × 8¾ in (35 ×
22 cm). London, courtesy of
Sotheby Parke Bernet

OPPOSITE:
81. *Manet at the races*, 1870–72.
Pencil, 12½ × 9½ in (32 × 24 cm).
New York, Metropolitan
Museum (Rogers Fund, 1918)

89

Nothing could be more interesting than the talks we had, with their perpetual clashes of opinion. Your mind was held in suspense all the time, you spurred the others on to sincere disinterested inquiry and were spurred on yourself, you laid in a stock of enthusiasm that kept you going for weeks on end until you could give final form to the idea you had in mind. You always went home afterwards better steeled for the fray, with a new sense of purpose and a clearer head.'[74]

Degas was an occasional visitor putting in short visits and on the whole refraining from joining in some of the arguments, perhaps from fear of losing his temper. The views he did express were quixotic and class-conscious. He liked to maintain that it was a bad idea to bring art to the poorer classes, that work should be kept expensive and out of their reach. Duranty referred to him on one occasion as the master of social chiaroscuro. His visits to the Café Guerbois, however, did have important effects: they widened his circle of acquaintance among other artists and thus brought him into contact with landscape painting. It was through the Café Guerbois that he came to know Monet, Pissarro and Renoir, colleagues with whom he joined in forming the first Impressionist exhibition, and it was thus that he became aware of their interest and theories about landscape.

Although he was primarily interested in depicting the human figure he did try his hand now and then at landscapes. On a trip to Boulogne in 1869 to join Manet he returned with over thirty-seven studies of the sea-shore and the sand dunes to be seen in that part of France (plate 82). Many of these studies look like Whistler's simplified seascapes of the mid-1860s; when Degas saw those, perhaps for the first time, on a trip to London in 1873, he commented to Tissot that Whistler 'has really found a personal note . . .[a] mysterious mingling of land and water'.[75]

Much of the café talk which Degas heard was not about art or the rights and wrongs of painting out-of-doors, but typical painters' worries, the difficulty in getting work accepted by the Salon, the over-crowding of these exhibitions, the obtuseness of the critics and the reluctance of collectors to buy their work. Zola listened to these talks with sympathy and in 1866 he persuaded Henri de Villemessant, the editor of *L'Evénement*, to allow him to review the forthcoming Salon, even though he had no previous experience of writing Salon criticism. His articles, and in particular his attack on the jury system, made him a hero within the Café Guerbois circle but caused a furore with the readers of *L'Evénement* and his series had to be stopped by the editor. The publication of his pamphlet on Manet in 1867, the support

which he gave to him in organizing his own independent exhibition outside the great Paris exhibition of 1867, all helped focus attention within the group on the need to join together and find alternative ways for exhibiting their work. The discussions which took place there, however, were brought to a swift end by the sudden war which broke out between France and Prussia in 1870.

The group went their separate ways. Monet and Pissarro left France for London, as did the dealer Paul Durand-Ruel; Bazille joined the forces formed in the south-west; and Degas and Manet joined a defence force formed in Paris after the defeat of Napoleon III and his armies at Sedan. Manet found himself serving under his Salon opponent Meissonier, who proved to be no less objectionable in uniform than he had been in civilian life. Degas enlisted in the infantry but when he was sent to Vincennes for rifle practice, it was found he could not see the target with his right eye. He was transferred to the artillery and found himself serving under his schoolfriend Henri Rouart; as a result they became the closest of friends, Rouart later forming one of the finest collections of Degas's work.

Degas was not inspired by his military experience to paint any pictures of soldiers in action. In fact he deeply disapproved of his colleagues who took time off from their duties to sketch or paint the events they witnessed. Jean-Louis Forain liked to recount an anecdote of Tissot coming up to Degas with a sketch of a sculptor friend, Cavelier, who had been seriously wounded at Le Bourget: 'I did a drawing of him –

82. *Beach at low tide with boat*, 1869. Pastel on paper, 8¾ × 11¾ in (22 × 30 cm). London, Courtesy of Lefèvre Gallery Ltd

83. *Children and ponies in a park*, 1867. Oil on canvas, 35 × 39¾ in (89 × 101 cm). New York, Collection of Mrs Vincent de Roulet

here, look.' Degas pushed the sketch away refusing to look at it. 'You would have done better if you'd picked him up,' he snapped.[76] The only works which the siege of Paris inspired were portraits of his colleagues in the battery (plate 69), depicted later in civilian dress.

Had Degas been killed in the fighting, as Bazille was, it is tempting to wonder what his reputation would be today. A great portraitist? A genre painter of great potential? A realist of the calibre of Tissot and Stevens? By 1870 he had produced a number of masterpieces which would ensure the survival of his name as a leading figure in the art of the mid-nineteenth century – the great portraits from 1860 on, the genre paintings and the sheets of beautiful drawings and studies for these paintings – but Degas had still to find the voice or the subjects which were to make him famous. The paintings of the next two decades are the ones which reveal his true originality as an artist.

Chapter 3

From the Commune to the first Impressionist Exhibition

On 29 January 1871 the city of Paris surrendered. 'There was no way to hold on,' Manet informed his wife on 30 January. 'We were dying of hunger.'[1] A month later the Prussians occupied the city for two days. It was a symbolic act, but for Frenchmen humiliating. The dramatist Arsène Houssaye described the scene:

'Wave followed human wave. We were pressed against the chains and stone of the Arc de Triomphe. Suddenly, the sounds of German martial music punctuated with the hoofbeats of galloping horses. The Prussians! The Uhlans! The Bavarians! They were coming up the Avenues de L'Impératrice and de la Grande Armée. Alas – where was the Grande Armée? All of us seemed enveloped in a nightmare. Suddenly, though the enemy's regiments were still at a distance, some horsemen emerged right next to the Arc de Triomphe. It seemed as if they had risen from the ground. . . .

They were soon followed by King William, proud to let the hooves of his horse resound on the victories of Napoleon. The military band was still playing its victorious music. I wished I could be a hundred feet under the earth, but I had to confront the spectacle – a forced confrontation because we could neither move forward nor backward.'[2]

But worse was to follow. On 18 March civil war broke out between the remnants of the civil defence force left in Paris and the French troops gathered round the Republican government, led by Adolphe Thiers, which was installed at Versailles. Dissatisfied with the peace terms negotiated by Thiers, humiliated by the German occupation of Paris, abandoned by their leaders, the citizen army took matters into their own hands, assembled their own command and ordered the election of a city government which repudiated the peace treaty and the government of Thiers. A Commune was declared and a situation soon developed that seemed like the Revolutions of 1789 and 1848 all over again. A number of artists joined the rebellion, including Courbet and, surprisingly, Degas's friend James Tissot – surprising because he had shown no interest in politics and was not the stuff from which revolutionaries are made.[3] Manet took no part, but he did witness the brutal suppression of the Commune when the Versailles troops entered Paris by the Porte de Saint-Cloud on 21 May. His sketches and lithographs of the executions and killings which took place over the next week – a week in which 20,000 men and women lost their lives – convey the horror of those days. By 29 May it was all over and Edmond de Goncourt wrote in his journal: 'All is well. There has been neither compromise nor conciliation. The solution has been brutal, imposed by sheer force of arms . . . the bleeding has been done thoroughly, and bleeding like that, by killing the rebellious part of the population, postpones the next revolution by a whole conscription. The old society has twenty years of peace before it . . .'[4]

Degas was spared this horrific episode of French history. He left Paris after the siege to visit his school-friend Paul Valpinçon at Ménil-Hubert, but as in the case of many of his countrymen, the French defeat at Sedan, the siege and the Commune left bitter memories and stiffened his sense of patriotism. In later life he became quite uncontrollable when questions of 'Country' and 'Honour' seemed to be at stake, having become the fiercest of anti-Dreyfusards, and retaining a lasting disillusionment with his country's politicians. He, who had relatives in America and in Italy, and who enjoyed the friendship of cultivated French Jews like the Halévys, became the narrowest of Frenchmen and even an antisemite.

Ménil-Hubert was a place of refuge. He could arrive without warning and always be sure of a warm welcome, and visits which were meant to last for a few days were stretched to a month or more. In addition to the friendship he enjoyed with Paul Valpinçon there was the pleasure of seeing his daughter Hortense, later Mme Fourchy, with whom Degas developed a close relationship. As a young girl in 1871, she posed for him wearing a straw hat, a white pinafore and a cashmere shawl around her shoulders (plate 89). It is perhaps the masterpiece of his paintings and drawings of children, ravishing in its balance of colours and perceptive in its understanding of child psychology. Children are never easy sitters, being naturally restless and easily bored. To hold her attention Degas gave her an apple divided into quarters. In the portrait she holds the last quarter in her hand and looks enquiringly at the artist as if to ask whether she can eat it. The composition follows Degas's usual practice of placing the figure off-centre. She is balanced by the basket of wools and needlepoint on the left, these objects acting rather like the vase of flowers in the picture of *A Woman with Chrysanthemums* (plate 59).

Another of Paul Valpinçon's children, his infant son Henri, became the subject of two further paintings inspired by Degas's stay at Ménil-Hubert. The first is the delightful small canvas of a *Carriage at the Races* (plate 84). Measuring $13\frac{3}{4}$ by $21\frac{3}{8}$ inches (35 x 54 cms), it is one of a number of small oils which Degas painted in the early 1870s and which in their detail and their refinement seem to refer back to the Dutch masters of the seventeenth century and to Chardin and Watteau in France of the eighteenth. A family outing to the races inspired this particular oil, and in the background a race is taking place, but the Valpinçon family is entirely occupied with the welfare of the baby; mother, father, nurse, even the

dog, are looking at him. With its fresh pale green colours Degas captured the atmosphere of a sunny summer day in the country. It could, as many writers have pointed out, almost be considered a snapshot, one in which the artist/photographer has not managed to fit everything in: a man in a trap on the left-hand side has been cut in two by the framing edge of the canvas and the Valpinçon coach and horses on the right have been 'cropped'. The same child and nurse are shown in another outdoor scene (plate 85), this time in a garden park near the château. The baby is sitting in a carriage attended by his nurse and in the background his sister and mother are playing in the sunlight.

Although both works were probably executed in the studio, they show that Degas at this stage was prepared occasionally to work out of doors. In a letter written to Tissot dated 30 September 1871 he writes: 'I have just had and still have a spot of weakness and trouble in my eyes. It caught me at the château by the edge of the water in full sunlight

84. *Carriage at the races*, 1871–2. Oil on canvas, $13\frac{3}{4} \times 21\frac{1}{2}$ in (36×55 cm). Boston, Courtesy Museum of Fine Arts (Arthur G. Tompkins Residuary Fund)

85. *Henri Valpinçon and nurse*, 1871–2. Oil, 12 × 16 in (30 × 40 cm). Private Collection

whilst I was still doing a watercolour and it made me lose nearly three weeks, being unable to read or work or go out much, trembling all the time lest I should remain like that.'[5]

For the rest of his life Degas was tormented by problems with his vision. The nature of his disease or failing has not been identified, but the effect was to produce a blind spot in his field of vision. Sickert, who himself suffered with his eyes, appreciated and sympathized with Degas's problem:

'It was natural that, during the years when I knew him, from 1883 onwards, he should sometimes have spoken of the torment that it was to draw, when he could only see around the spot at which he was looking, and never the spot itself. When we consider the immense output of the latter half of his life, the high intellectual value of it and the generous store of beauty that forms its contribution to the history of art, the debonair heroism of such a life, its

inspired adaptation to conditions apparently intolerable, must remain a monument for amazement and for respect.'[6]

Sickert believed that Degas's difficulties with his eyes led him to give up oil painting for pastel: 'Minute delicacies of detailed execution had to be abandoned. A very natural dread that the affliction might grow made, of the necessary delays that oil-painting exacts, an intolerable anxiety. A pastel is always ready to be gone on with.'[7]

After 1872 Degas began to dread spending any length of time in strong sunlight. In a letter written from New Orleans he complained: 'The light is so strong that I have not been able to do anything on the river. My eyes are so greatly in need of care that I scarcely take any risks with them at all.'[8] Painting out of doors in front of the subject, as practised by Monet, Pissarro, Renoir and Sisley, was a physical impossibility as well as being inconsistent with his belief that a painting was the product of the artist's imagination and his memory. In any case he was a city child, by birth attracted to its pleasures and its people; landscape, like still lifes, held little appeal for him.

After his stay at Ménil-Hubert he was no doubt pleased to return to the familiarity of Paris. In July 1871 he was seen once again at Manet's salon, which, according to Berthe Morisot's mother, had survived the war and the Commune unchanged:

'*I found the Manet salon in just the same state as before; it is nauseating. If people were not interested in hearing individual accounts of public misfortunes, I think little would have been said. The heat was stifling, everybody was cooped up in the one drawing room, the drinks were warm. But Pagans sang, Mme Edouard played and M. Degas was there. That's not to say that he flitted about; he looked very sleepy – your father seemed younger than he.*'[9]

The Opéra had also survived the upheavals of the last few months and during the summer of 1872 Degas gained access to the practice rooms where he was able to observe the ballet master and choreographer Louis François Mérante conducting a class.

From these visits two beautiful small oils emerged; one was bought by M. Brandon soon after it was painted (plate 86); the other was bought by Louis Houth at Paul Durand-Ruel's gallery in London in 1872 (plate 87).[10] Both works show a dancing class with one dancer poised ready to begin her steps, and both suggest that at this stage Degas was not ready to tackle the more complicated subject of dancers in motion; they stand, in a sense, as prologues to the ballet pictures to come.

Both pictures enchanted all who saw them. Degas's brother René wrote enthusiastically about one of the oils in a letter to his wife in New Orleans, and the London critic Sidney Collin was ecstatic about the other which he saw at Durand-Ruel's fifth exhibition of the Society of French Artists in New Bond Street. Sidney Collin became the first English critic to notice Degas's talents. In the *Pall Mall Gazette* of 28 November 1872 he wrote:

'*It is impossible to exaggerate the subtlety of exact perception, and the felicitous touch in expressing it, which reveal themselves in his little picture of ballet-girls training beneath the eye of the ballet-master. . . . It is a scheme of*

86. *The dancing class,* 1871-2. Oil on wood, $7\frac{3}{4} \times 10\frac{1}{2}$ in (19.7 × 27 cm). Lent by M. Brandon to the first Impressionist exhibition. Formerly called *Le Foyer.* New York, Metropolitan Museum (Bequest of Mrs H. O. Havemeyer, 1929)

various whites, gauzes and muslins, fluttering round the apartment, and the ballet-master in white ducks and jacket in the middle; and all the little shifts of indoor light and colour, all the movements of the girls in rest and strained exercise, expressed with the most perfect precision of drawing and delicacy of colour, and without a shadow of a shade of that sentiment which is ordinarily implied by a picture having the ballet for its subject.[11]

(ii)

Any plans he may have made to continue his ballet paintings were interrupted by his decision in October 1872 to set off on a journey to New Orleans with his younger brother René. His reasons for going are not immediately apparent. He may have wanted some distraction from worries about his eyesight, he may have suffered from the restlessness which affected many of his friends at the Café Guerbois, or he may simply have been curious to see the land of his mother. 'Louisiana must be respected by all her children of which I am almost one,' he wrote to a friend.[12] Travel itself was unlikely to provide him with new subjects. He believed good art could only come from long study and familiarity with the customs and ways of a people. 'It is not good to do Parisian art indiscriminately. It is liable to turn into the *Monde Illustré*,' he wrote. 'Nothing but a really long stay can reveal the customs of the people, that is to say their charm – Instantaneousness is photography, nothing more.'[13] And in the same letter he defined his artistic credo: 'I want nothing but my own little corner where I shall dig assiduously. Art does not expand, it repeats itself . . . In order to produce good

87. *Dance class at the Opéra*, 1872. Oil on canvas, $12\frac{1}{2} \times 18$ in (32×46 cm). Paris, Louvre (Jeu de Paume)

fruit one must line them up on an espalier. One remains thus all one's life, arms extended, mouth open, so as to assimilate what is happening, what is around one and alive.'

Degas was not a good traveller. Before leaving for America he tried to learn a few words of English. René reported that he had 'a mania for pronouncing English words; he has been repeating "turkey-buzzard" for a week'.[14] But it was to no avail; he never mastered the language and throughout the journey he relied on his brother to make all the necessary arrangements. They left for America via London and Liverpool. In London Degas had many artist friends, including Tissot and Whistler, and he hoped to find a market for his work there as they had done. Paul Durand-Ruel had established a London gallery, and it was during the Franco-Prussian war that he came to know the work of Monet and Pissarro. He organized a series of exhibitions under the banner title of the Society of French Artists and Degas, as mentioned earlier, arranged to have two of his oils included in the fifth of these exhibitions. He does not appear to have had complete confidence in Durand-Ruel, however, and while he was in London he looked around for other possibilities. The dealer Agnew was suggested and after his return from New Orleans some six months later he wrote to Tissot to tell him about his inquiries: 'I spoke about him [Agnew] casually to a few friends and what they told me is absolutely fascinating. They urge me to place myself in his redoubtable hands.'[15] Nothing, however, came of this plan and Degas went on showing with Durand-Ruel.

Degas was successful in England from the very beginning. The English public liked his paintings, particularly those of the ballet, and praised his 'real originality and indisputable talent',[16] and he was considered to be the leading figure in the new French school. Dante Gabriel Rossetti, who had a blind spot for most French art, nevertheless thought the ballet pictures showed 'surprisingly clever pieces of effect, of odd turns of arrangement, and often of character, too pertinaciously divested of grace'.[17] Degas also found collectors for his work. Of the two paintings in his first show in London one was sold to Louis Houth, as mentioned above; and Captain Henry Hill of Brighton built up a remarkable collection of his pictures, including six ballet paintings and L'Absinthe.

The language barrier prevented Degas from getting to know the English as a whole better. On the boat, which he caught from Liverpool on 12 October 1872, he found the English to be 'reserved, cold and conventional', and as a result he did not enjoy the crossing. When the boat docked in New York, Degas was able to spend thirty-six hours there. He was impressed by the vitality of the city. 'It has some charming spots,' he informed Tissot, '. . . What a degree of civilization! Steamers coming from Europe arrive like omnibuses . . . It's England in her best mood.'[18] 'New York, great town and great port. The townsfolk know the great water,' he wrote to another friend. 'They even say that going to Europe is going to the other side of the water. New people. In America there is far more disregard of the English race than I had supposed.'[19] He was impressed by the number of immigrants from Germany: '. . . Germans are arriving in their thousands, half the shops in Broadway have names like Eimar and Wolf, Shumaker and Vogel, etc. Texas is full of Germans. The other day a French maid whom René had engaged before leaving arrived on a small German boat. In the hold . . . were 621 German immigrants fleeing the Vaterland, misery and a new war with Russia or fair France.'[20]

Degas was full of compliments for Yankee ingenuity and drive and felt that the Creoles in New Orleans were no match for them. He was particularly impressed by American trains and the comforts of their sleeping cars. 'You cannot imagine what this marvellous invention is like,' he wrote to Désiré Dihau. 'You lie down at night in a proper bed. The carriage is as long as at least two carriages in France and is transformed into a dormitory. You even put your shoes at the foot of the bed and a kind negro polishes them whilst you sleep. – What luxuriousness you will say. No, it is a simple necessity. Otherwise it would be impossible to undertake such journeys at a stretch. And then the ability to walk all round your own coach and the whole train, to stand on platforms is immensely restful and diverting. Everything is practical and very simply done here, so simply that the trains leave almost without warning. – Well I was with René who is from these parts and I did not miss anything.'[21]

The train journey took four days which would place Degas's and his brother's arrival in New Orleans around 28 October. They were met at the station by Michel Musson who looked at them over his spectacles in much the same way as Degas later depicted him in the painting of the Cotton Exchange (plate 92). His cousins and their six children were there and he was soon thrown into family life. The Musson family was a large one, all living in a huge house on the Esplanade.[22] It consisted of Michel, brother of Degas's mother, a widower with three surviving daughters, Désirée, Mathilde, married to William Bell, and Estelle, who in 1869 had married René Degas. Mathilde and her husband had six

OVERLEAF, LEFT:
88. *Désirée Musson (La malade)*, 1872-3. Oil on canvas, $25\frac{1}{2} \times 18\frac{1}{2}$ in (65 × 47 cm). New York, Private Collection

OVERLEAF, RIGHT:
89. *Hortense Valpinçon*, 1871. Oil on canvas, $29\frac{3}{4} \times 44\frac{3}{4}$ in (73 × 110 cm). Minneapolis, Institute of Arts (John R. Van Derlip Fund)

children. Estelle had a daughter by her first husband who had been killed in the Civil War, a boy and a girl by her marriage to René and, when Degas arrived, she was expecting another child, who was to become Degas's god-daughter. Degas's middle brother Achille was also in New Orleans. He and René had set up a business as wine importers and commission merchants using funds which René had raised in France through his father's bank. Although these were difficult times – New Orleans was still recovering from the effects of the Civil War and the deprivations of the 'carpetbaggers' – the two brothers appeared, at any rate to Degas, to be doing well and he was proud of their success.[23]

Degas had scarcely finished unpacking when he set to work painting portraits of his Musson relatives. He was particularly struck by the plight of Estelle, René's wife, whom he had not seen since her trip to France accompanying her mother in 1863. She was now blind, but, he wrote: 'She bears it in an incomparable manner; she scarcely needs any help about the house. She remembers the rooms and the position of the furniture and hardly ever bumps into anything. And there is no hope.'[24] Degas depicted her sitting down, wearing a light muslin dress, staring into space with unseeing eyes (plate 93). She is also believed to have sat for another portrait, now in the Isaac Delgado Museum, New Orleans.[25] Neither work, however, gives any hint of the tragedies that were to befall her: René later abandoned her for another woman leaving his three children behind, then in the yellow fever epidemic which swept New Orleans in 1880 and 1881 her daughter by her first marriage died as well as two of René's children.

The other members of the Musson family to sit for him during the first two or three months of his stay were Mathilde, whom he showed sitting on the balcony of the house, Estelle's daughter by her first husband, Joanna, who posed for a young girl in *The Pedicure* (plate 90), and Désirée, who posed for the sick woman in the painting also called *La Malade* (plate 88). Although these pictures are for the most part unfinished, they show Degas's best qualities as a portraitist and reveal his tender affection for his sitters. He was, nevertheless, dissatisfied with them and complained, 'They have to be done more or less to suit the family taste, by impossible lighting, very much disturbed, with the models full of affection . . . and taking you far less seriously because you are their nephew or their cousin.'[26]

One side effect of these portraits was a new desire for a family of his own. 'I am thirsting for order,' he confessed to Rouart. 'I do not even regard a good woman as an enemy of this new method of existence.

A few children of my own, is that excessive too? No.'[27] To Tissot, who in the 1860s had become one of the most successful womanizers in Paris, Degas confessed that he longed to be free of 'the need of being gallant'.[28] Southern women, particularly the Creoles, caught his eye. He felt they had 'that touch of ugliness without which no salvation'. But he was worried that they were too empty-headed. He was particularly impressed by the black women:

'I like nothing better than the negresses of all shades, holding in their arms little white babies, so white, against white houses with columns of fluted wood and in gardens of orange trees and the ladies in muslin against the fronts of their little houses and the steamboats with two chimneys as tall as factory chimneys and the fruit vendors with their shops full to bursting, and the contrast between the lively hum and bustle of the offices with this immense black animal force, etc. etc. And the pretty women of pure blood and the pretty quadroons and the well-set-up negresses!'[29]

After five weeks Degas began to tire of his stay in New Orleans and he informed his friend Rouart that he would return to Paris the following January. 'One does nothing here,' he complained. 'It lies in the climate. Nothing but cotton. One lives for cotton and from cotton.'[30] Degas no doubt listened to his uncle and his friends talk about cotton. Its price was of acute concern to all businessmen in New Orleans as the prosperity of the city depended upon it. Despite the upheavals of the Civil War New Orleans was still the centre for cotton exports to other parts of America and to Europe. Visiting his uncle and his partners at the Cotton Exchange (then at 231 Carondelet Street, above Canal Street, in the American quarter of the city), he was able to see how cotton was bought and sold. The sight of the office, with its tables covered with the bales spread out for inspection, gave him the idea for a picture in which he could combine the art of portraiture with the skills of genre painting, in much the same way as he combined these talents in his portrait of Désiré Dihau and the members of the orchestra at the Opéra (plate 64). The subject, he felt, would appeal to the English, particularly to the rich cotton manufacturers in Manchester who were clients of Agnew, and on 18 February 1873 he wrote to Tissot to tell him that he had abandoned painting his relations, 'in the worst lighting conditions that I have ever found or imagined', to settle down on 'a strong composition' which he intended Agnew to sell: 'If a textile manufacturer of cotton ever wished to find his painter, I would make quite an impression,' he wrote.[31] Nothing came of his plan, however, and he had the painting sent to Paris. In 1878 it was purchased by the city of Pau in the south of France for its museum, and it

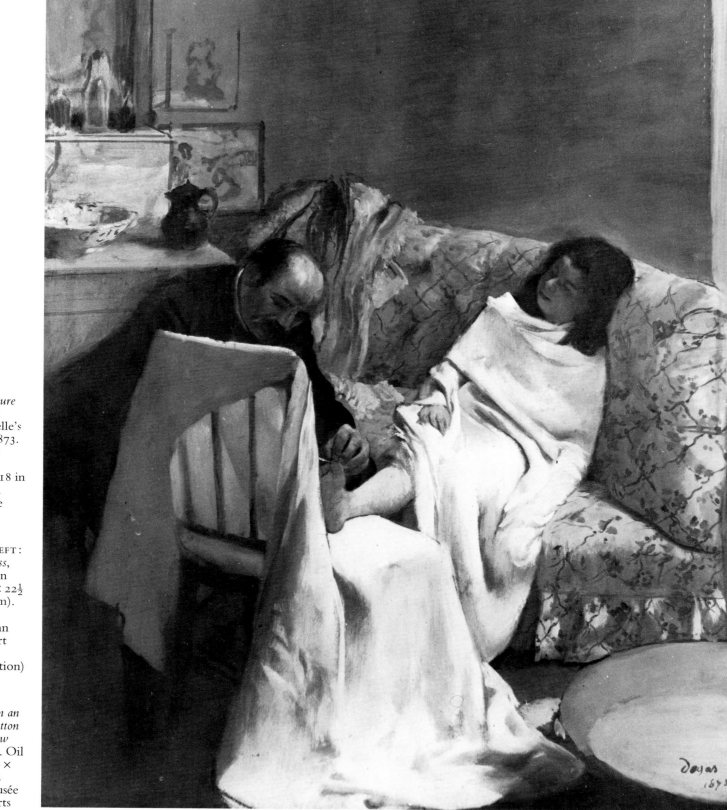

90. *The pedicure* (with Joanna Balfour, Estelle's daughter), 1873. Oil on paper mounted on canvas, 24 × 18 in (61 × 46 cm). Paris, Louvre (Cabinet des Dessins)

OVERLEAF, LEFT:
91. *Dance class*, c.1876. Oil on canvas, $16\frac{3}{4} \times 22\frac{1}{2}$ in (43 × 57 cm). Washington, DC, Corcoran Gallery of Art (William A. Clark Collection)

OVERLEAF, RIGHT:
92. *Portraits in an office – the Cotton Exchange, New Orleans*, 1873. Oil on canvas, 29 × 36 in (73 × 92 cm). Pau, Musée des Beaux-Arts

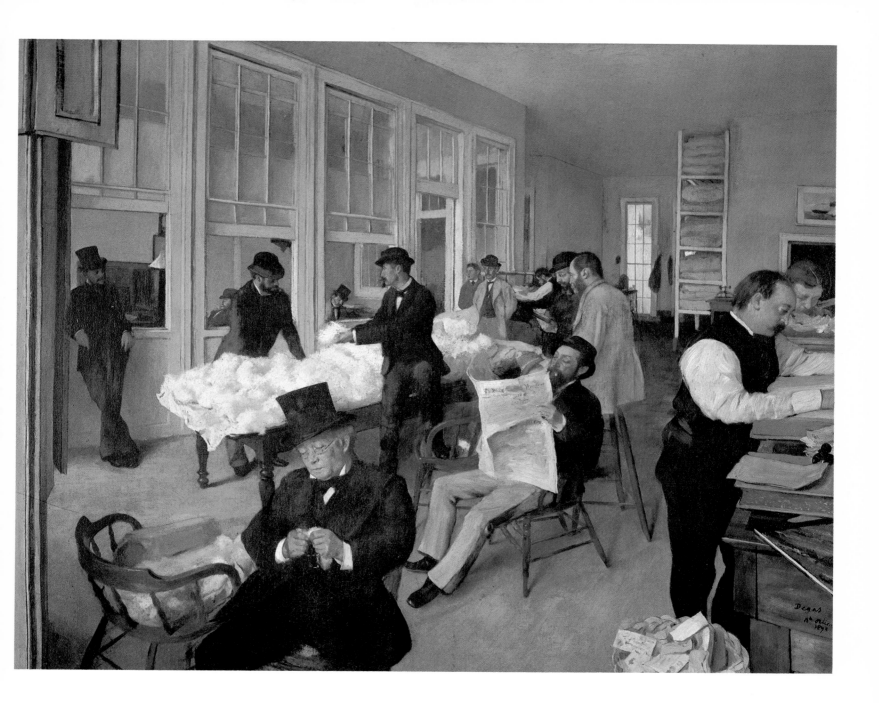

became the first work by Degas to enter a public collection.

The 'strong composition' referred to is *Portraits in an Office – The Cotton Exchange, New Orleans* (plate 92). It is the masterpiece of his American trip, a group portrait which rivals his picture of the orchestra, a work which is in the tradition of the group portraits of Guild officers painted by the seventeenth-century Dutch artists (it has been compared to Rembrandt's *The Sampling Officials of the Drapers' Guild* in the Rijksmuseum, Amsterdam), and which marks one of the high points of his Realist phase. The picture succeeds both as a collection of portraits and as a description of a particular world. The figures in the composition have been identified by John Rewald on the basis of his researches in New Orleans.[32] Michel Musson sits in the foreground examining a sample of cotton, his partner John Lavaudais inspects the ledgers at a desk to his left. Between the two men sits Degas's brother René, reading the *Times-Picayune*. Achille leans casually against a window-sill on the left of the picture. In the middle distance Michel Musson's other son-in-law William Bell shows cotton to a potential buyer. Achille and René appear to be taking little interest in what is going on, but then this was not their own but their uncle's place of business.

The tempo, however, of life in this office (before the invention of the telephone) is unhurried; decisions are reached slowly and recorded methodically. The picture is full of the atmosphere of the South: one can almost feel the humidity in the air, hear the swish of a fan and smell the distinctive New Orleans odour of coffee and chicory from a nearby café.

The detail in this painting is impressive; it is hard to see why Zola later criticized it for its weak drawing when he saw it at the second Impressionist exhibition in 1876. 'The result lies halfway between a marine painting and an engraving in an illustrated newspaper,' he wrote.[33] Did he mean the picture was vague in parts and detailed in others? Each figure, however, in the painting is the result of careful

93. *Estelle Musson de Gas*, 1872–3. Oil on canvas, 28½ × 36¼ in (73 × 92 cm). Washington, DC, National Gallery of Art (Chester Dale Collection)

OPPOSITE:
94. *Cotton merchants*, 1873. Oil on canvas, 23 × 28 in (60 × 73 cm). Cambridge, Mass., Courtesy of the Fogg Art Museum, Harvard University (Gift of Herbert N. Straus)

OVERLEAF:
95. *Dance class with
M. Mérante*, c.1875.
Oil on canvas, 30 ×
39 in (66 × 100 cm).
Glasgow Art
Gallery, Burrell
Collection

observation and reveals Degas's uncanny eye for character conveyed by pose as much as by facial expression. Equally impressive is the skill with which the composition is tied together by an overall colour scheme of black and white – black clothes and top hats, white shirts, cotton and newspaper – set against a background of pale greens and browns. The blacks are spaced evenly across the canvas like notes on a musical score, giving the picture a visual rhythm which catches and pleases the eye.

No preparatory drawings have survived to tell us how the picture evolved. Degas did, however, inform Tissot that he planned a second version which would be less complicated and more spontaneous and, he added, 'better art'.[34] The oil sketch (plate 94) may be a study for this second version of which otherwise no record remains. From his vantage point in New Orleans Degas began to see that the Realist movement was branching in two directions: one, the highly detailed, polished work of Tissot, Millais and the pre-Raphaelites which appealed to the English market; the other, the looser, more spontaneous style of French artists such as Manet and Monet. He believed that his colleagues in France were producing 'better art' than those in London, and he wrote to Tissot, in the letter mentioned above: 'Our race will have

something simple and bold to offer. The Naturalist movement will draw in a manner worthy of the great schools and then its strength will be recognized. This English art that appeals so much to us often seems to be exploiting some trick. We can do better than they and be just as strong.'

(iii)

With renewed vigour, his head crammed with ideas, Degas set sail for France, arriving back in Paris by the end of March 1873. 'What a lot of good this absence from Paris has done in my case,' he wrote to Tissot. 'I have made the most of it. I have made certain good resolutions which (you will laugh) I honestly feel capable of carrying out.'[35] His absence seems to have whetted his appetite for Parisian subjects. In New Orleans he had confessed that one Parisian laundry girl with bare arms was worth all the beauties he had seen on his journey,[36] and now that he was back he began a series of canvases which showed women ironing and carrying heavy baskets of laundry. Nearly one year later, when Edmond de Goncourt visited his studio in February 1874, he noticed a pile of these works and he was most impressed by Degas's

96. *Laundry-girl*, pastel. Paris, Louvre (Cabinet des Dessins)

knowledge of the laundry-girls' skills, watching him demonstrate the different ways to iron, using the pressing stroke for some articles of clothing and the circular stroke for others. Paris, it should be said, was famous for its laundries and many rich European families, like the Poniatowskis in Poland, used to send their linen all the way there for washing and pressing. The girls working in the laundries were a familiar sight in most districts, but until Degas and Zola began to study them at work they had been overlooked by French painters and writers. It is true that Fragonard and Boucher painted buxom peasant girls washing clothes in the river in picturesque settings, but Degas's approach was more matter-of-fact, more in the tradition of such Dutch artists as Pieter de Hooch. This type of subject, like those of many of his works, from the portrait of the Bellelli

97. *Laundry-girl*, 1873-4. Oil, $9\frac{3}{4} \times 7\frac{1}{2}$ in (24.7 × 19 cm). William Beadleston Inc.

98. *Laundry-girls*, 1882. Oil on canvas, 31 × 28¾ in (79 × 73 cm). Paris, Collection Durand-Ruel

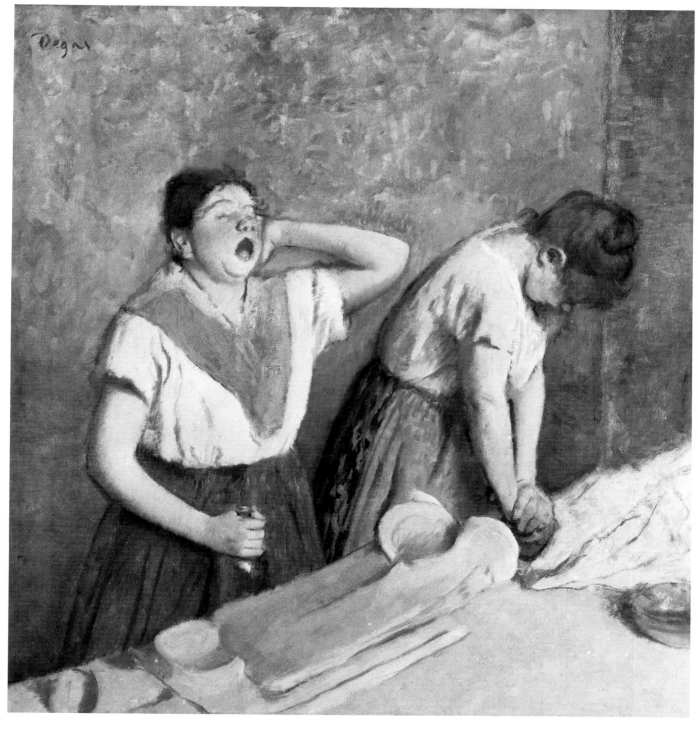

OVERLEAF, LEFT: 99. *Laundry-girls ironing*, c.1884. Oil on canvas, 34¼ × 29½ in (87 × 75 cm). Los Angeles, Norton Simon Foundation

OVERLEAF, RIGHT: 100. *Two ballet girls*, c.1879. Pastel on paper, 18 × 26¼ in (45 × 65 cm). Vermont, Courtesy of the Shelburne Museum

family to *The Cotton Exchange*, belongs to a Northern tradition. He treats all these subjects, however, with a French sensibility, with a light palette and cool clear colours. Unlike Manet, who visited Holland in 1872 and returned to paint the Hals-like portrait, *Le Bon Bock* – he was accused of 'watering his talent with Haarlem beer'[37] – Degas remained true to his heritage and his training.

The laundry provided Degas with numerous opportunities: there were the work rooms piled with freshly-ironed shirts (plate 99), baskets stacked with washing, sheets hanging up to dry. There were the girls themselves (plates 96–98) bathed in sweat, singing, yawning, stretching their aching arms and tired backs, showing many of the same gestures of physical fatigue as the young ballet dancers that he was also painting in the 1870s. Compare plate 99 with plate 100; in the former they can be seen from the back of the shop silhouetted against the daylight coming in through a window and a doorway. They

102. *The rehearsal of the ballet on stage*, 1873-4. Oil colours with turpentine, watercolour and pastel over pen and ink drawing on paper mounted on canvas, 21½ × 28¾ in (53 × 72 cm). New York, Metropolitan Museum (Gift of Horace Havemeyer, 1929)

OPPOSITE:
101. *Dance lesson*, 1874-5. Oil on canvas, 33½ × 29½ in (85 × 75 cm). Paris, Louvre (Jeu de Paume)

are massive creatures compared with the young dancers whom he also liked to paint against a backdrop of light, but they are alike in the sense that they both earned their living by physical effort.

Goncourt had also noticed at Degas's studio 'the curious silhouette of a dancer's legs coming down a staircase, outlined against the light of a window.' He was presumably referring to the picture in the Burrell Collection (plate 95), as he goes on to mention 'a ridiculous ballet-master serving as a vulgar foil'. Goncourt was impressed by Degas's grasp of dancing technique and was amused to see him, 'up on his toes and with arms curved, blending the aesthetics of the dance-master with the aesthetics of the painter'. He concluded his account of his visit by adding: 'An original fellow, this Degas, sickly, neurotic, and so ophthalmic that he is afraid of losing his sight; but for this very reason an eminently receptive creature

and sensitive to the character of things. Among all the artists I have met so far, he is the one who has best been able, in representing modern life, to catch the spirit of that life.'[38]

The Burrell picture is one of a series of related pictures of dancers which Degas began after his return to Paris in 1873. Many of these pictures exist in pairs or threes. There are the two dance classes with girls descending a staircase (plates 91 and 95), the two versions of the dance class taken by the famous dancer and ballet master Jules Perrot in a distinctive pose resting on a thick wooden stick (one in the Louvre, plate 101, and one in a private collection, plate 109); and then there are the three versions (two in the Metropolitan and one in the Louvre) of the rehearsal on stage (plate 102) which show young dancers illuminated by the stage footlights rehearsing before the watchful eyes of the director seated in the

Degas

PAGE 114:
103. *Elena Carafa*,
c.1873-4. Oil on
canvas, $27\frac{1}{2} \times 21\frac{1}{2}$ in
(70×55 cm).
London, National
Gallery

PAGE 115:
104. *Girl in red*,
1873-5. Oil on
canvas, $38\frac{1}{2} \times 31\frac{1}{2}$ in
(98×80 cm).
Washington, DC,
National Gallery of
Art (Chester Dale
Collection)

105. *A ballet dancer in
position*, 1872. Pencil with
black crayon and white
chalk on pink paper, $16 \times
11\frac{1}{4}$ in (41×28.5 cm).
Cambridge, Mass.,
Courtesy of the Fogg Art
Museum, Harvard
University (Bequest of
Meta and Paul J. Sachs)

PAGE 118:
107. *Before the start*, c.1875
-8. Oil, $12\frac{1}{2} \times 16$ in ($31.75
\times 40.5$ cm). Switzerland,
Private Collection

PAGE 119:
108. *Racehorses at
Longchamp*, 1873-5. Oil on
canvas, $12 \times 15\frac{3}{4}$ in (30×40
cm). Boston, Museum of
Fine Arts (S.A. Denio
Collection)

106. Study for
*Portrait of Jules
Perrot*, 1875.
Essence on grey-
green paper, 18¾ ×
11¼ in (47.5 × 30
cm). Philadelphia,
Henry P. McIlhenny
Collection

tions or rehearsals. Ronald Pickvance has demonstrated[39] how Degas would make use of the same
figure in different pictures: a drawing of Mlle
Gaujelin served as a study for a picture of *Three
Dancers*, silhouetted against a window, which in
turn is related to the Corcoran Gallery's *Dance Class*
(plate 91).[40] Similarly Degas made multiple use of
the figure of Jules Perrot, showing him in the two
dance classes mentioned above, in a rehearsal on
stage, in a monotype and in a portrait sketch on his
own (plate 106).

These pictures have several features in common
which distinguish them from the two small oils done
in 1872, discussed earlier (plates 86, 87). They show a
greater interest in movement and in more complex
lighting – the effect of footlights on figures on a stage
and the effect of backlighting on figures standing in
front of a window (plate 91) – and a greater freedom
in the use of colour, with the dancers wearing bigger
and brighter sashes (plate 95). In general the paintings
are more animated than the earlier works; some show
ballerinas in mid-dance, standing on points, with
arms raised, in arabesque. The floors remain carefully
defined with the floor-boards helping to underline
the perspective of the rooms. As Valéry remarked:
'Degas is one of the rare painters who gives due
emphasis to the *ground*. His floors are often admirable.
Sometimes he will view a *danseuse* from a fair height,
projecting her shape against the plane of the stage,
just as we see a crab on the beach, a standpoint which
gives him novel angles and interesting juxtaposi-
tions.'[41]

The ballet pictures painted in the two or three years
after 1873 are among the most popular and most
widely reproduced of all his works – and with good
reason: they are pretty without being sentimental,
and full of carefully observed detail. Once the eye has
taken in the overall effect, it can roam around these
pictures and delight in their individual components –
a girl scratching her back, another tying on her
slipper, a member of the chorus yawning, a director
leaning back in his chair watching a rehearsal in
apparent boredom, a watering-can used to sprinkle
the floor to keep the dust down, even a small dog
standing at the feet of a dancer watching M. Perrot's
class. These works are now so familiar that it is easy
to overlook their originality. But in the mid-1870s
they made an abrupt break with the pictures of the
ballet then in circulation. For the most part these
consisted of coloured prints showing the great
ballerinas of the day, Fanny Elssler and Marie
Taglioni, in the costumes of their best-known roles,
striking graceful poses. They were artificial and
sentimental, distant forerunners of the glossy photo-

wings. The starting point for these pictures was a
group of sketches dated 1873, bearing the name of
Mlle Gaujelin, a retired dancer-turned-actress who
had served as a model for Degas in the 1860s. With
their help it is possible to trace Degas's working
methods at this time; he first studied the figure in
isolation, usually in his studio, before building up a
kind of pattern book for the more complex compositions with several figures in dance classes, examina-

graphs of Hollywood stars issued a century later. The actual steps of the ballet dancer, her training, her life behind the stage went unrecorded. After Degas the world of the ballet has never been the same; his observations have proved so just and so telling that it has been nearly impossible for any later painter to tackle the subject without appearing to imitate him.

There is the same striking originality in Degas's racing scenes of this period, which separates them from the mass of those which were then in such demand. These works, like their ballet counterparts, are small in scale and delicate in colour, the silks worn by the jockeys corresponding to the costumes and ribbons worn by the dancers. The horses and their riders, like the ballet dancers, are anonymous and the racecourses have generally proved hard to identify. One work, which shows a twin steeple on the horizon, was at one time thought to have been painted on the outskirts of New Orleans, but it is now believed to show a racecourse in the suburbs of Paris.[42] The course at Longchamp, which opened in 1857, however, provided the setting for a work painted around 1874 (plate 107). This is perhaps the masterpiece of his racing pictures. It shows the jockeys and their mounts in an informal group walking or trotting their horses down to the start, the colours of the silks – lemon-yellow, mauve, azure blue – glistening in the sunlight, standing out in contrast to the pale greens of the turf and the mottled browns of the hillside in the distance. The picture has a quiet mood and is reminiscent of those small-scale landscapes with horsemen and figures which Dutch artists such as, for example, Cuyp painted. The riders are relaxed, concentrating on the feel of their horses in preparation for the hectic moments ahead. In its relative calm this work can be contrasted to a painting done two or three years later (plate 108), which shows the horses and riders grouping themselves in front of the starter, with one jockey on the left desperately trying to bring his horse under control.

(iv)

The year 1874 marks a turning point in Degas's life: his father died on 23 February, the first Impressionist exhibition opened on 15 April, and on 19 July he was 40. The death of his father had unfortunate repercussions: the affairs of the small bank were found to be in disarray with large sums owed to other banks, including a sum of 40,000 francs owed to the Banque d'Anvers which had been used by René to start his business in New Orleans. If the Degas bank was to remain in business René would have to pay back what he owed; but he was in no position to do this and further credit had to be arranged to allow him to repay it in three instalments spread over a year. Achille returned to Paris and with his uncle Henri Musson (Michel's younger brother) they attempted to sort out the family's affairs; but to no avail. The cotton market slumped (the price of cotton fell from around 17 cents a pound in 1874 to around 10 cents a pound in 1876), René was unable to pay back his debts, and the bank slid further into debt. To make matters worse the year 1874 saw the beginning of a worldwide economic depression, as severe as that of the 1930s, with stock-markets crashing simultaneously in Germany, France, England and America.[43]

By August 1876 the Degas business affairs showed no signs of improvement. In a letter written on 31 August Achille summed up the situation:

'You know the condition in which father's firm was placed at the time of his death; only on credit have I been able to support an enormous uncovered balance during two years, but that credit is at last exhausted, the firm's business was nearly at a standstill and we have, so to speak, no more clients. It was at last necessary to call a halt . . . We are obliged, Edgar, Marguerite and I, to live altogether on a bare subsistence, in order to honour the promises we have made.'[44]

Eventually Degas and his brother-in-law Henri-Gabriel Fèvre (who was married to Marguerite), in order to stave off a suit threatened by the Banque d'Anvers, settled the debts of the family bank out of their own pockets. Degas sold his house, his collection of Old Masters, including some eighteenth-century pastels inherited from his father, and he found himself forced to sell his own work as well. For someone brought up in the secure bourgeois world of mid-nineteenth-century Paris this represented more than financial hardship: it meant loss of status, loss of freedom and loss of self-confidence. Degas became extraordinarily sensitive on the subject of his family's affairs. Although he behaved in a dignified and responsible manner in meeting the family debt, going beyond what was legally necessary, yet he resented any mention of his actions. George Moore was rash enough to write in one of his memoirs that: 'It is rumoured that he [Degas] is a man of some private fortune, and a story is in circulation that he sacrificed the greater part of his income to save his brother, who had lost everything by imprudent speculation in American securities.'[45] Degas was furious and refused to speak to Moore again.

Degas was more fortunate than many of his colleagues in that his work proved fairly easy to sell. Even in those difficult economic times Durand-Ruel was able to find buyers for him both in London and in Paris. In England, as mentioned earlier, there was Captain Henry Hill, and in Paris in 1875 a young American, Miss Louise Elder, the future Mrs Havemeyer, bought her first Degas. She was brought to Durand-Ruel's gallery by another young American, Mary Cassatt, who made her look at a pastel of a ballet rehearsal. 'I scarcely knew how to appreciate it,' she wrote later, 'or whether I liked it or not, for I believe it takes special brain cells to understand Degas. There was nothing the matter with Miss Cassatt's brain cells, however, and she left me in no doubt as to the desirability of the purchase and I

bought it on her advice.'[46] Mrs Havemeyer subsequently built up the largest collection of Degas's work outside the artist's own.

The most important collector for Degas, however, in the 1870s was the baritone Jean-Baptiste Faure. He was a popular figure at the Opéra and earned large sums for his appearances in spite of the economic depression. He was a vain and difficult man but had an eye for painting. He was among the first to collect Manet's work; in 1872 he bought five pictures from him all at one time, and paid 6,000 francs for *Le Bon Bock* – a large sum by Manet's standards, but very little in comparison with the prices charged by a

109. *Ballet lesson on stage*, c.1875. Monotype, pastel and gouache, 21½ × 27 in (55 × 68 cm). Los Angeles, Norton Simon Foundation

110. *Ballet scene from 'Robert Le Diable'*, c.1876. Oil on canvas, 29½ × 32 in (75 × 81 cm). London, Victoria and Albert Museum

successful Salon artist like Meissonier or Bouguereau. He discovered Degas about the same time as he discovered Manet, and soon after meeting him he purchased the *Carriage at the Races* for 1,500 francs and a *Dance Class* for 5,000 francs. In about 1874 he commissioned four large canvases from Degas, pictures of dancers, racehorses and laundresses, and *The Ballet Scene from Robert le Diable* (plate 110), which showed the dance of the nuns in a scene from Meyerbeer's very popular opera. In addition to a sum paid directly to Degas he agreed to buy back a group of paintings from Durand-Ruel which Degas had been forced to sell earlier and which he believed were not properly finished. Degas delivered two paintings to Faure in 1876, but the remaining two were still incomplete ten years later. Faure lost patience and

sued Degas for them and won the case. Even without this difficulty, theirs was not an easy relationship: Faure was egotistical and demanding, and Degas not suited to the role of flatterer. One evening he went to the singer's dressing-room to compliment him on his performance but found the room full of well-wishers all exclaiming their admiration for the singer with cries of 'Magnificent! Admirable! Sublime!' Degas could not resist adding, 'And so simple!'[47]

Even under the best conditions, Degas disliked selling his work, partly because he felt the whole business was demeaning and took his mind off his researches, and partly because he was never satisfied that he had finished a work. In his studio his paintings lived with him and grew old with him; he added to and changed them at will. Once a picture was sold it

OPPOSITE:
111. EDOUARD MANET, *Head of Jean-Baptiste Faure*. Oil on canvas, 18 × 15 in (45.7 × 38 cm). New York, Metropolitan Museum (Gift of Mrs Ralph J. Hines, 1959)

was beyond his grasp, that is unless it had been sold to a friend like Henri Rouart. Ernest Rouart tells the revealing story of the fate of one of the many Degas pictures bought by his father:

'Whenever he came upon some more or less early work of his own, he always wanted to get it back on the easel and rework it. Thus, after seeing again and again at our house a delightful pastel my father had bought and was very fond of, Degas was seized with his habitual and imperious urge to retouch it. He would not let the matter alone, and in the end my father, from sheer weariness, let him take it away. It was never seen again.

Often my father would ask him about his beloved pastel; Degas would put him off in one way or another, but in the end he had to confess his crime: the work entrusted to him for a few retouches had been completely destroyed. Imagine my father's despair; he never forgave himself for being party to the destruction of something he was so fond of.

It was then that Degas, to make up to him for his loss, sent him one day the famous "Danseuses à la barre".

The comic part of it was that for years and years afterwards we would hear Degas, whenever he saw this picture, say to my father: "That watering can is definitely idiotic, I simply must take it out!" I believe he was right, and that the effect of the picture could only have been improved by the removal of that utensil. But having learned from experience, my father would never allow him another try.'[48]

(v)

Degas's difficulties in finishing his works may also have had their origin in the many disruptions he experienced in the 1870s: the various trips and excursions he made to the country and abroad, his financial worries, the sale of his house, and also the eight Impressionist exhibitions in which he took an active part. All these activities interrupted his flow and encouraged him to put aside an uncompleted oil to be finished later.

The first Impressionist exhibition opened in April 1874, but plans for it had been made over the previous year. The idea for the exhibition was first proposed by Monet and Pissarro, whom Degas knew at the Café Guerbois. Both artists were tired of having their work rejected by the official Salon which was still the same reactionary force that it had been during the Second Empire. In 1837 they approached Degas, asking him to join in forming an independent exhibition, to be held before the Salon opened, to be selected by artists and hung by artists. Degas agreed to take part, not because he sympathized with their revolutionary ideas, but because, as previously discussed, he disliked the atmosphere of the Salon and because he felt the Realist movement, of which he now felt a part, needed a forum. 'The Realist movement no longer needs to fight with the others,' he explained to Tissot in an attempt to win him over to the cause. 'It already *is*, it *exists*. It must show itself as something distinct. There must be a Salon of Realists.'[49] But Degas felt that it was important that the independent exhibition should not appear to be made up of Salon rejects. He agreed to take part only if the exhibition was broadened to include successful artists as well as some who exhibited regularly at the Salon. The others reluctantly agreed, not because they welcomed the inclusion of Degas's friends, but because it made economic sense to defray the cost of the exhibition by increasing the number of exhibitors, each of whom had to pay an entrance fee. On 27 December 1873 Degas and his friends Ludovic Lepic, Léopold Levert and Henri Rouart signed a charter to set up the first Impressionist exhibition, together with Monet, Pissarro, Renoir, Edouard Béliard and Armand Guillaumin.[50]

During the next four months Degas set out to persuade more of his friends to take part. He tried hard to encourage Manet to join the enterprise but learnt that Manet, who at last, after many years of trying, had found success at the Salon with his *Bon Bock*, preferred to stay with the Salon, his eyes now set on winning an honourable mention or a prize. 'I definitely think he is more vain than intelligent,' was Degas's opinion. The relationship between the two artists, never easy, now began to deteriorate. In about 1878 Manet tried to explain to Degas how important it was for the artist to seek recognition while he was still alive: 'In this beastly life of ours, which is wholly a struggle, one is never too well armed. I know I have not been decorated. But it is not my fault, and I assure you that I shall be if I can and that I shall do everything necessary to that end.' Degas was contemptuous; shrugging his shoulders he replied: 'Naturally, I've always known how much of a bourgeois you are.'[51]

Degas thought he stood a better chance of persuading his friends in London, Tissot and Legros, to take part, but once again he was unsuccessful. A long enthusiastic letter to Tissot, explaining the venture, went unheeded. Despite the fire at the Opéra on 28 October 1873, which struck him as a personal loss, and despite the illness of his father and his subsequent death in February, Degas entered into the arrangements for the exhibition with energy and enthusiasm. 'I am really getting worked up and running the thing with energy,' he told Tissot, adding, 'and, I think, a certain success.'[52]

The place chosen for the exhibition was the studio of the photographer Félix Nadar, which overlooked the boulevard des Capucines, then as now one of the busiest streets in Paris. It was a corner site with direct access from the street below. The rooms were large, well-lit and hung in russet-coloured cloth, a reflection of Nadar's taste – he adored everything red, had red hair, wore red clothes, gave red borders to his prints and signed his name in red ink. Degas inspected the rooms and declared himself pleased.

The exhibition opened on 15 April. There was a last-minute dispute when the organizers attempted to find a title for their group. Degas proposed 'Les Capucines' after the boulevard, Renoir objected and finally a name was selected without any overtones and the group was called the Société Anonyme des Artistes, Peintres, Sculpteurs, Graveurs, etc. But the critics who came to review the exhibition found the title too anonymous; the group was called by some Intransigents and by Louis Leroy, in the satirical magazine *Charivari*, Impressionists, after the title of one of Monet's pictures in the show, *Impression, Sunrise*.[53]

Degas was represented by ten works, including the *Dance Class* of 1872 (plate 86), *Carriage at the Races* (plate 84), a *Dance Class* belonging to Faure and a picture of laundresses. On the whole they were well received. The main fire of the critics was directed elsewhere, at Monet, at Renoir (who exhibited a charming picture of a young dancer) and above all at Cézanne, who was represented by a turbulent fantasy, a kind of spoof on Manet, called *A Modern Olympia*.

The exhibition, which has been so well documented by John Rewald,[54] need not be discussed in detail here, but it is worth stressing that it made much less impact than is commonly supposed. It was the subsequent exhibitions which brought in the crowds and set the critics searching for new terms of abuse. At the first exhibition the attendance was modest: 3,500 people saw it in four weeks, 175 on the first day and 54 on the last. In the evenings there were times when there were only two or three people in the rooms. The exhibition generated few sales and, when the accounts were closed, it was found to have run at a deficit and the charter members decided to abandon their society and start again.

The most prominent critics of the day ignored the exhibition, saving themselves for lengthy reviews of the Salon. Jules Castagnary, however, an early supporter of Courbet and the Realist movement, did write a review in *Le Siècle*, in which he applauded the artists' initiative in organizing the exhibition, but doubted whether the group would be able to hold together:

'*Within a few years the artists who today have grouped themselves on the boulevard des Capucines will be divided. The strongest will have recognized that while there are subjects which lend themselves to a rapid impression, to the appearance of a sketch, there are others in much greater numbers that demand a more precise impression . . . Those painters who, continuing their course, will have perfected their draughtsmanship, will abandon impressionism as an art really too superficial for them.*'[55]

Castagnary was proved right. Degas had little in common with the 'Impressionists' in the group. He was primarily interested in painting the human figure; his colleagues in the exhibition, Monet, Pissarro, Sisley and to some extent Renoir, were mainly occupied with landscape. He was at heart a draughtsman and they were painters, colourists. He believed that a work of art stemmed from the painter's imagination and should be done from memory in the studio; they believed that a work of art should accurately reflect what the painter sees and should be done directly in front of the subject or motif. He believed in perception; they believed in observation. The sketchiness of his pictures stemmed from his training as a draughtsman, a discipline which encourages the rapid sketch and allows the artist to be spontaneous in the way he first puts down his ideas on paper. The landscape artists in the exhibition appeared 'sketchy' to Castagnary and others because of the system of painting in dabs of pigment, short comma-like brushstrokes, in an attempt to capture the fleeting colours they saw in 'light'; their sketchiness stemmed from being painters, not draughtsmen.

Gradually the differences between Degas and the Impressionists became more pronounced, and future exhibitions divided into two groups: Degas and his friends on the one side; Monet, Pissarro, Sisley and Renoir on the other. But despite these differences Degas, unlike Monet, Renoir and Sisley, remained committed to the idea of an independent exhibition held outside the Salon and he took part in seven of the eight exhibitions. (Only one artist took part in all eight and that was the kind and tolerant Pissarro.)

Chapter 4

1874 to 1884

IN THE MID-1870s the Café de la Nouvelle-Athènes on the place Pigalle replaced the Café Guerbois as the favourite haunt of the writers and painters in the Impressionist circle. With its marble-top tables and hat-stands it looked like many Parisian cafés of the period and was probably not much different from the Café Guerbois, but it left a vivid mark in the memory of one of its habitués, George Moore, who regarded it and the conversations he heard there as his university. 'I can recall the smell of every hour,' he wrote. 'In the morning that of eggs frizzling in butter, the pungent cigarettes, coffee and bad cognac; at five o'clock the fragrant odour of absinthe; and soon after the steaming soup ascends from the kitchen; and as the evening advances, the mingled smells of cigarettes, coffee and weak beer.'[1] Degas used to arrive at the café at ten o'clock in the evening and sit at a table to the right of the entrance reserved for him and his friends. Moore described him wearing a pepper-and-salt suit and a large necktie, round-shouldered, his eyes small, and his words 'sharp, ironical and cynical'. Sometimes Degas was very argumentative, and he was accused by Gustave Caillebotte, a wealthy engineer-turned-painter, of spending his time at the Nouvelle-Athènes haranguing his colleagues:

'[He] would do much better to paint a little more. That he is a hundred times right in what he says, that he talks with infinite wit and good sense about painting, no one doubts (and isn't that the outstanding part of his reputation?). But it is no less true that the real arguments of a painter are his paintings and that even if he were a thousand times right in his talk, he would still be much more right on the basis of his work.'[2]

The figure that Degas cut at this time was neatly caught by Marcellin Desboutin's etching of about 1876 (plate 112), in which he is shown standing in an imperious fashion, elbows thrust behind him, hands on hips. It is a forceful stance, but it is also one adopted by a man with back-ache. He had in fact a tendency to stoop, as the drawing by F. Mathey (plate 113) done six years later makes clear. In his forties he must have looked old for his age; his hair had thinned on top, his face was pale from long hours spent in the studio and when he ventured out, he usually protected his ailing eyes against the glare by wearing tinted glasses or a pince-nez straddling his rather short nose.[3]

He lunched every day with rare exceptions at the Café de la Rochefoucauld. On Mondays he went to the Opéra to which he had a season ticket and a pass which allowed him to go backstage. On Tuesdays he went to Alexis Rouart's house and on Fridays to his brother Henri Rouart. The people he saw socially, away from the Nouvelle-Athènes, tended to come from the same world as himself. Besides the Rouarts these included Ludovic Halévy, the playwright who together with Henri Meilhac was responsible for the libretto of Bizet's *Carmen* and of many of Offenbach's

112. MARCELLIN DESBOUTIN, *Portrait of Degas*, c.1876. Etching, $8\frac{3}{4} \times 5\frac{3}{4}$ in (22.8 × 14.6 cm). New York, Metropolitan Museum (Rogers Fund, 1922)

operettas, the sculptor Paul-Albert Bartholomé, Albert Cavé, whose eminence, according to Daniel Halévy, lay in the fact that he did nothing all his life, but whose wit 'spangled many of the light comedies written during the Second Empire'[4] (he can be seen standing with Ludovic Halévy backstage in plate 158); and Charles Ephrussi, connoisseur, the founder and editor of the *Gazette des Beaux-Arts* magazine and one of the models for Proust's Swann. Although immensely hard-working himself, contrary to what Caillebotte said, Degas seems to have enjoyed the company of men of leisure, social ease, wit and good looks. Like Proust he was much intrigued by the elegant man-about-town Charles Haas, another model for Swann. Proust in turn took an interest in Degas of whom he had heard from his schoolfriend Jacques-Emile Blanche, and he may have had Degas in mind when he later wrote of the painter Elstir: 'Lacking society that was endurable, he lived in isolation with a savagery which fashionable people called pose and ill-breeding, public authorities a recalcitrant spirit, his neighbours madness, his family

113. F. MATHEY,
Edgar Degas,
February 1882.
Pencil, 18¾ × 12¼ in
(48 × 31 cm).
Present whereabouts
unknown

selfishness and pride.'[5] Degas, who admired the social ease of such men as Cavé, Ephrussi and Haas, and for that matter Manet, was seldom at ease in society himself. He was happiest in the company of a few close friends, many of whom he had known since his childhood, and when he met people outside that group he often seemed brusque and bad-tempered. Quite a number, like Ludovic Halévy, were Jews, which makes his subsequent behaviour over the Dreyfus affair all the harder to understand.

His artist friends did not belong to the immediate Impressionist circle, partly because many of the collaborators on the first Impressionist exhibition were now settled outside Paris and partly because he seems to have regarded them as rough company. 'Do you really invite those people to your house?' he once asked Caillebotte, referring to Monet and Renoir.[6] Several of the artists whom he saw regularly in the second half of the 1870s were Italians or had Italian connections – Federico Zandomeneghi, a Venetian who came to Paris in 1874; Jean-François Raffaëlli, son of an Italian father, an actor-turned-painter whom Degas invited to exhibit with the Impressionists; Giuseppe de Nittis from Barletta; Carlo Pellegrini (plate 147) from Capua, a cartoonist who spent some time in Paris before establishing himself in London; and Marcellin Desboutin, who returned to Paris in about 1874 after many years in Florence. Through these Italian artists, through the Italian critic Diego Martelli (plate 148) and the occasional visit to Florence and Naples on family business, Degas kept in touch with the Italian Realist movement and the work of the Macchiaioli, a group of artists named after the word *macchia* or spot, because their pictures were painted in patches of colour accenting the contrast of light and dark.

Many of his friends were chosen for their conviviality and social background; on the other hand he was drawn to Mary Cassatt, whom he met in 1877, and Walter Sickert, to whom he was introduced by Whistler in 1884, because of their artistic talent. According to Renoir, Degas liked to 'mystify' people with his artistic enthusiasms:

'I have seen him amuse himself like a schoolboy by puffing up a great reputation for some artist or other whose fame, in the ordinary course of events, was certain to perish the following week.

He fooled me badly once. One day I was on the driver's box of an omnibus, and Degas, who was crossing the street, shouted to me through his hands: "Be sure to go and see Count Lepic's exhibition!"

I went. Very conscientiously I looked for something of interest. When I met Degas again, I said: "What about your Lepic exhibition?"

"It's fine, isn't it? A great deal of talent," Degas replied. *"It's too bad he's such a light weight!"* [7]

Although there was an element of snobbery in his friendships, his cultural tastes were catholic. His taste in opera was regarded by, for instance, the Halévys, father and son, as rather low. He resisted the enthusiasm for Wagner whose music was the subject of a revival of interest in Paris in the early 1880s and of whom he used to say, 'He's a bore. He's a bore. With his Grail and his Father Parsifal.'[8] He seems to have been just as much at home in the humbler and somewhat vulgar café-concerts as at the Opéra, listening to the singers and their comic songs about dogs, landlords and cuckolded husbands. He liked the circus and the Pantomime Anglais which enjoyed a vogue in Paris in the 1870s.[9] His friend and biographer Paul Lafond tells us that he had a special liking for the clowns and prized their irony, their cruelty and their buffoonery.[10] There was in Degas himself a touch of the clown, and Sickert remarked on Degas's 'rollicking and somewhat bear-like sense of fun'.[11]

Although it has been said that in his pictures of working women he shows an aloofness and an aristocratic disdain – a criticism also levelled at the Goncourt brothers – many of his remarks reveal a different aspect of his character. 'I like to see the families of the working men in the Marais,' he once remarked to the Halévys. 'You go into these wretched-looking houses with great wide doors, and you find bright rooms, meticulously clean. You can see them through the open doors from the hall. Everybody is lively; everybody is working. And these people have none of the servility of a merchant in his shop. Their society is delightful.'[12] In the last years of his life he enjoyed travelling around Paris in an omnibus, which he much preferred to a *fiacre* or cab, because it allowed him to look at his fellow passengers.

It was his interest in working-class life which inspired an idea for a series on bakers, a project which he never carried out, but which would have complemented the paintings of laundresses. His eye was caught by the decorative possibilities suggested by the sight of bakers working in their cellars, glimpsed through an air vent leading up to the street, and he made a note of the colour of the flour (*couleur de farine rose*): 'Lovely curves of pie, still lifes on the different breads, large, oval, fluted, round, etc. Experiment, in colour, on the yellows, pinks, grey-whites of breads. Perspective views of rows of breads. Charming layout of bakeries. Cakes, the wheat, the mills, the flour, the sacks, the market-porters.'[13]

Indeed his head teemed with ideas, many of which

he was not able to realize. Some, such as an idea for a series on mourning and different degrees of blacks, were very much his own, others, like his note to study 'smoke, smoke of smokers, pipes, cigarettes, smoke of locomotives, of high chimneys, factories, steamboats, destruction of smoke under bridges, steam',[14] were shared by his Impressionist colleagues. Manet, for example, had studied the effect of smoke from trains in his painting *The Railroad* (1874), and in 1877 Monet set up his easel and canvas at the Gare St Lazare to study the effect of trains shunting in and out of the station, letting fly great puffs of steam and smoke as they gathered power.

Like many of his Impressionist colleagues, he enjoyed occasional visits to the seaside. In Dieppe he stayed with Ludovic Halévy who used to take a summer villa there, and in the early 1880s he became friendly with a group of sophisticated artists, mainly portrait painters, who were at home on both sides of the channel and moved freely in the fashionable Anglo-French society that gathered at resorts like Dieppe in the summer months. These included Jacques-Emile Blanche, mentioned above, the son of an eminent physician, the writer Henri Gervex, who according to Georges Rivière was a 'sympathetic fellow, possessing a distinguished manner, full of warmth',[15] and Sickert. In 1885 in Blanche's studio in Dieppe Degas painted a group portrait of his friends (plate 114) which included Cavé in the foreground and behind him Gervex, Blanche and Ludovic Halévy. The young Daniel Halévy, wearing a straw boater, pokes his head out between his father and Blanche; and Sickert, the English visitor, stands separate from the group on the right, holding his hat in his hand, wearing an overcoat with the collar half turned up. They are a worldly group of men, the sort who can be found later in Proust's *Remembrance of Things Past,* visiting the seaside resort of Balbec.

Earlier in 1876 Degas painted a picture which in many ways is the essence of a summer holiday at such a resort, *Beach Scene* (plate 137). It shows a young girl having her hair combed by a nurse, and in this respect it stands as a distant forerunner of those pictures a decade later (plate 174) of models having their hair combed by maids. But above all it is a picture full of sunlight and the atmosphere of the seaside, based, one feels, on direct close observation; Degas was, however, at pains to point out that the painting was done from memory in the studio, and when Vollard asked him how, he replied: 'It's quite simple. I spread my flannel vest on the floor and had the model sit on it.'[16]

It was the sort of subject which would also have

114. *Six friends*,
1885. Pastel and
black chalk on grey
paper now yellowed,
$45\frac{1}{4} \times 28$ in (113×70
cm). Providence,
Museum of Art,
Rhode Island School
of Design

115. *Dancer with a bouquet*, c.1878. Pastel and wash over black chalk on paper, $15\frac{1}{2} \times 19\frac{3}{4}$ in (40×45.4 cm). Providence, Museum of Art, Rhode Island School of Design (Gift of Mrs Murray S. Danforth)

appealed to Renoir; without each other realizing it, they were both attracted to the same subjects almost simultaneously, though from very different points of view. They both, for example, painted child dancers, the *rats* of the Opéra; they both were drawn to theatrical subjects – Renoir painted the *First Outing* (plate 117) in 1875 and Degas the view from a box in 1878 (plate 115); both painted scenes based on visits to the Cirque Fernando in 1879, Renoir showing two young jugglers standing in the ring holding oranges in their arms, and Degas painting the mulatto Miss La La suspended from the ceiling, gripping a rope with her teeth (plate 116). While Renoir dwells on the prettiness of the two little circus girls, Degas captures the way in which the spectators crane their necks to look up at the performers above them.

In many of his pictures of the 1870s Degas managed to catch an unusual angle from which to view his subject; his notebooks of the period explain his intentions: 'Having done portraits seen from above, I will do them seen from below – sitting very close to a woman and looking at her from a low viewpoint . . .',[17] and in the same notebook he wrote a reminder to himself to draw something simple, such as a profile, taking up his position at different levels. To do this he planned to set up a number of benches in his studio to help him get used to drawing from different levels. In composing his pictures he often looked for the unexpected effect produced by objects cutting into his field of vision, a flagpole at a racecourse (plate 138), the pillars of a café (plate 140) or a mirror at the milliner's (plate 144). This use of the unexpected was, as Duranty noticed, 'one of the great delights of reality'.[18]

After the age of forty (1874) Degas's style began to change. He became increasingly interested in technique, in means rather than ends, and this interest was matched by a gradual shift from the particular to the general, from the individual to the universal, from Realism to a new form of Classicism. The pictures

'It is the movement of people and things that distracts and even consoles, if there is still consolation to be had for one so unhappy. If the leaves of the trees did not move, how sad the trees would be and we too.'[19] It was the movement of the female figure which most delighted him and which drew him to the ballet. It was there that he found all that survived of the 'movement of the Greeks', the note of grace that he had observed in Greek statues as a young student in Paris and Rome. The pictures he now began brought him right back to his beginnings, to the study once again of the human figure.

(ii)

After thirteen years of construction Charles Garnier's huge new Opéra opened in January 1875. The building became a second home for him and its opening seems to have inspired him to study with greater depth the life and training of ballet dancers. At this time the great proportion of his work was devoted to the ballet, and the subject assumed such importance in his life that he himself remarked in a letter of 1886: '. . . even this heart of mine has something

117. AUGUSTE RENOIR, *The first outing*, 1875–6. Oil on canvas, 25½ × 19¾ in (64.7 × 50 cm). London, National Gallery

116. *Miss La La at the Cirque Fernando, Paris*, 1879. Oil on canvas, 46 × 30½ in (117 × 77.5 cm). After cleaning and restoration. London, National Gallery

became simplified, the number of figures were reduced from those of the early ballet pictures with ten or more dancers to works with three or four at the most. And as he moved closer to his subject, he began to lose interest in the individual quality of the face; his heads became generalized, and the pictures we see, for example, of the ballet stand for any dancer, in any ballet, at any time. Another important pre-occupation was to find ways of capturing movement, whether it be the pirouette of a dancer or the gait of a thoroughbred. Movement, he believed, gave beauty to people and objects. In 1886 he wrote to a friend:

118. *Dancer at the bar*, 1880.
Pastel, $26\frac{1}{4} \times 18\frac{1}{2}$ in (66 × 46 cm).
Vermont, Courtesy of the
Shelburne Museum

practising, painted in subdued colours heightened here and there by a splash of pink or scarlet ribbon, gradually became transformed into a subjective exercise, an endless search for the means to convey the dancer's movements and positions.

While the early paintings, such as those of the rehearsals and the dance classes of M. Mérante and M. Perrot, give the impression that he placed himself at a discreet distance from his subjects, either standing in the wings or at the back of the classroom, the pictures he now began to do suggest that he placed his drawing board quite close to the dancers, so as to study every straining muscle, every gesture, every grimace. Most of the studies were done in his studio using a model and, to judge by a letter sent to Albert Hecht written around 1880, Degas seldom went to the practice rooms at the Opéra itself: 'I have done so many of these dance examinations without ever having seen them,' he wrote, 'that I am a little ashamed.'[22]

From his position close to the girls he began to understand the physical effort and the mental concentration required for dancing. From 1875 onwards his pictures concentrate on the dancers' long hours of training and exercise and show an increased understanding of their off-duty moments, as they fuss with their clothing and make sure their slippers are properly tied on. He watched the young *rats* do their first exercises at the bar; he listened to the bumps and squeaks of the older girls practising their *pointe* work, he heard their groans and gasps as they finished their exercises and he saw them raising their hands to their foreheads in pain (plate 131) or sitting slumped on benches around the classroom (plate 124). The more familiar he became with their movements, the more confident and spontaneous became his drawing, and the colours of his pictures began to glow with a new warmth. His work became increasingly expressive, personal and emotional.

Several writers have noted[23] that one of the reasons why Degas identified so closely with the dancers is that their training was as long and as arduous as that of the artist. The hours of practice and rehearsal correspond to the hours Degas believed the artist should spend drawing and studying. He recognized in the rehearsal room the agonies he suffered in the studio. He could also identify with the artifice of the ballet: he watched relatively plain girls, with aching backs and bruised feet, become transformed by the stage lights into weightless creatures, the embodiment of female grace and allure. He believed too that painting involved artifice, that it was a conjuring trick performed by the artist in the privacy of his studio. 'Art is falsehood', he once remarked in the

119. *Dancer at the bar*, c.1885. Black chalk with touches of pink and white, $12\frac{1}{2} \times 9\frac{1}{2}$ in (31.2 × 23.7 cm). Cincinnati Art Museum

artificial. The dancers have sewn it into a bag of pink satin, pink satin slightly faded, like their dancing shoes';[20] and Zola, when it was suggested that Degas might be considered as the leader of the Realist school of the 1860s and 1870s, dismissed the idea as preposterous: 'I cannot accept a man who shuts himself up all his life to draw a ballet-girl as ranking co-equal in dignity and power with Flaubert, Daudet and Goncourt,' he remarked.[21] The view that Degas painted nothing but pretty pastels of dancers, first expressed by Zola, has persisted and to some extent still tends to obscure Degas's achievement in other fields. It is true, however, that in his forties Degas's interest in the dance amounted to an obsession. What started as an objective study of a certain world, beginning with pictures of large rooms illuminated by a cool even light filled with girls exercising or

120. *Dancers in yellow*, 1878–80. Pastel over monotype, $11\frac{1}{2} \times 10$ in (29 × 26 cm). Paris, Collection Ernest Rouart

presence of Mallarmé, and to a young admirer he said: 'A picture is something which calls for as much cunning, trickery and vice as the perpetration of a crime.'[24] He believed that paintings must seem mysterious, that they must make people pause and wonder how they were done, and he bitterly resented the attempts of writers and journalists to explain the mystery of art:

'*I want to succeed where I want, when I want, and how I want. My God! People crowding around our pictures, why? Do they crowd into a chemist's laboratory? You have read how Manet used a black mirror to gauge values.*

All that is very complicated. What can they understand about it? Nothing! A chemist works in peace. We, we belong to everybody! What anguish!'[25]

The little *rats* of the ballet provided him with a subject within a subject. They mostly came from poor families and, according to Lillian Browse,[26] they arrived at the theatre wearing other people's discarded clothes, insufficiently fed and always begging for a few sous with which to buy sweets. They entered the Opéra between the ages of seven and eight and they grew up with little or no education but a desire to succeed. At ten, if they showed promise,

121. *Three dancers*, 1880.
Pastel, 31 × 19¾ in (81 × 51
cm). Paris, Collection
Durand-Ruel

135

they were given a salary of 900 francs a year, a fortune for many of the girls, and they spent the next eight or nine years taking classes and preparing to become members of the chorus or, if they were lucky, *petits sujets*.

Degas possessed a special knack for portraying young girls. He did not sentimentalize them as Renoir was apt to do, and yet he showed great insight into their characters and ambitions. Indeed the theme of young girls runs like a leitmotif throughout his career, from his sketches of Giulia Bellelli (plate 13) to his portrait of Hortense Valpinçon (plate 89) and

the pictures of his friends Lepic and Rouart with their respective daughters. He was still studying them in his old age when he could no longer paint, but could photograph them (plate 195), and he himself was photographed by an unknown hand standing at a window with a young girl at his side (plate 194). Young girls perhaps appealed to an avuncular side, or perhaps in their company he felt sexually secure: there was no need to be gallant and no need for any pretence. One work, however, perhaps unintentionally, does betray a strange sexual undercurrent, *The Little Dancer of Fourteen* (plate 172). The tilt of her

122. *Henri de Gas and his niece Lucy*, c.1876. Oil on canvas, $39\frac{1}{4} \times 47$ in (96×113 cm). Chicago, Art Institute (Mr and Mrs L. L. Coburn Collection)

123. *The ballet class*, c.1880. Oil on canvas, 32 × 30 in (81 × 76 cm). Philadelphia Museum of Art (W. P. Wisbach Collection). Formerly in the collection of Mary Cassatt

OVERLEAF, LEFT: 124. *Dancers resting*, c.1880. Pastel on paper mounted on cardboard, 19¾ × 23 in (50 × 58.5 cm). Boston, Museum of Fine Arts (Juliana C. Edwards Collection)

OVERLEAF, RIGHT: 125. *Ballet dancers in butterfly costumes*, c.1880. Pastel and tempera on paper, 27 × 19 in (69 × 48 cm). Los Angeles, Norton Simon Foundation

head, the forward thrust of her body, the half-closed eyes, suggest yearning. Seen full face she reminds one of those restless virgins whom Edvard Munch painted in the 1890s, holding their arms behind their backs, lifting up their heads, and forcing forward their breasts (for instance, the young girl in the painting called *The Voice*). It was perhaps the adult expression on the face of the young dancer which shocked many when it was exhibited in 1881 (see pp. 179–83).

Although Degas liked to maintain that he had a cold heart, it is evident that he came to sympathize with the dancers' struggles to get on. A letter to Ludovic Halévy survives in which he asks him to help arrange the re-engagement of a young nineteen-year-old dancer, Mlle Chabot, who had been at the Opéra since she was eight:

'*You must know what a dancer is like when she wants you to put in a word for her. She returns twice a day to find out whether you have seen anybody or whether you have written. Are you better? If you have the courage and strength write a word to Vaucorbeil or to Mérante, not about her salary, which would be wrong, but about her dancing, her past and her future. I have never known anybody so worked up. She wants everything done immediately. She would wrap you up and carry you to the Opéra if she could.*'[27]

Degas's paintings and drawings of the 1870s show a greater awareness of the reality of women's lives and ambitions than that of any artist of his time. Womanizers like Manet and Renoir, for example, could not help glamorizing their models, drawing attention to their physical charms rather than to their social position. Degas observed them with a colder eye, getting nearer to the truth, showing them using their physical gifts to earn a living – *working* in the laundry, *working* at the Opéra, *working* as singers in cafés, or *working* in a brothel.

Nineteenth-century Paris could boast an unusually rich supply of brothels and more prostitutes per head than any city in Europe. In 1870 it was estimated that there were 145 official brothels in Paris, called *maisons de tolérance*, which were under police surveillance and subject to medical inspection. But there were many more clandestine ones and many cafés which served as annexes to dubious hotels. The numbers of prostitutes working in Paris were recorded in the official statistics: between 1871 and 1903 the police arrested 725,000 women as suspected prostitutes and in the same period there was a total of 155,000 women registered with the police as licensed prostitutes.[28]

126. *The curtain*, c.1881. Pastel over monotype, $10\frac{3}{4} \times 12\frac{3}{4}$ in (27.3 × 32.4 cm). Washington, DC, Collection of Mr and Mrs Paul Mellon

127. *The entrance of the masked dancers*, c.1879. Pastel, 19¼ × 25½ in (49 × 64.7 cm). Williamstown, Mass., Sterling and Francine Clark Art Institute

OVERLEAF, LEFT:
128. *The dance lesson*, 1879. Pastel on paper, 25½ × 22¼ in (67 × 59 cm). New York, Metropolitan Museum (anonymous gift in memory of Horace Havemeyer, 1971)

OVERLEAF, RIGHT:
129. *Three ballet dancers*, 1879. Oil on canvas, 8 × 6¼ in (20 × 16 cm). London, Courtesy of the Lefèvre Gallery Ltd

There were women for all classes of customer; at the top end of the scale there were the great courtesans of the Second Empire, women like Blanche d'Antigny and the English girl Cora Pearl, who became the mistress of Prince Napoleon, and at the bottom there were the *grisettes* or working girls to be found with the students in Henri Murger's *Bohème*. But the great supporters of the system were the middle classes who often seemed to prefer prostitutes to sexual relations with their wives.

The habit of going to the brothel was formed early in the life of most Frenchmen. We learn from the confessions of young people recorded by Abbé Timon-David, and published in 1865[29], that visits to prostitutes often began at school, and this precociousness was often encouraged as a way of prevent-ing what was considered the much more dangerous vice of masturbation. Eyewitnesses report that on holidays and the Thursday half-day the brothels swarmed with schoolboys. Still, it is hard to imagine someone as shy and serious as the young Degas joining in this sport and it is equally hard to imagine the forty-year-old man making regular appearances at the local brothel. Besides, if he wanted sex, it could be found nearer at hand with his models; here again he did not follow the usual custom but kept his models at a distance. We are told that 'he was prey to an adolescent shyness, a fear of refusal, a pre-liminary embarrassment and shame, that kept him from moving along the amorous way. His tentative questing, with his models, would be checked, then turned to jesting; so that Degas grew to be known

not as a lover but as a prankster, and all the practical jokes of the bohemian quarter were attributed to him.'[30]

If Degas had little or no direct experience of brothels, or perhaps even of sex, how did he come to produce the fifty-odd surviving monotypes of brothels? A starting point was almost certainly the watercolour by Constantin Guys (plate 130) which showed prostitutes waiting for clients and gossiping with each other. Not only did Degas depict similar scenes, he also used a generalized style similar to Guys which lies half-way between caricature and realism.

Degas, like Guys, worked from memory and imagination rather than from direct observation of the model, and it was the universal look of these monotypes which appealed to Renoir and which in this painter's view made Degas's work superior to Toulouse-Lautrec's pictures of the same subject:

'Just compare their paintings of "cocottes . . ." Why, they're worlds apart! Lautrec just painted a prostitute, while Degas painted all prostitutes rolled into one. Lautrec's prostitutes are vicious . . . Degas's never. Have you ever seen "The Patronne's Birthday?" It's superb! When others paint a bawdy house, the result is usually

OPPOSITE:
131. *Dancer with left arm raised*, 1887. Pastel on grey paper, $18\frac{3}{4} \times 11\frac{3}{4}$ in (47.6 × 29.8 cm). Fort Worth, Kimbell Art Museum

130. CONSTANTIN GUYS, *Conversation galante (Brothel scene)*. Watercolour. Paris, Musée Carnavalet

132. *La fête de la Patronne* (*The party for Madame*), 1878–9. Pastel over monotype, $10\frac{1}{2} \times 11\frac{1}{2}$ in (26.5 × 29.5 cm). Present whereabouts unknown

pornographic – always sad to the point of despair. Degas is the only painter who can combine a certain joyousness and the rhythm of an Egyptian bas-relief in a subject of that kind. That chaste, half-religious side, which makes his work so great, is at its best when he paints those poor girls [plate 132].'[31]

It was perhaps the human qualities of Degas's monotypes of brothels, the absence of moral tone, which appealed to Picasso, who in the 1960s bought some to add to his collection.

Degas may have had the opportunity to see Guys' watercolours in the collection of Manet, who was a friend of the artist and once painted his portrait. Doubtless too Degas was aware of Baudelaire's famous essay on Guys, *The Painter of Modern Life*, published in 1863, which drew attention to the artistic opportunities presented by prostitutes:

'*Among them there are some examples of an innocent and monstrous conceit, who carry in their boldly raised heads and eyes an obvious air of happiness at being alive (why, indeed?). At times, and without searching for them, they find poses so bold and noble, that they would delight the most fastidious sculptor, if the modern sculptor had the courage and the sense to pick up nobility, wherever it may be, even in the mire. At other times they show themselves prostrate in the hopeless attitudes of weariness, in the sluggishness of the "estaminet", with masculine cynicism smoking cigarettes to kill time, with the resignation of Oriental fatalism; sprawling, or rolling about on sofas, their skirts rounded behind and in front in double fan shape, or balancing on stools and chairs.*[32]

Many of these suggestions Degas seems to have carried out to the letter. Some of the girls in his brothel pictures do seem happy creatures and others

LEFT:
133. *The client (Le client sérieux)*, c.1879. Monotype in black ink on wove or china paper, 8¼ × 6¼ in (21 × 15.9 cm). London, Estate of William Peploe

RIGHT:
134. *Woman at her toilet in a brothel.* Universités de Paris, Bibliothèque d'Art et d'Archéologie (Fondation Jacques Doucet)

BELOW:
135. *Bordel*, c.1879. Monotype in black ink on cream paper, with pale ochre watercolour, plate: 6¼ × 8¼ in (16 × 21.4 cm), sheet: 8¼ × 10¼ in (21 × 26 cm). Universités de Paris, Bibliothèque d'Art et d'Archéologie (Fondation Jacques Doucet)

OVERLEAF, LEFT, ABOVE:
136. *Nurses on the beach*, c.1875. Oil on pale mauve paper, 17½ × 23 in (46 × 62 cm). Los Angeles, Norton Simon Foundation

OVERLEAF, LEFT, BELOW:
137. *Beach scene*, c.1876. Oil on paper mounted on canvas, 18½ × 32½ in (47 × 82.5 cm). London, National Gallery

OVERLEAF, RIGHT:
138. *Jockeys before the start with flag-pole*, c.1881. Oil on paper, 42½ × 29 in (108 × 74 cm). Birmingham, Barber Institute of Fine Arts

147

loll around on sofas in various states of decay and weariness. *Women on the Terrace of a Café*, 1877 (plate 140) shows a group of street-walkers gossiping among themselves and justifies Degas's claim that 'In a single brushstroke we can say more than a writer in a whole volume.'[33] The work was admired by Zola who for ten years had nurtured plans for a novel about the demi-monde,[34] and in 1879 after much effort his novel about a young actress and former laundry girl, *Nana*, began to appear in serial form.

About the same period as he was painting brothels, Degas began to study another popular place of entertainment in Paris, the café-concerts, which also catered for all classes and all pockets, and were the forerunners of the music halls and strip-tease palaces of the twentieth century.[35] At their most primitive level they consisted of a small stage erected at one end of a café. (It was one of these establishments, the Palais du Travail, which encouraged Maurice Chevalier to embark on his career as an entertainer.) The

OPPOSITE, ABOVE:
139. *Pauline and Virginie conversing with admirers* (for *La Famille Cardinal* by Ludovic Halévy), c.1880–3. Monotype in black ink on white laid paper mounted on cardboard, plate: 8 × 9½ in (16 × 21 cm). William Beadleston Inc.

OPPOSITE, BELOW:
140. *Women on the terrace of a café*, 1877. Pastel over monotype, 16 × 23½ in (41 × 60 cm). Paris, Louvre

141. *Young woman at a café*, c.1877. Pastel over monotype in black ink, 6¼ × 4¾ in (15.9 × 12.1 cm). New York, Mrs Donald S. Stralem

OVERLEAF, LEFT:
142. *Chez la modiste* (*At the milliner's*), c.1883. Pastel, 29¾ × 33¼ in (75.9 × 84.8 cm). Switzerland, Collection Thyssen-Bornemisza

OVERLEAF, RIGHT:
143. *Chanteuse au gant* (*Singer with glove*), 1878. Pastel on canvas, 21 × 16¼ in (53 × 41 cm). Cambridge, Mass., Courtesy of the Fogg Art Museum, Harvard University (Bequest of Maurice Wertheim, 1906)

café-concerts of Degas's day mainly catered for the working classes, but in time they became more elaborate and attracted a richer class of clientele, one of the reasons for their wider popularity and increasing sophistication being the removal in 1865 of an ordinance limiting theatrical costume to a few licensed theatres. The performers could now dress up as they saw fit. The managements of the cafés, many of which were out in the open, tried to employ as many pretty singers as possible, and the performers were chosen as much for their looks and their costumes as for their voices. An American visitor to Paris at this time noted:

'The object of the manager seems to be to keep as many of them as possible constantly before the gaze of the audience, and as soon as the performer is through with her part, she returns to her seat on the stage. . . . You notice that all of the women have bouquets. The establishment does not provide these bouquets – they are gifts of the admirers of the "artistes". A person wishing to make the acquaintance of one of these fair demoiselles, sends a bouquet with his card to her. If she appears with it on the stage, she thereby signifies her willingness to accept Monsieur's attentions.[36]

According to the visitor, the Alcazar (one of the cafés which Degas used to frequent) had the prettiest singers. Degas recommended it to his friend Henri Lerolle: 'It is near the Conservatoire and it is better.' He particularly enjoyed the singing of a certain Theresa whom he thought should be persuaded to sing Gluck. 'She opens her large mouth and there emerges the most roughly, the most delicately, the most spiritually tender voice imaginable. And the soul, and the good taste, where could one find better. It is admirable.'[37]

Most of these places were rowdy: the audience was allowed to do what it liked, to eat, drink, smoke (which they could not do in the regular theatres), join in the singing or carry on a conversation with their friends. To make themselves heard the singers had to project strong voices. Degas caught them as they leant over the footlights to capture the audience's attention, or opened their mouths wide to bellow out their songs (plates 143, 145, 146, 149).

Degas was interested in every aspect of women's life. He observed their gestures and movements down to the last detail. In the early 1880s he accompanied them to the dressmaker's and the milliner's and he

144. *At the milliner's*, 1882. Pastel on paper, 30 × 34 in (76.2 × 86.4 cm). New York, Metropolitan Museum (Bequest of Mrs H. O. Havemeyer, 1929). Mary Cassatt is believed to have posed for the woman trying on a hat

145. *Café-concert*, c.1875-7. Pastel over monotype, 8½ × 16 in (23.5 × 43 cm). Washington, DC, Corcoran Gallery of Art, William A. Clark Collection

watched how they tried on a hat and looked at themselves in a mirror (plates 142, 144). He was not the
dispassionate observer that he is sometimes made out
to be: according to Berthe Morisot he professed the
'liveliest admiration for the intensely *human* quality
of young shop girls'.[38] Later in his life, when his
eyesight prevented him from painting, he continued
to observe feminine mannerisms, and gave a delightful performance for Valéry's benefit of a woman
taking a seat on an omnibus:

'*He described the precautions she took to be well arranged
and comfortably seated. She ran her fingers over her dress
to uncrease it, contrived to sit well back so that she fitted
closely into the curve of the support, drew her gloves as
tightly as possible over her hands, buttoned them carefully,
ran her tongue along her lips which she had bitten gently,
worked her body inside her clothes, so as to feel fresh and at
ease in her warm underwear. Finally, after lightly pinching
the end of her nose, she drew down her veil, rearranged a curl
of hair with an alert finger, and then, not without a lightning
survey of the contents of her bag, seemed to put an end to
this series of operations with the expression of one whose
task is done, or whose mind is at rest, since all that is
humanly possible in the way of preparations has been done,
and the rest must be left to providence.*

The tram went rattling along. The lady, finally settled,

149. *Le concert des Ambassadeurs (café-concert)*, c.1875–7. Pastel over monotype, 14½ × 10½ in (37 × 27 cm). Lyons, Musée des Beaux-Arts

150. Two studies of Mary Cassatt in the Louvre. New York, Mrs Siegfried Kramarsky

151. *Woman on a sofa*, 1875. Oil sketch on pink paper, $18\frac{3}{4} \times 16\frac{1}{2}$ in (48 × 42 cm). New York, Metropolitan Museum (Bequest of Mrs H. O. Havemeyer)

remained for about fifty seconds in this state of total well-being. But at the end of what must have seemed to her an interminable period, Degas (who mimed to perfection what I am describing with great difficulty) saw dissatisfaction appear: she drew herself up, worked her neck inside her collar, wrinkled her nostrils a little, rehearsed a frown; then recapitulated all her adjustments of attitude and dress – the gloves, the nose-pinching, the veil. . . . A whole routine, intensely "personal", followed by another apparently stable condition of equilibrium, which lasted only for a moment.

Degas, for his part, went through his pantomime again. He was charmed with it. There was an element of misogyny in his enjoyment.[39]

(iii)

It was his powers of observation, combined with a prodigious visual memory, which made him such a great portraitist. Sometimes these powers proved too telling and he offended his female sitters, but with his men friends there was less risk of causing offence, and the portraits of Desboutin, Lepic, Duranty and Martelli are among his greatest works, fulfilling his father's prediction that one day portraiture would become one of the jewels in his son's crown.

Perhaps the most famous of these portraits, and the one which in its day caused most controversy, is the work which was once called *Au Café* and is now better known as *L'Absinthe* (plate 154). It shows

154. *L'absinthe*,
c.1876. Oil on
canvas, 36¼ × 26¾
in (92 × 68 cm).
Paris, Louvre

Marcellin Desboutin sitting at a café table with a woman at his side, to whom he pays not the slightest attention. Desboutin, as mentioned earlier, had returned to Paris in the mid-1870s, having lived for many years in Florence. He was a friend of de Nittis and of Manet, having been a student with the latter in the studio of Thomas Couture. Degas shared with him an enthusiasm for engraving, but he seems to have found Degas's zeal a little excessive. In a letter to Mme de Nittis in Florence he described Degas's antics:

'[*He*] *is no longer a friend, he is no longer a man, he is no longer an artist! He is a "plate" of zinc or copper blackened with printer's ink, and this plate and this man are rolled together by his press, in the meshing of which he has disappeared completely! – He is in the metallurgic phase for the reproduction of his drawings with a roller [au rouleau] and runs all over Paris in his zeal to find the equipment which corresponds to his fixed idea! – It is altogether a poem!*[40]

One of Desboutin's favourite haunts was the Café de la Nouvelle-Athènes, and he is sometimes given the credit for bringing it to the attention of Manet, Degas and their followers. It was therefore only natural for Degas to show his friend sitting at a café table in a work which is only in part a portrait of the artist and deals principally with café life, its piquancy, the long hours that people can spend nursing a drink, waiting for friends, people-watching or laying up plans for the future. His model for the woman who sits at Desboutin's side was the actress Ellen André. He used her on a number of occasions and, judging by the roles she played in his work, she was a capable performer. Renoir also used her as a model, and late in his life he spoke warmly of her talents as a panto-mime artist. In *L'Absinthe* she was undoubtedly playing a part and was probably dressed especially for the occasion. In this painting she stands for one of the anonymous women, down on their luck, who find refuge and maybe a customer in a Paris café. She sits close to Desboutin and appears even to be sharing the same table; but his mind is elsewhere.

The composition shows Degas at his best; the figures are placed off-centre, and their situation in space is conveyed by the zig-zagging lines of the café tables. Duranty's article on the 'New Painting' at the time of the second Impressionist exhibition, where this work was exhibited, explained Degas's method (although he did not mention him specifically by name):

'*If one now considers the person, whether in a room or in the street, he is not always to be found situated on a straight line at an equal distance from two parallel objects; he is more confined on one side than on the other by space.*

In short, he is never in the center of the canvas, in the center of the setting. He is not always seen as a whole: sometimes he appears cut off at mid-leg, half-length, or longitudinally. At other times, the eye takes him in from close-up, at full height, and throws all the rest of a crowd in the street or groups gathered in a public place back into the small scale of the distance.[41]

Café life was a subject which was also dear to Manet's heart: a year after Degas painted *L'Absinthe*, Manet painted a similar scene in *The Plum*. Again the work deals with a forlorn young girl sitting over a glass with a sugary plum; there is a touch of sadness in her expression, but the effect is softened by mouth-watering pinks and yellows so that the spectator is drawn to the charms of the girl rather than to the sadness of her plight. Degas's work, by contrast, is more bitter and more penetrating: the colouring is subdued and there is a feeling of hopelessness about the situation of the woman. It was this which seems to have upset the English public. Shortly after the second Impressionist exhibition the picture was acquired by Captain Hill and joined his collection in Brighton. The painting was included in his sale in 1892 and according to its purchaser Arthur Kay, 'When *Au Café* [*L'Absinthe*] was placed on the easel, it was hissed – *sifflé*, say the French.'[42]

In March 1893 the painting was exhibited at the Grafton Gallery; the reaction of the critics both for and against has been documented by Douglas Cooper. The critic D. S. MacColl described it as an 'inexhaustible picture, the one that draws you back and back again'. A writer calling himself 'The Philistine' attacked 'this rhapsody over a picture of two rather sodden people drinking in a café'. W. B. Richmond commented on its 'literary' qualities and wrote, 'It is not painting at all. It is a novelette – a treatise against drink,' and a chorus of critics joined in the fray and the picture was called 'vulgar', 'boozy', 'sottish', 'loathsome', 'ugly', 'be-sotted', 'degraded' and 'repulsive'. As Cooper points out: 'Moore, MacColl and others made ranting replies and this conflict assumed an importance not far short of the Whistler-Ruskin lawsuit of 1877.'[43]

While Degas was painting Desboutin, he was also engaged on a picture which contains a portrait of his friend Vicomte Lepic, with whom he collaborated on his first monotype. Lepic had many interests: he was an anthropologist, a dog-breeder and an engraver who took an interest in the technicalities of his craft – in 1876 he published a book on his experiments out-lining different ways of inking plates. He was also the father of two spirited girls, and Degas painted a lively portrait of father and daughters, accompanied by one of his hounds, crossing the place de la Con-

155. *Place de la Concorde* (*Vicomte Ludovic Lepic and his daughters*), c.1876. Oil on canvas, 31 × 46½ in (79 × 118 cm). Destroyed

corde (plate 155). Unfortunately the painting has disappeared and is believed to have been destroyed in the Second World War. It was an arresting composition and one of the very few pictures of Paris streets painted by Degas. For such a confirmed Parisian it is surprising that Degas, unlike his colleagues Manet, Monet, Renoir, Pissarro and Caillebotte, does not seem to have been at all interested in the topography of Paris, its boulevards or fine prospects. This painting, however, shows Degas at his most daring, and the cropping effect, so noticeable in this work, seems to suggest that we are looking at a still from a film: within a few frames the figures will disappear from view.

His gift of finding unexpected angles and situations for his portraits, and of conveying character as much through posture as through facial expression, is perhaps seen most clearly in his portraits of two critics, Edmond Duranty and Diego Martelli (plates 152 and 148). Both were painted in 1879 and both by coincidence have come to rest in Scotland. Both

writers wrote enthusiastically about Degas's work and their portraits belong to the tradition of Manet's portrait of Zola done a decade earlier. But whereas Manet's treatment of the writer at his desk is flat, with the figure placed parallel to the surface of the picture, Degas's treatment of space is more ambitious and more lively, the space conveyed by a cunning use of diagonals formed by tables and papers in the rooms in which the sitters are posed.

Degas came to know Duranty in the 1860s when he was an aspiring novelist and essayist. His contemporaries suggest that by the 1870s he was an unhappy man, dissatisfied with his achievement. Although he possessed an air of great dignity, and spoke softly and slowly in well-thought-out sentences, there was a trace of bitterness in his voice. 'How many disillusions one felt hidden behind his always discreet cheerfulness,' wrote his early friend and writer on the Impressionists, Armand Silvestre.[44] His aloofness, his mordancy and his sense of disillusionment were qualities which Degas and he shared in common and there developed a close bond between them. When he died unexpectedly a few days after the opening of the fifth Impressionist exhibition in 1880, in which his portrait by Degas appeared (plate 152), the painter was among the first to come to the aid of his widow and took an active part in organizing an auction of paintings for her benefit. So close was the bond between the two men that it has sometimes been argued that Degas was largely responsible for the arguments Duranty put forward in his defence of the Impressionists, *The New Painting*, in 1876. Certain passages do indeed seem close to Degas's views and the paragraphs on portraiture seem to predict, and to be fulfilled by, the portrait which was finished three years later:

'By means of a back, we want a temperament, an age, a social condition to be revealed; through a pair of hands, we should be able to express a magistrate or a tradesman; by a gesture, a whole series of feelings. A physiognomy will tell us that this fellow is certainly an orderly, dry, meticulous man, whereas that one is carelessness and disorderliness

itself. An attitude will tell us that this person is going to a business meeting, whereas that one is returning from a love tryst. "A man opens a door; he enters; that is enough: we see that he has lost his daughter." Hands that are kept in pockets can be eloquent. The pencil will be steeped in the marrow of life.[45]

In this work Degas suggests the man's life by means of the piles of books and papers which surround him. But the gesture which catches Duranty's nervous intelligence is the position of his fingers, which seem to be drilling a hole in his temple. It was this which caught Huysmans's eye when he reviewed the exhibition:

'Those slender and nervous fingers, those piercing and mocking eyes, that penetrating and acute look, that expression of wryness one finds in English comedy, that small dry smile into the stem of his pipe, rise before me again when I look at this painting in which the character of this curious analyst is so well rendered.[46]

Diego Martelli was another critic who admired Degas's work and wrote enthusiastically about it,

156. FEDERICO ZANDOMENEGHI, *Portrait of Diego Martelli*, 1879. Florence, Galleria d'Arte Moderna di Palazzo Pitti

becoming the first to publicize Degas's name in Italy.[47] Martelli was a Florentine and in his youth he met the Macchiaioli group of painters and writers who used to gather at the Café Michelangelo in the 1850s and 1860s. Degas may have been introduced to him in Florence in 1859, but their friendship really developed when Martelli came to Paris for two long stays in 1878 and 1879. In 1879 both Degas and their mutual friend Zandomeneghi painted portraits of the critics (plates 148 and 156). Zandomeneghi was also a capable photographer and he portrayed Martelli in close-up and, to continue the photographic metaphor, in sharp focus. Degas's picture, on the other hand, is in softer focus; his viewpoint is also more unusual, as he has placed himself above and at a distance from Martelli, a position which enabled him to show a table strewn with papers, and to convey Martelli's robust good nature through his facial expression and rotund body.

Duranty's belief that 'by means of a back', a social condition could be revealed, was carried out by Degas in a number of portraits and sketches of this period. The figure of the dance-master Jules Perrot (plate 106), the portrait of Carlo Pellegrini (plate 147) and the portraits of Halévy and Cavé on stage (plate 158) all convey character and even their social standing as much through their figures and deportment as

157. *At the Bourse*, 1879. Oil on canvas, 39½ × 32¼ in (100 × 82 cm). Paris, Louvre

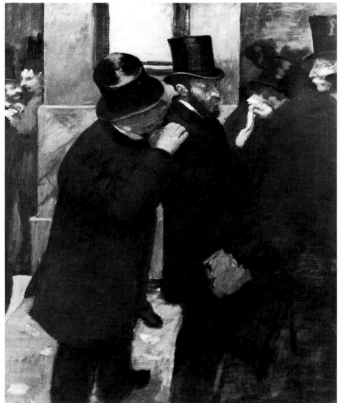

through facial expression. In many cases their faces can hardly be seen and yet it is entirely possible to sense what kind of people they were. And one of the most expressive portraits of this period, as well as being one of the most dramatic, is Degas's picture of Mary Cassatt's back (plate 159). Degas met Mary Cassatt in 1877, but they were both aware of each other's work before then. Degas had had the opportunity to see her paintings at the Salons of 1872, 1873, 1874 and 1876 and he is supposed to have once remarked: 'There is someone who feels as I do.'[48] Mary Cassatt saw her first Degas in the window of Durand-Ruel's gallery shortly after her move to

158. *Halévy and Cavé on stage*, 1876. Pastel and tempera on paper, 31 × 21½ in (79 × 55 cm). Paris, Louvre

159. *Mary Cassatt in the Louvre*, 1880. Pastel on grey paper, 25 × 19¼ in (60 × 47 cm). Philadelphia, Henry P. McIlhenny Collection

Paris in 1873. She later remembered: 'I used to go and flatten my nose against that window and absorb all I could of his art. It changed my life. I saw art then as I wanted to see it.'[49] Even before meeting Degas she had persuaded her friend from Philadelphia, the future Mrs Havemeyer, to buy one of his pastels (see page 121). Thus when Degas was brought by their mutual friend M. Tourny to meet her and he asked her to give up sending her work to the Salon and exhibit with him and his friends, she accepted 'with joy'. 'Finally I could work with absolute independence without concern for the eventual opinion of a jury. Already I recognized those were my true masters. I admired Manet, Courbet and Degas. I detested conventional art. I began to live.'[50]

Mary Cassatt now lived in Paris with her parents and her sister. They were a wealthy family, originally from Pittsburgh, and their house in Paris was run with a certain style. Mary was a capable hostess: she dressed well and entertained a wide variety of visitors from France, England and America – Clemenceau, Mallarmé, Moore and Whistler among them. Her servants were well turned out, the family kept a coach and she was an excellent horsewoman. She was one of the few examples of an artist who was able to lead two lives: one as a well-brought-up daughter of a rich family and one of a very determined artist.

For a woman in her position it was of course considered unsuitable to go to the Nouvelle-Athènes, but her studio was a few minutes' walk from the place Pigalle and regulars noticed her walking by the café every day. We are told that 'she favoured, when *en promenade*, sober-toned, often russet-brown pleated frocks with white frills at wrists and neck, and carried a parasol with an air'.[51] It was in these day-clothes that Degas showed her trying on a hat at the milliner's (plate 144) and visiting the Louvre with her sister. It was a version of this last picture that Sickert noticed in Degas's studio, and it is interesting to learn that one of Degas's intentions was 'to give the idea of that bored, and respectfully crushed and impressed absence of all sensation that women experience in front of paintings.'[52]

There soon developed a warm friendship between them. Originally Degas had assumed the role of teacher and Huysmans, when he reviewed the fourth Impressionist exhibition, spoke of her as Degas's pupil. He worked on the background of one of her paintings, *Little Girl in a Blue Armchair* (1878), he encouraged her to take up print-making and he stimulated her interest in Japanese art, fostering a respect for clear precise line. Although she soon broke free of the master-pupil relationship, she continued to respect and fear his judgement. When she undertook the painting of a huge mural for the building devoted to women's achievements at the Columbian Exhibition in Chicago in 1893, she wanted to ask his advice:

'*I have been half a dozen times on the point of asking Degas to come and see my work, but if he happens to be in the mood he would demolish me so completely that I could not pick myself up in time to finish for the exhibition. Still, he is the only man I know whose judgement would be a help to me.*'[53]

Degas in turn had something to learn from Mary Cassatt. He enjoyed her company, accompanied her out shopping, appreciated her sense of elegance and, probably, he respected her tongue. In her own way she could be as brutally frank, where art was concerned, as he was. The American critic Forbes Watson wrote:

'*She had to the end a sense of elegance that encompassed both her art and her living. Yet from no lips have I heard less ingratiating language when her passionately-held artistic beliefs were threatened. The elegance that was Mary Cassatt's had its limitations. This was due to a fierce love of truth which made it impossible for her to say a gracious word to the conniving or to flatter the painter who had been untrue to himself. Miss Cassatt sent more than one inelegant message to those of her contemporaries who allowed their gifts to become tainted by worldliness. And upon stupid visitors who came to see her from idle curiosity, she could exercise a bitter tongue.*'[54]

The same writer once heard Degas remark: 'I would have married her, but I could never have made love to her.' Although there has been some speculation of an affair between them, it hardly seems likely. Theirs was undoubtedly a platonic friendship, a relationship based on mental sympathy, a common sense of style and art.

There was, however, a vain streak in Mary Cassatt and her eagerness in later life to deny any relationship with Degas[55] – she is supposed to have called him 'a common little man' – and the fact that she destroyed his letters to her may have sprung from resentment at his indifference to her physical charms. She certainly behaved very oddly in her attempts to banish the portrait that Degas painted in 1880, showing her holding some cards. Although the woman in this picture is not beautiful, the face is lively and intelligent. But in 1912 Mary Cassatt asked Durand-Ruel to find a buyer outside America for it:

'*I particularly want to get rid of the portrait Degas made of me which is hanging in the room beside the drawing room (my studio) . . . I don't want to leave this portrait by Degas to my family as one of me. It has some qualities as a work of art but it is so painful and represents me as such a repugnant person that I would not want anyone to know that I posed for it. . . . If you think my portrait saleable I should like it sold to a foreigner and particularly that my name not be attached to it.'*[56]

Women can be difficult sitters, as Degas discovered when in about 1879 he agreed to do a portrait of Mme Dietz-Monin, probably the only occasion on which he accepted a commission. He adopted a stance looking up at her, showing her wearing an extravagant hat and a magnificent boa. Mme Dietz-Monin seems to have tired of the sittings and offered to send over her boa and hat so that Degas could work on the portrait without her. He, it need hardly be said, was deeply offended and a letter was found in his papers in which he expressed his feelings:
'Dear Madame,

Let us leave the portrait alone, I beg of you. I was so surprised by your letter suggesting that I reduce it to a boa and a hat that I shall not answer you.

Must I tell you that I regret having started something in my own manner only to find myself transforming it completely into yours? That would not be too polite and yet . . .

But, dear Madame, I cannot go into this more fully without showing you only too clearly that I am very much hurt.

Outside of my unfortunate art please accept all my regards.'[57]

After his fiftieth birthday Degas did fewer portraits and those that he did lack the animation and psychological insight of the earlier work. This may have been due partly to troubles with his eyesight, which forced him to give up detailed observation for the study of more generalized shapes and masses, and partly because he became less interested in individuals and more concerned to find the universal. The eclecticism of his work in his forties was replaced by a narrowing focus: he confined himself to the exploration of a few set themes, with the same subjects drawn and redrawn. The studio became even more the centre of his work and of his world.

(iv)

The studio for Degas was the equivalent of the laboratory for the alchemist – a place for experiment, for concentrated activity and for retreat, a place from which outsiders were barred lest they discover the magician's secret formulas. Paul Valéry was one of the privileged few to be admitted to the studio he kept at the top of his house at 37 rue Victor-Massé. If Degas was in a good mood, he took him into a long attic room, with a wide but dirty bay window where light and dust mingled gaily:

'The room was pell-mell with a basin, a dull zinc bathtub, stale bathrobes, a "danseuse" modelled in wax, with a real gauze tutu, in a glass case, and easels loaded with charcoal sketches of flat-nosed, twisted models, with combs in their fists, held around thick hair gripped tight in the other hand. A narrow shelf ran under the window where a ghost of sunshine lingered; it was piled with bottles, flasks, pencils, bits of pastel chalk, etching needles, and all the nameless odds and ends that may come in handy one day. . . .'

Valéry concluded:

'It sometimes seems to me that the labor of the artist is of a very old-fashioned kind; the artist himself a survival, a craftsman or artisan of a disappearing species, working in his own room, following his own homemade empirical methods, living in untidy intimacy with his tools, his eyes intent on what is in his mind, blind to his surroundings; using broken pots, kitchenware, any old castoffs that come to hand.'[58]

Although his subject-matter gradually became narrower, during his forties the painter began to experiment with a great variety of techniques. He used new shapes – fans and canvases which were twice as long as they were high; he worked in pastel, gouache, and oil soaked in turpentine to form a kind of wash; he became fascinated with all forms of print-making and experimented with etching, lithography and monotypes. He also turned his hand to sculpture and began modelling figures in wax and clay. But pastel became his favourite medium and it dominated his output for the rest of his life. He found in it new riches of colour and expression which no artist before or since has been able to achieve.

Pastel consists of powdered chalk and pigment mixed into a paste; it is held as one would a stick of charcoal and is generally applied to paper with a smooth or glossy finish in short even strokes. The paste crumbles easily and one of the main problems is to find a way of fixing the pastel to the surface of the paper. Degas tried various methods, eventually using a solution given to him by the Italian Luigi Chialiva – a secret formula, he believed – and this allowed him to layer his pastels, putting one colour on top of another.[59] It is a medium which above all is associated with the French artists of the eighteenth century, Maurice Quentin de la Tour and Jean-Baptiste Perronneau being among the most famous. Degas was able to see examples of both artists' work in his father's collection and in the homes of his father's friends Eudoxe Marcille and Louis LaCaze, who were both enthusiastic collectors.

At the beginning of the nineteenth century pastel

had fallen into disfavour, perhaps because it was associated with the fripperies and frivolities of the rococo age; but the activities of Marcille and LaCaze, and the enthusiasm of the Goncourt brothers for the art of the eighteenth century, helped to stage a revival. Delacroix sometimes used pastel, and Degas was much impressed by the sight of one of his pictures of a tiger, which under glass looked like a watercolour. 'It is pastel', he wrote, 'put on very lightly on a slightly glossed paper. It is very vibrant, it is a lovely method.'[60]

In the 1860s Degas used pastel occasionally as, for example, in the portrait of Berthe Morisot's sister and his own sister Thérèse. He also used it in the series of seascapes of about 1869. But it was in the 1870s that he really began to explore the possibilities of the medium, at first adding it to a drawing which had been coloured with oil colours thinned in turpentine, to give highlights to the dancers' costumes (see, for example, plate 102). These early works are mostly on smooth paper and the technique follows traditional procedures, but by the end of the 1870s he was experimenting with different textures of paper and different tints. He also began to use it in conjunction with prints, particularly monotypes, adding colour to what were otherwise monochrome works.

After 1880 he began to vary his strokes to create an atmosphere and a sense of depth by 'juxtaposing strokes of contrasting or related tones running in several directions.'[61] His pastel technique has also been discussed in a recent publication by Alfred Werner,[62] but our basic information about his methods remains Denis Rouart's *Degas à La Recherche de sa Technique*.[63] From him we learn that Degas invented a way of steaming his pastels to form a semi-liquid paste; he would then spread it with a brush, sometimes to form a wash. He used this often to give an even tone to the background of his pictures and, as Rouart points out: 'He took great care not to spray the water vapour all over his picture, so as to give variety. He would not treat the flesh of the dancer in exactly the same way as her tutu, or the scenery might be given a different quality from the floor.'[64]

Parallel to his experiments with pastel was his increasing enthusiasm in the late 1870s for all forms of print-making. He began to employ a wide variety of techniques, sometimes combining etching, aquatint and electric crayon all on the same plate. He aimed to show the results of his researches in the magazine *Le Jour et la Nuit*, which he hoped to start with his colleagues Mary Cassatt and Pissarro with funds provided by Caillebotte, but the project never got under way. His interest in etching went back to his

161. *Woman getting out of the bath*, c.1882. Etching, electric crayon, drypoint and aquatint, 5 × 5 in (12.7 × 12.7 cm). New York, Metropolitan Museum (Rogers Fund, 1921)

OPPOSITE:
160. *Mary Cassatt in the Louvre*, 1879-80. Etching, aquatint, drypoint and electric crayon, 11¾ × 5 in (30.1 × 12.5 cm). Chicago, Art Institute (Gift of Walter S. Brewster)

thickness. *When the plate is bitten, you are left with a grained effect that is dark or pale according to the depth of the bite. This is necessary if you want to obtain even tints. Less regular effects can be obtained by using a stump or the fingertip or any other form of pressure on the paper that is placed over the soft ground.*[65]

In a notebook in use around 1875-77 he noted that lavender oil dissolves transfer ink better than turpentine, and he recorded in his curious semi-scientific style a reminder to 'Apply flowers of sulphur mixed with oil on a copperplate, this gives a delicate tone.'[66] Many of the effects he discovered through a process of trial and error, and he lamented in one letter the need for professional advice. To Bracquemond he wrote: 'You were supposed to teach us instead of letting us go all over the place.'[67] One morning in 1882 at Alexis Rouart's, when sleet prevented him from leaving, he began to use the carbon filament of a light bulb, which Rouart found in the factory next door, to make an etching of a *Woman Leaving Her Bath* (plate 161).[68] The effect pleased him and he used an electric crayon in several prints of this period. The resourcefulness which he showed in his prints, his willingness to try new techniques and new combina-

162. *Portrait of a woman*, c.1880. Monotype with brown ink, 8¼ × 6¼ in (21.6 × 16 cm). Chicago, Art Institute (Mrs Potter Palmer Memorial Fund)

youth. As a student he had called on his father's friend, Prince Nicolas Soutzo, a Greek collector and amateur engraver. A notebook in use around 1856-59 records an 'extraordinary conversation' with the prince, who undoubtedly encouraged him to make his first etchings. In Rome he became a friend of Joseph Tourny, who had won a Prix de Rome for engraving in 1847, and it was he who helped him with the etched self-portrait of 1857 (plate 5). In the early 1860s Degas had received further encouragement from Félix Bracquemond and Manet; but it was not until the mid-1870s, when he came in contact with Desboutin, Lepic, de Nittis and Alphonse Hirsch, that he began to produce prints in any number.

The notebooks and letters after 1875 are full of references to his experiments. Some, like the tips he sent Pissarro, read like a cook's recipe:

'Take a really smooth metal plate (this is essential, you understand). Remove every trace of grease with whiting. You have previously dissolved some resin in a strong concentration of alcohol. You pour this liquid, in the same way as photographers pour the collodion over their glass plates, taking care just as they do to tilt the plate and let it drain thoroughly; the liquid evaporates and leaves the plate covered with a layer of little grains of resin, of varying

tions, puts one in mind of another painter-print-maker, Picasso.

Perhaps the most interesting result of his experiments with prints, a field in which he produced some of his most original work, was his discovery of monotype. A monotype is a simplified form of print: greasy ink is applied to a smooth non-absorbent surface, such as zinc, copper or glass. Paper is then laid over it and pressed down either by means of a roller or by placing it in a press. The monotype removes the necessity of etching or engraving the plate but, since the plate remains smooth, it is not possible to make more than one or two or, very occasionally, three impressions as the plate soon loses its coating.

There are two basic methods of making the image printed in this way: the dark field method which involves covering the plate completely with ink and then using a rag or a brush to wipe away the design; and the light field method in which the ink is applied to a clean plate to form the design. In about 1876 with his friend Lepic he made his first monotype (using the dark field method), which they both signed.[69] The subject was a dance rehearsal on stage and he used the familiar figure of Jules Perrot resting on his stick. It soon occurred to him that it was an ideal medium for recording the shadows and shafts of light to be observed on the stage and in the twilight world of the brothel.

Since the technique does not allow a fine precise line, it forced Degas to compose in generalized masses of light and dark. Smearing the ink around and wiping it away with a rag, he began to do pictures with a spontaneity and freedom often denied to him when holding a pencil in his hand. As Eugenia Janis observed in her account of Degas's monotypes, the manual freedom presented by such a technique must have come as a revelation:

'Degas could quickly create textures and half tones in the ink. He even began using his own finger prints to grey the black and white contrasts. Large broad shapes could be changed quickly and easily by adding or wiping away ink here or there at will. What is more, the artist could work at a leisurely pace. Making a monotype requires speed only in the printing because, once the paper has been dampened, the artist must go about transferring the ink to the paper with pressure quickly before the paper dries. The ink on the plate, consisting mostly of oil, does not dry quickly and can be worked over and over again by the artist before he prints. The greasy ink, slow to dry, and therefore always in a potential state of change on the plate, plus the occasional use of transparent celluloid plates (Degas could lift the plate and see his design in reverse as it would look when it was printed without stopping actually to print it) allowed Degas to keep the monotype sketch in a flexible state for a longer period of time.'[70]

There are many parallels between the monotype process and photography: both involve the recording of light on to a sensitized plate, one using mechanical means, the other requiring the hand and eye of the artist. About the same time as he was making his first monotypes, Degas was also taking an interest in the developments of photography, and although at this stage he did not take photographs himself he often made use of their visual information. In a letter to Faure written in 1876 he asked: 'Do not forget to remind Mérante [ballet master at the Opéra] about the photographs he offered me yesterday. I am eager to see them and work out what I can make of this dancer's talent.'[71] He was probably referring to the small cartes-de-visite which photographers such as Disderi took of dancers and which provided a useful aide-mémoire for a dancer's steps and positions.[72]

But of even greater significance is an entry in a notebook dated 1878–9 which refers to the journal La Nature.[73] He was perhaps referring to the issue of 14 December which contained an article by the editor Gaston Tissandier, a scientist and keen photographer, recounting the results of Eadweard Muybridge's experimental photographs in California of horses galloping and trotting, and including reproductions of the photographs. The article attracted widespread interest, and its implications for artists were enormous. Muybridge's experiments showed that the traditional mode of suggesting the horse's gallop – the flying position with front legs stretched out and the hind legs stretched backwards, giving the impression that the horse is suspended in mid-air, a position which Degas himself had employed in the background of Carriage at the Races (plate 84) – was no longer scientifically acceptable. The distinguished French scientist Etienne-Jules Marey,[74] who had himself been studying animal movement, was quick to point out that painters would have to revise their thoughts, although Muybridge himself seems to have realized that an arbitrary notion which had grown up in people's minds from infancy would take some dislodging. Meissonier, for instance, who prided himself on the accuracy of his paintings, was astonished when he first saw Muybridge's work, and according to one contemporary accused the camera of 'seeing falsely'.[75] Degas, for all the intransigence he showed in social life and for all his hatred of modern inventions, was quick to absorb the new lessons, and the results can be seen in the sculpture of horses modelled in the 1880s as well as in the pastels of the 1870s. Degas perhaps mentioned his interest to Valéry who wrote that he was 'one of the first to study the true

163. *Woman leaving the bath*, c.1880. Monotype with black ink, $6\frac{1}{4} \times 4\frac{3}{4}$ in (15.7 × 11.8 cm). Paris, BN, Cabinet des Estampes

164. *Jockey (Vicomte Lepic)*, 1882. Pencil, 12 × 9 in (30.5 × 22.9 cm). New York, Mr and Mrs David L. Loew

165. Photograph by Muybridge of Annie G. in canter. Courtesy of Professor Aaron Scharf

166. *Horse and jockey*, 1887–90. Red chalk on white paper, $11\frac{1}{4} \times 16\frac{1}{2}$ in (28.3 × 41.8 cm). Rotterdam, Museum Boymans-van-Beuningen

forms of the noble animal in movement by means of the instantaneous photographs of Major Muybridge',[76] and François Thiébault-Sisson, who was acquainted with Degas, maintained that it was these photographs which whetted his appetite again for racing scenes that 'occupied him for a fairly long time after intimate scenes and portraits, or ironers, milliners and laundresses.'[77] Indeed, after a lapse of some six or seven years, Degas did begin to paint racing scenes again, and in about 1882 he returned to the racetrack itself and made a series of drawings of jockeys, perhaps an indication that he felt in need of a refresher course.[78] Later he made more sketches of horses, as well as models of horses galloping, and many of these were based, as Aaron Scharf has pointed out, on the photographs of 'Annie G in Canter' published by Muybridge in his famous work *Animal Locomotion* (1887)[79] (plate 165).

It would be interesting to know if Degas was aware of the demonstration which Muybridge performed at the reception given for him by Meissonier

in November 1881, attended by a number of distinguished writers and artists, including Degas's acquaintance Gérôme. At this reception Muybridge used an invention called a 'zoopraxiscope' which enabled him to project a moving image of a horse in motion. In any case the event was reported by *Le Figaro* and Degas probably also heard of it on the artistic grapevine. A few years later he performed his own demonstration of movement to the young Sickert, using a technique borrowed from the panto-mime theatres which were then so popular. 'He showed me a little statuette he had on the stocks,' reported Sickert, 'and – it was night – he held a candle up, and turned the statuette to show me the succession of shadows cast by its silhouette on a white sheet.'[80] According to Charles Millard, who duplicated the

experiment, the effect is 'as if a dancer were behind the screen executing movements recorded by her cast shadow', and he noted that the projected figure is life-size, 'giving an impression of startling vitality'.[81]

In his quest for ways of rendering movement Degas went beyond Muybridge, and it may have been a dissatisfaction with the two-dimensional nature of his photographs (which were essentially silhouettes) that propelled him to seek a solution in sculpture. One of the interesting side-effects of his photographs is that each frame, if taken singly, freezes movement: it is as if the men and animals he studied played 'grandmother's footsteps' with the camera. Rodin noticed this effect and maintained: 'If the artist succeeds in producing the impression of movement which takes several moments for accomplishment,

167. *Jockeys in the rain*, 1881. Pastel, $18\frac{1}{2} \times 25\frac{1}{2}$ in (47 × 65 cm). Glasgow Art Gallery, Burrell Collection

OPPOSITE:
168. Sketch for *Pagans and Degas's father*, c. 1874. Pastel on paper, $18\frac{3}{4} \times 24\frac{1}{2}$ in (47 × 61 cm). Philadelphia Museum of Art (Mr and Mrs Carrol S. Tyson Collection)

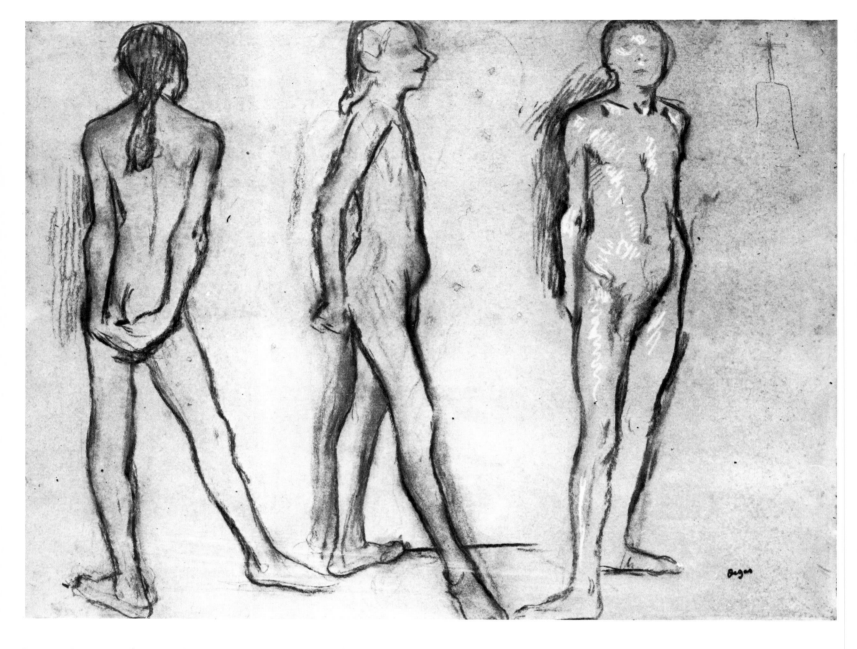

169. Studies for the *Little dancer of fourteen*. London, Private Collection

his work is certainly much less conventional than the scientific image, where time is abruptly suspended.'[82] Referring to Géricault's use of the 'flying gallop' in his picture of the Epsom Derby he added, 'Now I believe that it is Géricault who is right, and not the camera, for the horses *appear* to run.' This remark closely resembles Degas's celebrated axiom, 'Drawing is not the same as form, it is a way of seeing form.'[83] He might also have said of his sculpture that 'sculpture itself does not move, it is a way of seeing movement'.

He began to make sculpture in the mid-1870s.[84] It has been suggested that his interest may have been aroused by the sight of Daumier's sculpture which was revealed for the first time at a retrospective exhibition at the Durand-Ruel gallery in 1878. That

same year on 17 February Marie van Goethem, a ballet student at the Opéra, became fourteen, and he began modelling a wax figure of her in a position which, when seen from the side, does indeed correspond to the backward-leaning figure of Daumier's most famous sculpture *Ratapoil*. Degas made a number of drawings of the young dancer from different angles (plate 169), and together with the little wax figure (which was unclothed) (plate 170) they became the starting point for a more elaborate work (plate 172) of her dressed in a bodice, tutu and slippers, which after a great deal of effort and many false alarms was eventually displayed at the fifth Impressionist exhibition in 1881, having failed to appear the previous year.[85] Even then Degas was late. Jules Claretie in *Le Temps* of 5 April noted that the

OVERLEAF, LEFT:
171. *Before the race*,
1882. Oil on panel,
10½ × 13¾ in (26.5 ×
34.9 cm). Williams-
town, Mass.,
Sterling and
Francine Clark Art
Institute

OVERLEAF, RIGHT:
172. *Little dancer of
fourteen* (front and
side views). London,
Courtesy of Lefèvre
Gallery Ltd

glass vitrine for the sculpture was still empty and visitors to the exhibition in the opening days had to make use of the sketches which Degas had sent in preparation. But the wait seems to have whetted the appetite and when the *Little Dancer of Fourteen* was shown, its appearance stunned or shocked all who saw it. Huysmans was bowled over:

'The terrible reality of this little statue produces an evident unease in him; all those ideas about sculpture, those cold inanimate whitenesses, those memorable stereo-types copied again and again for centuries, are upset. The fact is that, with his first blow, M. Degas has up-ended the traditions of sculpture as he has long been shaking the conventions of painting.'[86]

Nina de Villars wrote: 'Before this statuette I experienced one of the most violent artistic impressions of my life.'[87] Whistler is reported to have been seen, 'carrying a bamboo maul-stick by way of a cane, uttering sharp cries and gesticulating in front of the case which enclosed the wax figurine.'[88] Renoir said on several occasions that he regarded Degas as the greatest sculptor of the age. 'After Chartres I see but one sculptor,' he once remarked. 'It is Degas.'[89]

The effect of the figure seems to have induced in many of the critics who reviewed the exhibition a frisson of pleasure mixed with pain. Paul Mantz was shocked by the ugliness of the girl, as were many others; he seems to have seen in this a determination to carry out the philosophy of Baudelaire and he ended his article by observing: 'M. Degas is implacable. If he continues to make sculpture and if he maintains [this] style, he will have a small place for himself in the history of the cruel arts.' Mantz also seems to have detected a moralizing element, a sculptural version of the warning 'Don't put your daughter on the stage, Mrs Worthington'. 'Why is she so ugly?' Mantz asked in the same article. 'Why is her forehead, half concealed by her hair, already marked like her lips by a nature so profoundly vicious? M. Degas is without doubt a moralist; he

170. *Little dancer of fourteen, nude.* Bronze.
London, Courtesy of Sotheby Parke Bernet

perhaps knows things about the dancers of the future which we don't know. He has plucked from the arbours of the theatre a precocious blossom of depravity, and he shows it to us withered before its time. The intellectual result is achieved. The ordinary people, admitted to study this waxen creation, stand for a moment stunned, and you can hear fathers crying: "Heaven forbid my daughter becoming a dancer!"'[90]

One reason why people were shocked by their first sight of Degas's sculpture was its arresting realism. The figure was modelled in wax, but dressed in a linen bodice, a gauze tutu, satin slippers, and her hair was real, bought from a supplier to puppet theatres and tied with a silk ribbon. The real-life elements – a technique which has become commonplace in the twentieth century – struck many, conditioned to see their sculpture in the form of marble and bronze, as peculiar, and critics detected a connection with medieval polychromed wood sculpture. Nina de Villars, for instance, drew her readers' attention to the ornaments, fabrics and jewellery often covering these works and asked: 'I wonder why a great artist has not had the idea of applying this process to a work which is modern and powerful, and *voilà*, I find my idea realized and it is a true joy.'[91]

But she could have found a precedent for Degas's technique nearer at hand. As Reff points out,[92] wax-work figures were given real clothes and real hair, and were very popular in the 1870s. Degas had had the opportunity of seeing them on his visits to London, where Madame Tussaud's museum attracted large crowds, and later he could see them in a similar museum founded in 1882 in Paris by Alfred Grévin, a famous caricaturist and designer of the theatrical costumes to whose 'frenzied drawings' Degas refers in a letter of 1880.[93]

The choice of an adolescent figure to mark his début as a sculptor was interesting but not without precedent. Many sculptors of the day made statues of young figures, including one whom Degas admired, Paul Dubois,[94] whose bronze model of a young Florentine singer of the fifteenth century was praised when exhibited in 1865. Degas himself had drawn Donatello's *David*[95] as a student in Florence, and there was a vogue in France for work in the Donatello mould, provided the youthful limbs were idealized and not made to seem too bony or awkward. Degas's wax figure was based on observation of his model, and some critics even accused him of distortion:

'The proof that your little girl of fourteen is not realistic is that she has nothing youthful about her; her slenderness is the shrinking, the skinniness and the wrinkles of old age and not of childhood. Could you really have found so

horrible and repulsive a model? And, even if one admits you did find her, why did you choose her? I don't ask of art that it should always be graceful, but I don't believe that its role is to be biased in favour of representing ugliness. Your opera "rat" has something of the monkey, the Aztec, the manikin about her. If she were smaller one would be tempted to shut her up in a specimen spirit jar.'[96]

But Degas had his defenders. Huysmans and others expressed their admiration for Degas's innovations and de Villars wrote: 'The work that is misunderstood today will one day be in a museum looked upon with respect as the first formulation of a new art.'[97] Although Degas liked to claim that success had no meaning for him, he was probably inwardly pleased by the reaction (which was mostly favourable) and felt encouraged to embark on further sculptural experiments. Perhaps he also enjoyed 'shocking the bourgeoisie'. In any event in the summer of 1881, after the close of the exhibition, he began modelling a clay relief, about three feet square, called *The Apple Pickers*, using his cousin from Naples, Lucy, and his niece Anne as models. Again he seems to have been attracted to boyish and youthful figures but when Lucy returned to Naples and he lost the use of her replacement, he became discouraged and appears to have allowed the clay to dry out and crumble into dust. Besides he had to earn his living, and he felt that he was spending too much time on his sculpture at the expense of his 'articles', the pictures he produced for sale.[98] Although all that is now left of this work is a version much smaller in scale, and a few preparatory drawings, it was evidently an impressive work and Renoir, who saw it in Degas's studio, commented that it was 'as handsome as the antique'.[99]

Despite this failure Degas was encouraged by the Valpinçons to embark on another ambitious sculptural project while staying with them for the summer of 1884. Degas's fiftieth birthday had thrown him into a fit of depression, and the weather at Ménil-Hubert was bad. To his friend Henri Rouart he wrote on 22 August:

'One should believe in nothing but rain, in France. Here we are in a hollow. Large park, very high dense trees and water which rises everywhere from under your feet. There are some pastures where it is like walking on sponges. Why do the animals that feed and do their business in these damp pasturing grounds not get rheumatism and why do they not pass it on to us who eat them?'[100]

He seems to have suffered from the city-dweller's pessimistic belief that the weather in the country is always bad, but then to his surprise the sun came out. At the same time Mme Valpinçon, in an effort to jolt him out of his depression, had jestingly asked him to look again at her daughter Hortense, the girl

OPPOSITE:
173. *Rearing horse.* Bronze, ht 12¼ in (31.1 cm). New York, Metropolitan Museum (Bequest of Mrs H. O. Havemeyer, 1929)

he had painted fourteen years earlier. She was now an attractive young woman, soon to marry, and romance was in the air. Degas accepted the challenge, making two Holbeinesque drawings of her seen in profile[101] and a portrait bust, modelled in clay mixed with pebbles. He soon found himself in the same kind of situation as the one he faced when he arrived in New Orleans and began by painting family portraits. Again the family followed his progress with what he called 'malignant curiosity', and what had started as a jest became for him a full-scale challenge. He felt spurred on 'to a frantic effort on my part to obtain a likeness and even something more'.[102] He explained to Ludovic Halévy the need to extend his stay in Normandy:

'But! this bust! so you think it is nothing, you do not believe that "I am fanatically keen about it with (style Goncourt) a family bending over my talent?" You want me to take advantage of the fine weather and leave, and they put it forward to make me stay. And then there is the bust, I swear to you that it is a bust with arms and that I want to press on with it. If I leave it, it is lost.'[103]

After many weeks of work Degas felt ready to have his model cast in plaster. But he was impulsive: instead of getting professional help, he decided to do the casting himself, and without waiting for the proper materials, he used common plaster which could be found locally. It was a disaster. Bust and cast broke during the operation and all that remained of his labours was the back of the figure, which he preserved in his studio for a few months until it too fell apart.[104] After these two defeats a lesser man might have given up sculpture but, as will be seen in the following chapter, he continued to model figures of dancers and horses, albeit on a smaller scale, throughout his fifties and sixties. He never had much regard for the permanence of his work, and on his death his studio was found to be littered with broken and unsalvageable sculptures. The bust of Hortense, although destroyed, does, however, show Degas's inspiration, his desire to experiment for the sake of experiment, and in this respect his work stands as a distant precedent for the sculpture of Picasso, who also liked to work with anything that came to hand.

As he approached fifty Degas seems to have been infected with a burst of creative energy. His letters and notebooks contain snatches of poetry. It was as if all the visual means at his disposal were not sufficient to convey the wealth of his ideas; he bought a treatise on poetry, a copy of Ronsard and a dictionary of rhymes. Eventually he produced the group of sonnets which will be discussed in the next chapter. This search, however, for new means of expression had its drawbacks: work in his usual mediums went un-

finished, projects were abandoned and he was apt to fall into deep depressions. In a letter written on 21 August 1884, a few weeks after his fiftieth birthday, he shared his feelings with Henri Lerolle:

'I have made too many plans, here I am blocked, impotent. And then I have lost the thread of things. I thought there would always be enough time. Whatever I was doing, whatever I was prevented from doing, in the midst of all my troubles and in spite of my infirmity of sight, I never despaired of getting down to it some day.

I stored up all my plans in a cupboard and always carried the key on me. I have lost that key.'[105]

(v)

His colleagues were made only too aware of his black moods, his fits of anger· and his intransigence. Caillebotte, who had joined the Impressionist group for the second exhibition in 1876, and who greatly admired Degas's talent, began to think that he suffered from a persecution complex, and in a letter to Pissarro of 1881 he asked: 'Before his financial losses was he really different from what he is today? Ask all who knew him, beginning with yourself. No, this man has gone sour. He doesn't hold the big place that he ought according to his talent and, although he will never admit it, he bears the whole world a grudge.'[106] Degas's relations with the Impressionists soon deteriorated. He believed in rules and failed to understand his colleagues' predicament. Once he had decided that an artist could not exhibit both at the Salon and at the independent exhibitions (a complete reversal of his original position), he became quite inflexible. He thought Monet, Renoir and Sisley were disloyal and self-seeking, failing to understand the poverty which drove them back to the Salon. At the same time he burdened the exhibitions with his friends – artists like Rouart, Zandomeneghi, Raffaëlli, and Mme Bracquemond – who were light-weight and who lowered the standard. This had the effect of alienating Monet who maintained: 'The little clique has become a great club which opens its doors to the first-come dauber.'[107]

He took part in all eight Impressionist exhibitions except the seventh, and would have been in that too if a palace revolution had not been staged against him. Although the quality of the work he submitted was uneven (and in Caillebotte's view disappointing), and although he often promised more than he delivered, he seems to have regarded the exhibitions as a means for showing new work. At the second exhibition he unveiled his series of laundresses; at the fourth he and Pissarro exhibited a series of fans; at the sixth he showed his sculpture and at the eighth he displayed a series of bathers, painted, he believed, from a new and original point of view, the 'keyhole'.[108] Zola believed that there was a more basic reason for Degas's loyalty to the independent exhibitions:

'M. Degas alone has derived a true benefit from the private exhibitions of the Impressionists; and the reason for this must be sought in his talent. M. Degas was never one of those persecuted by the official Salons. He was accepted, and even relatively well shown. But since his artistic temperament is a delicate one, since he does not have an impressive power, the crowd passed before his pictures without seeing them. Quite understandably the artist was annoyed and realized that he would gain certain advantages by showing with a small group, where his fine, carefully executed paintings could be seen and studied by themselves. And indeed, as soon as he was no longer lost in the crowd of the Salons, he was known to everyone: a circle of fervent admirers gathered round him.'[109]

There was an element of truth in this comment. The subtleties of Degas's art would not have been appreciated in the Salon. He was temperamentally opposed to the idea of putting all his efforts into one eye-catching statement, as Manet could; thus Zola was right in his review of the second Impressionist exhibition when he said, 'his best pictures are among his sketches', although he was wrong in his conclusion that 'his brushes will never become creative'.[110] These remarks can hardly have endeared Zola to Degas, and although they shared so many subjects in common, friendship never developed between them. Later in his life Degas was equally dismissive about Zola's talents. 'He gives me the impression of a giant studying the telephone directory,' he once remarked to George Moore,[111] and to Halévy he said, 'Zola's idea of art, cramming every-thing about a subject into a book, then going on to another subject, seemed to me puerile.'[112]

Degas did indeed benefit by taking part in the Impressionist exhibitions. Through them his work reached the attention of a discriminating group of admirers, and on the whole the criticism he received was favourable. Duranty wrote with sensitivity about his paintings following the second Impressionist exhibition; Mallarmé also wrote enthusiastically about him in an article sent in 1876 to the London magazine The Art Monthly, in which he described him as 'A master of drawing; he has sought delicate lines and movements exquisite or grotesque, and of a strange new beauty, if I dare employ towards his work an abstract term, which he himself will never employ in his daily conversation.'[113] At the fourth show in 1879 Degas's work caught the eye of Huysmans who became over the next few years one of his keenest admirers. Among the essentially antagonistic reviews of the Impressionist exhibitions Albert Wolf, critic for the widely-read newspaper Le Figaro, singled out Degas for praise,[114] and as a result of these and other writings he came to be regarded as the leader of a new school (much to the irritation of the other exhibitors). The story of the eight Impressionist exhibitions can be found in Rewald's History of Impressionism,[115] and it is in many ways a sad one; an enterprise which started with optimism and good-will ended in division and bitterness. In the views of both Gauguin and Caillebotte Degas was largely to blame for the rows which split the group, and Gauguin predicted: 'You will see that Degas is going to end his days more unhappy than the others, wounded in his vanity for not being the first and only one. A time will come when . . . he will complain about all humanity.'[116]

Chapter 5

1884 to 1917

IN 1885 BERTHE MORISOT wrote to her sister Edma about her plans for another Impressionist exhibition, the eighth:

'I am working with some prospect of having an exhibition this year: everything I have done for a long time seems to me so horribly bad that I should like to have new, and above all better, things to show to the public. This project is very much up in the air, Degas's perversity makes it almost impossible of realization; there are clashes of vanity in this little group that make any understanding difficult. It seems to me that I am about the only one without any pettiness of character; this makes up for my inferiority as a painter.'[1]

Her efforts and those of her husband Eugène Manet proved unsuccessful, but the following year they tried again. This time Pissarro proved to be the stumbling block. In 1885 he had come under the influence of Georges Seurat whose system of painting in small dots of complementary colour, later called 'Pointillism', impressed the older artist as being more scientific than the Impressionist method of painting in dabs and comma-like brushstrokes, a technique which he now thought of as 'romantic'. He was particularly struck by Seurat's large canvas *La Grande Jatte*, which in the course of 1886 Seurat completely reworked in his Pointillist manner. Pissarro now adapted Seurat's technique to his own paintings, and when he was approached by the Manets to take part in the eighth Impressionist exhibition, he agreed on condition that his new friends Seurat and Paul Signac could show at the same time. Eugène Manet, however, was less receptive (as was Monet) to Seurat's ideas than Pissarro; the issue was further complicated by the size of *La Grande Jatte*, which threatened to take up too much room. A fierce argument ensued between Pissarro and Manet. 'You may be sure I rated Manet roundly – which will not please Renoir,' Pissarro informed his son. *'But anyhow, this is the point: I explained to M. Manet, who probably didn't understand anything I said, that Seurat has something new to contribute which these gentlemen, despite their talent, are unable to appreciate, that I am personally convinced of the progressive character of his art and certain that in time it will yield extraordinary results. . . . M. Manet was beside himself! I didn't calm down. They are all underhanded, but I don't give in. Degas is a hundred times more loyal. I told Degas that Seurat's painting was very interesting. "I would have noted that myself, Pissarro, except that the thing is so big!"'*[2]

In the end a compromise was reached and Pissarro and the Pointillists exhibited their work in a room to themselves. Monet, Renoir, Caillebotte and Sisley decided to abstain, but Degas, Mary Cassatt and Berthe Morisot took part, as did a number of their friends.

Degas was keen to take part in the exhibition,

175. *Portrait of George Moore*, drawing. 19½ × 12¾ in (49.7 × 32.8 cm). Oxford, Ashmolean Museum

despite Seurat's presence, perhaps because he had been working for some time on a series of nudes which he believed represented something of a new departure in the treatment of a time-honoured subject. 'Hitherto the nude has always been represented in poses which presuppose an audience,' he explained to George Moore. 'But my women are simple straightforward women, concerned with nothing beyond their physical existence. Just look at this one: she is washing her feet.'[3] To break free from the traditional self-conscious poses in which the model stood or lay on a dais in goddess-like positions, Degas adopted a stance outside the model's field of awareness, as though he were looking at her 'through a keyhole'. This last phrase, which Moore used in an article published in 1890,[4] caused a great stir in England because it seemed to imply a 'voyeuristic' element in Degas's paintings of nudes. Huysmans, however, argued that never before had pictures of nudes been so free from sexual implications:

'Among the people who visited this exhibition, some, in the presence of this woman who is seen squatting, in front-view, and whose belly does not need the usual deceits, cried out, indignant at this frankness, struck all the same by the life flowing from these pastels. In the end they exchanged some doubtful or disgusted comments and upon leaving, their parting shot was: "It's obscene".

Ah! If ever works were less so, if ever they were without fussy precautions, without subterfuge, completely, decisively chaste, it is above all these. They even glorify the disdain of the flesh, as no artist since the Middle Ages has ever dared to do.'[5]

The eighth Impressionist exhibition opened on 15 May, the same day as the Salon. The most discussed picture was, as expected, Seurat's *La Grande Jatte* and there was a steady stream of visitors led by Alfred Stevens from the Café Tortoni opposite the rooms where the exhibition was held, who persuaded his friends to come and see how low Degas had fallen in welcoming such an oddity.[6] When Moore arrived, he found the room with the Pointillist pictures full of people laughing, 'exaggerated laughter intended to give as much pain as possible'.[7] The sight of Degas's series of ten bathers, described in the catalogue as 'women bathing, washing, drying, rubbing down, combing their hair or having it combed', seems to have sobered and even shocked the critics, although the flow of words unleashed by Huysmans and the new advocate for the avant-garde, Félix Fénéon, was not stemmed. Huysmans, as already mentioned, believed that Degas was out deliberately to shock the bourgeoisie, that in addition to a special accent of 'scorn and hate', there was 'the unforgettable veracity of the drawing, so rich in its lucid and controlled

ardour and its icy fever', and he concluded that 'M. Degas arouses in each of his pictures the sensation of a calculated strangeness, of such insight that we are surprised and almost blame ourselves for being astonished.'[8] Moore too was surprised when he first saw the bathers, but once he had recovered from the initial shock, he confessed that he was profoundly moved by the sight of their humble and unglamorous bodies.[9] Fénéon's description of the pictures emphasizes the extreme realism of Degas's approach:

'Women crouched, like melons, swelling in the shells of their bath-tubs; one, chin against her breast, scrubs her neck, another's whole body is sharply contorted, her arm clutches her back and she addresses her coccygeal regions with a soapy sponge. A bony spine sticks out; upper arms shoot past juicy pear-shaped breasts and plunge straight down between the legs to wet a facecloth in the tub of water where the feet are soaking. There's a collapse of hair on shoulders, bosom on hips, stomach on thighs, limbs on their joints, and viewed from above as she lies on her bed, with her hands plastered against her buttocks, the slut looks like a series of bulging jointed cylinders. Seen from the front, kneeling, thighs apart, head drooping towards the flaccid torso, a girl is drying herself. And it is in obscure furnished hotel rooms, in the humblest circumstances, that these richly patinated bodies, bodies that bear the bruises of marriages, childbirth and illness, divest themselves and spread their limbs.'[10]

Degas's painter friends were impressed by his new pastels. Berthe Morisot went to see some further studies of bathers the following year at Goupil's gallery, and wrote to Monet, 'I went to see the nudes of that fierce Degas, which are becoming more and more extraordinary.'[11] Renoir was particularly struck by his use of pastel which he himself regarded as very disagreeable to handle, but which in Degas's hands achieved results which had 'the freshness of fresco'. To Vollard he remarked: 'If Degas had died at fifty, he would have been remembered as an excellent painter, no more. It is after his fiftieth year that his work broadens out and that he really becomes Degas.'[12]

Although his 'keyhole' approach was to some extent a new departure in figure painting, the theme of women bathing was by no means new. Degas himself said on one occasion that two centuries earlier he would have been painting 'Susannah at the Bath'. It was a subject painted several times by Rembrandt, and it is interesting to find a Rembrandt with this title belonging to Louis LaCaze, a friend of Degas's father, whose collection was bequeathed to the Louvre in 1869, to an enthusiastic reception. But perhaps the greatest painting in the LaCaze bequest, and certainly one of Rembrandt's greatest

OPPOSITE:
176. *Woman drying her hair*, c.1905–7. Pastel on paper, $24\frac{1}{2} \times 28$ in (62.2 × 71 cm). Los Angeles, Norton Simon Foundation

nudes, was *Bathsheba with King David's Letter* (plate 177), which shows a nude woman sitting on a divan having her feet washed by an attendant. Degas's *A Woman Having Her Hair Combed* (plate 178) seems to have been conceived in much the same light as the Rembrandt: both nudes are absorbed in their thoughts and appear to be oblivious of any onlooker except their attendants who go about their business in unselfconscious fashion. Their attitude reminds one of the dresser in Zola's *Nana* (which presumably Degas read shortly after its publication), whose 'shrivelled hands pass over Nana's naked charms without any sign of emotion, as if completely uninterested in her sex.'[13]

The difference between Rembrandt's and Degas's nudes, however, is that whereas Rembrandt's have a spiritual quality (as well as a Biblical connotation), Degas's exist on a purely physical plane; as he explained to Moore, 'I show them deprived of their airs and affectations reduced to the level of animals cleaning themselves,' and pointing to one of his bathers, he remarked that the woman was like 'a cat licking itself'.[14] The animal quality of his women has been noted by several writers beginning with Moore, and recently Françoise Cachin has drawn attention to the many visual and verbal associations which existed for Degas between horses and women.[15] She points out that he often chose his models like a horse-breeder and wrote their names and addresses in his notebooks with short descriptive reminders: 'Eliza Richard – blonde – well built', 'Catherine Essler – brunette – elegant – white teeth'. The great proportion of Degas's nudes feature heads of hair and buttocks, the parts of the body which correspond to the horse's mane and hind-quarters. The faces of his models, their individual characters, can seldom be seen, and are either hidden from view or swathed in flowing hair. The woman in the Hill-Stead Museum's *The Tub* (plate 180) is remarkably like an animal and appears to be almost on all fours, with her face, breasts, waist and thighs hidden, leaving the spectator with a view of her head of hair and her long back.

The bathroom, or the bath-house, was a setting which many of Degas's favourite artists used in their work. Ingres had chosen a Turkish bath as the setting for one of his most exotic and even erotic works, *Le Bain Turc*. Women bathing or being washed were recurring subjects of Japanese prints, which were exhibited in Paris and collected by Degas.[16] Gavarni, a caricaturist much admired by Degas, had depicted a woman in a bath (similar to the ones in Degas's pictures) being watched by another woman, a print of which was also in his collection.[17] Many of Degas's contemporaries and friends in the early

1880s seem to have been simultaneously drawn to this theme. A passage in Zola's *Nana* illustrates this fascination with women attending their toilette:

'*Nana undressed in the dressing-room. To be quicker about it, she took her thick mass of blonde hair in both hands and began shaking it above the silver wash-basin, so that a shower of long hair-pins rang a chime on the shining metal.*'[18]

At the eighth Impressionist exhibition Mary Cassatt showed *The Morning Toilette*, a painting of a young girl dressed in a chemise, standing in front of a marble wash-stand, plaiting her hair; it later became part of Degas's collection.[19] During the early 1880s Renoir also began a number of canvases of bathers, but he chose to put them in a more Classical setting, bathing in a river or adopting Ingres-like poses on the river-bank. In Aix-en-Provence Cézanne too was painting bathers in a river setting, a theme which occupied him at frequent intervals over the next twenty years. Both Cézanne and Renoir found themselves moving away from Impressionism, from the direct representation of nature painted on the spot to a more Classical art which could be executed in the privacy of the studio. Renoir turned back to the example of Raphael whose frescoes had so impressed him on a visit to Rome in 1881, and Cézanne looked to Poussin. Degas, in spite

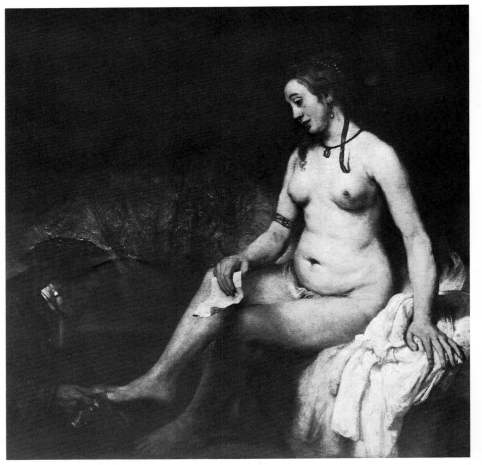

OPPOSITE:
178. *Woman having her hair combed*, c.1885. Pastel on paper, 29 × 24 in (74 × 60·6 cm). New York, Metropolitan Museum (Havemeyer Collection)

177. REMBRANDT, *Bathsheba with King David's letter*, c.1654. Oil on canvas, 56 × 56 in (142 × 142 cm). Paris, Louvre

OPPOSITE:
179. *After the bath*, c.1890. Pastel on brown cardboard, 28 × 22½ in (70.8 × 57.2 cm). Cambridge, Mass., Courtesy of the Fogg Art Museum, Harvard University (Gift of Mrs J. Montgomery-Sears)

180. *The tub*, c.1885–6. Pastel, 27½ × 27½ in (70 × 70 cm). Farmington, Conn., Hill-Stead Museum

of, or even because of, his Classical training, felt no desire to return to the past. Having perhaps a more original mind, he felt compelled to find new poses for the female body and new positions from which to observe it. In some of the pictures, such as *The Tub* (plate 180), he adopted the same position, looking down on his models from above, as he had in his portraits. At the same time he began to employ colour with a freedom and power which astonished even such a strong colourist as Renoir.

Two pastels of bathers reproduced in colour in this book (plates 187 and 188) give an indication of the richness of Degas's palette in his middle and old age.

They show how he built up colour layer upon layer, applying it in scrawls and scribbles in some areas and in cross-hatching composed of straight lines in others. They also show how he often ignored traditional theory of colour perspective, which placed bright hues in the foreground and cool colours in the background, and in fact did the reverse; his bathers were painted in fairly cool tones, while the backgrounds – the curtains, the wallpapers, draperies and towels – gleam in vivid fireworks of reds, yellows, purples and greens. It was a colour technique that Bonnard employed in his bathroom pictures half a century later. Denis Rouart has observed that Degas adapted

to pastel 'the technique of making colors play against each other by superimposition and transparency rather than merely by the opposition of color areas. Transparency could not, of course, be obtained in pastel as it could be with glazes in oil paint; so he arrived at an analogous effect by working in successive layers, not covering the lower layer entirely but letting it show through.'[20]

The technique was in part an attempt to find an equivalent to the Venetian artists' use of underpainting and glazing to produce rich glowing colour. The more interested he became in colour, the more he began to wonder how the Old Masters had achieved their effects, and as his pupil Ernest Rouart observed: 'He had a set of theories about colouring and its function in a picture which he would expound with great relish, but they were not always easy to grasp, and certainly not easy to make clear to an open-mouthed disciple, pondering on groundwork in *camaieu* [a method of painting in monochrome] glazes and so on.'[21]

The Impressionist exhibition of 1886 was the last. As a group the Impressionists were, and had been, hopelessly divided, but their exhibitions had served a purpose in breaking the Salon's hold on the career, and even the minds, of artists in France. Their example encouraged other artists to mount their own independent exhibitions; as a result the Salon des Indépendants and the Salon d'Automne were formed where not only the next generations, the Pointillistes, the Nabis and the Fauves, showed their work, but also the post-Impressionists, Van Gogh, Gauguin and Cézanne, first became known to a wide public.

Degas showed a large body of his work only once again, at Durand-Ruel's gallery in 1893; otherwise one or two pastels could be seen at dealers' galleries,

OPPOSITE:
181. *Dancer: developpé en avant.* Bronze, ht. 16 in (40.5 cm). New York, Metropolitan Museum (Bequest of Mrs H. O. Havemeyer, 1929)

182. *Prancing horse.* Bronze, ht. 10½ in (26.5 cm). Private Collection

mainly Durand-Ruel but also Goupil and Vollard. The relative scarcity of his work, combined with a growing demand, helped raise the price of his canvases and pastels. Some of the artist friends to whom he had given paintings as gifts took advantage of the market and sold them. Tissot was one and Degas was deeply offended that 'that old friend I lived with so long, had such fun with, knew so well' could do such a thing, but he admitted: 'Practically every-one I have given pictures to has sold them . . . Well, I can take my vengeance. I shall do a caricature of Tissot [who late in life had given up his pictures of society women for Biblical scenes] with Christ behind him, whipping him, and call it "Christ Driving his Merchant from the Temple". My God!'[22]

As the prices for his work began to rise, Degas enjoyed greater prosperity, but it made very little difference to his way of life; he continued to live parsimoniously on the rue Victor-Massé and was annoyed when he once lost his ticket on the omnibus and was forced to pay again. He began, however, to spend larger sums on buying the work of other artists. In the years following 1886 his collection grew rapidly; the result was that the first sale after his death consisted of 247 items, with 93 paintings and 154 pastels, watercolours and drawings, and the second 264 items including over 300 engravings and prints.[23] Degas was an avid collector, excited by a bargain but equally liable to be carried away in the salerooms. He often bought pictures for emotional reasons or from loyalty to an artist friend, and it was in this spirit that he acquired works by Gauguin, 'a lad who is dying of hunger and whom I esteem profoundly as an artist',[24] who in 1894 sold a group of his pictures

183. Parody of Ingres's *Apotheosis of Homer*, 1885. Photograph posed by Degas. Paris, BN

at auction to raise money for his journey to Tahiti. Halévy was astonished by Degas's intensity in the saleroom and watched him bidding and allowing himself to be carried away by prices that frightened even him, Halévy. 'What's more,' he wrote, 'he couldn't even see the pictures he bought. He would ask me, "What is it?" and then remember. He bought a copy of the *Olympia* that he had never seen. He would lean over to his neighbour and ask, "Is it beautiful?" '[25] It was, for instance, out of loyalty to the memory of Manet that Degas bought the fragments of his large composition *The Execution of Emperor Maximilian* (now in the National Gallery, London).

In forming his collection Degas's greatest enthusiasm was, as might be expected, for the work of the two masters whom he had held in such respect since his youth – Ingres and Delacroix. He owned a great many paintings and drawings by both. He had four portraits by Ingres, including two magnificent pictures now in the Metropolitan Museum, sixteen oils and oil sketches and ninety drawings, including a beautiful study for the *Large Odalisque*. These drawings were among his most cherished possessions and when Moore called on him in about 1888, Degas showed him his latest acquisition and said: 'Ah! look at it, I bought it only a few days ago; it is a drawing of a female hand by Ingres; look at those finger-nails, see how they are indicated. That's my idea of genius, a man who finds a hand so lovely, so wonderful, so difficult to render, that he will shut himself up all his life, content to do nothing else but indicate finger-nails.'[26]

His Delacroix collection was no less impressive: it included the portrait of *Baron Schwiter* (now in the National Gallery, London), battle scenes, a copy after Rubens, studies of landscapes, animals, the beautiful *Interior, The Comte de Mornay's Apartment* (now in the Louvre) and 190 drawings. Among the Old Masters that he had collected there were several which cast a revealing light on his taste and his development: a painting after Cuyp, which points to his having taken in his youth 'the road from Holland'; a Perronneau, a tribute to his early enthusiasm for the French pastellists of the eighteenth century; and El Greco's *Saint Ildefonso Writing at the Virgin's Dictation* (now in the National Gallery, Washington), an indication that he shared his countrymen's enthusiasm for the Spanish master whose work, after a long period of neglect, was rediscovered in the second half of the nineteenth century.

Among nineteenth-century artists, he owned pictures by Millet and Corot, an enormous collection of lithographs and drawings by Daumier, an equally large collection of caricatures by Gavarni and, of course, a group of paintings by his fellow Impressionist exhibitors, such as Pissarro (with whom Degas maintained a cordial relationship despite their differences of opinion on politics and art), Sisley, Armand Guillaumin, Mary Cassatt and Berthe Morisot. He had, however, no Monet, who represented all that he most disliked about Impressionism, the artist who more than any other, he felt, slavishly copied nature. He was forever making cracks about his work: 'His pictures always were too draughty for me,' he once remarked, and added that if he saw any more he would have to turn up his coat collar.[27] On meeting him at one of his exhibitions at Durand-Ruel, he is supposed to have said: 'Let me get out of here. Those reflections in the water hurt my eyes!'[28]

Degas's collection also reveals that he had an eye for and an understanding of the Impressionists' successors, whose art was so different from his own. He had been an admirer of Gauguin from his first meeting with him in the late 1870s and was even prepared to overlook the fact that to gain attention for his work Gauguin was ready to court publicity; among other paintings by Gauguin he owned *La Belle Angèle* (now in the Louvre). More surprisingly, he also admired the work of Cézanne and bought not the landscapes but the more romantic and expressive work of the 1870s, a small *Venus and Cupid*, a still life of apples, a self-portrait of about 1879-82 and Cézanne's portrait of Victor Chocquet, one of the early defenders and collectors of Impressionism. But perhaps the most unexpected pictures in his collection were two still lifes of 1887 by Van Gogh, unexpected because these fiery and turbulent paintings with their heavy pigment and rough lines seem at first glance so far removed from Degas's refined and disciplined taste. If, however, one remembers Degas's increasing use of expressive colour and spontaneous line in the late pastels, their similarities become more apparent. All the same it is interesting to speculate on how he came to know Van Gogh's work, whether Gauguin mentioned his friend's name or whether Vollard, who dealt in Van Gogh, was the first to draw his attention to the Dutchman's paintings. Apart from his interest in these three artists (he had none for one much closer in style to his own work – Toulouse-Lautrec), it is worth mentioning that all three lived outside society and were passionately devoted to their calling, putting their art above all other considerations. In addition all three had problems with women – Gauguin was aggressive and excessively masculine, Cézanne was almost as shy and as reticent as Degas, and Van Gogh, rejected by women of his own class, was only able to find a temporary relationship with a woman who

184. Scenes from a charade, photographs posed by Degas at Ménil-Hubert. Paris, BN

was a prostitute.

Degas's reluctance to entertain any friendship with Toulouse-Lautrec, and his somewhat reserved attitude to his work, are at first rather surprising. Toulouse-Lautrec came from an aristocratic family, he was a distant cousin of Degas's old friends the Dihaus, and he studied under another old friend, Léon Bonnat. Soon after his arrival in Paris in 1882 he became a passionate admirer of Degas; he shared his artistic interest in brothels and popular entertainment, and, more importantly, his respect for line, for original composition and for portraits in which deportment of the body is given as much weight as facial expression. His adulation of Degas was such that when he did portraits of Désiré and Marie Dihau (both were painted by Degas some twenty years earlier), Lautrec inquired 'timidly and humbly whether they did not look ridiculous beside those of Degas'.[29] Early one morning Lautrec took a group of friends, still dressed in their evening clothes, to Marie Dihau's apartment in which the portrait of her brother and the members of the orchestra (plate 64) still hung, and, once admitted, Lautrec ordered his friends to their knees to worship the master's work.[30] Yet despite the respect Lautrec showed for the older artist, thirty years his senior, Degas was reluctant to see him, perhaps because he was so much younger, perhaps because he disliked his unruly antics, or more probably because he recognized that of all the artists to come under his influence, including Jean-Louis Forain, Zandomeneghi and even Cassatt, Lautrec was the most talented and the one most likely to steal his secrets which, as he grew older, he guarded more closely in his fortress-like studio.

185. *Rocks beside a river*, 1890–3. Monotype and pastel on paper mounted on cardboard, $11\frac{3}{4} \times 15\frac{3}{4}$ in (30 × 42.5 cm). Paris, Private Collection

OVERLEAF, LEFT: 186. Study for the maid in *The cup of tea*. London, courtesy of Lefèvre Gallery Ltd

OVERLEAF, RIGHT: 187. *The cup of tea (Le petit déjeuner à la sortie du bain)*, 1883. Pastel on paper, $47\frac{1}{2} \times 36\frac{1}{4}$ in (120 × 92 cm). London, courtesy of Lefèvre Gallery Ltd

Toulouse-Lautrec's admiration for Degas is echoed in Moore's article on Degas published in 1890, of which its author was justly proud, being the first, as Pickvance has noted,[31] to evaluate Degas's work by reference to his life and his convictions. Moore concluded his article by pointing out:

'*Degas now occupies the most enviable position an artist can attain. He is always the theme of conversation when artists meet, and if the highest honour is to obtain the admiration of your fellow-workers, that honour has been bestowed on Degas as it has been bestowed upon none other. His pictures are bought principally by artists, and when not by them by their immediate entourage.*'[32]

Moore was right. Through Whistler and through another old friend, Alphonse Legros, Degas's work began once again to enter English collections in the 1890s, as, for instance, *The Ballet Scene from Robert Le Diable* (plate 110), brought from Faure by the painter and collector Constantine Ionides.[33] Whistler's pupil Sickert owned a *Dance Rehearsal on Stage* and through Mary Cassatt, who herself owned several Degas, a number began to enter America besides the many bought by her old friend Mrs Havemeyer; the painter Jacques-Emile Blanche was immensely proud of the Degas in his collection; and in Germany, the *pièce de resistance* of the painter Max Liebermann's collection was the great 80-inch wide 'frieze' of a dancer adjusting her shoe in a sequence of four different positions (now in the Cleveland Museum).[34] The high regard in which Degas's work was held by artists has continued: Picasso owned several monotypes of brothels; more recently David Hockney has expressed his admiration for Degas:

'*On the other hand, you have painters like Barnett Newman; if you compare Newman as a painter to, say, Degas, I think you can see that Newman is concerned more with ideas – obsessively so, because he's not as good an artist as Degas. He is more concerned with theory as well, though Degas was too – any good artist is, actually; you can't ignore it. But it's Degas's eye and attitudes that matter, the responses he got, the responses he in part "felt". In Barnett Newman's work it isn't like that at all. I'm not praising one over another, we all know who is the better artist, I'm sure Barnett Newman wouldn't say he was as good as Degas. He loved Degas, actually, as I do.*'[35]

Degas collected around him a group of young admirers, and as his beard grew and his hair turned white and his eyesight faded he even began to resemble the popular image of an Old Testament prophet. These admirers were often sons of old family friends, or their friends. They included the youthful Daniel Halévy, whose notes of Degas's conversation provide one of the major sources for documenting Degas's sayings, Ernest Rouart, painter

son of Henri Rouart (who married the daughter of Berthe Morisot and Eugène Manet), and the poet Paul Valéry, also an amateur painter, who came to know Degas around 1893. Valéry's *Degas, Dance, Drawing* is another major source of information about Degas's opinions and personality and remains the one which comes closest to understanding Degas's unique qualities as an artist.

Degas's attitude to the young people whom he met at the Halévys' and the Rouarts' varied between the friendly and the ferocious. 'He was kind to me', wrote Valéry, 'in the way one is to people who scarcely exist. I was not worth his shot.[36] Arriving at the Halévys' one evening, Degas reported on his dinner the previous night at Henri Rouart's (a dinner at which Valéry may have been present): 'There were his sons and some young people – all talking art. I blew up. What interests me is work, business and the army.'[37]

With Degas at their tables not even his closest friends knew what to expect. He could be moody, silent, rude, bitter, aggressive, depressed; at other times he was gay and according to Valéry was often the soul of the evening:

'*A constant, brilliant, unbearable guest, spreading wit, terror, and gaiety. A piercing mimic, with an endless fund of whims, maxims, banter, anecdotes, brilliantly unfair in his attacks, infallible in his taste, narrow-mindedly yet lucidly passionate, he was always throwing mud at writers, at the Institut, at the aloof poseurs, and the artists who were bent on "getting there" – quoting Saint-Simon, Proudhon, Racine, and the weird pronouncements of "Monsieur" Ingres. . . . I can still hear him.*'[38]

The years when Degas was at his best were those before his sixtieth birthday (1894), before the Dreyfus affair, before the death of many of his friends, before his eyesight made his work almost impossible to complete, and before his ill-health, attacks of bronchitis, put him in mind of his own death. The photographs taken of, and sometimes posed by, Degas in his fifties, reveal a man who was capable of enjoying himself, with a strong sense of fun. In Dieppe staying with Ludovic Halévy in 1885, Degas appears to have become quite friendly with a local photographer who took a picture of the painter standing next to Halévy and Albert Cavé, all dressed similarly in hats, cravats, high-winged collars, frock-coats, waistcoats and with almost identical beards. On Degas's instructions he also took a posed photograph (plate 183) which was a parody of Ingres's *Apotheosis of Homer* (he owned four preparatory drawings for this work) which can be interpreted as a prophesy of his own blindness: Degas played the part of the blind poet, with Halévy's sons Elie and

Daniel at his feet.

But the photographs which perhaps capture Degas in some of the happiest moments of his life are the group of pictures of him and Paul-Albert Bartholomé in a Tilbury carriage on their travels through Burgundy in October 1890. On 30 September the two friends set off from Ludovic Halévy's house at Montgéron, south-west of Paris, with the object of reaching Diénay where another artist, Georges Jeanniot, lived. Throughout the journey Degas kept Halévy informed of his progress and the state of the horse which pulled the carriage and whose appetite for oats even surpassed that of Degas and Bartholomé for the country food they enjoyed at their various stops. Degas's letters are full of jokes, asides and comments and include some of the menus encountered: at Montereau, lunch at the Hôtel du Grand Monarque consisted of sheep's foot, fried gudgeon, sausage and mash ('admirable') and beefsteaks with cress, and at the Hôtel de la Poste at Villeneuve-la-Guyard dinner consisted of panada (bread boiled to a pulp with sugar and nutmeg) with milk, brains in melted butter, jugged hare, and leg of mutton with mixed beans ('famous'). As a footnote to his letter he adds, 'No more thoughts, one eats too much. Each meal three francs.'[39] The journey pleased Degas enormously and for once his letters contain no complaints about the weather or the state of his eyes.

Four days later the two travellers arrived at their destination, and their host Jeanniot later described their reception:

'We were warned of the exact time at which the white horse was to appear on the road. All our friends were there, the young girls with their baskets of flowers, Edmond Couturier, as an inspector carrying the keys of the village on a silver dish. I myself, as a policeman, represented the public services. When the moment came the young girls advanced with their flowers, with which they covered the horse and the travellers. The keys were offered to Degas who was very touched by it. Our little band, escorting the carriage, entered the village slowly, with all the dignity worthy of the occasion.'[40]

The journey through the Burgundy countryside seems to have whetted Degas's appetite for landscape. As soon as he arrived at Jeanniot's, he asked for copper or zinc plates and a rag cloth, explaining that he had wanted for a long time to do a series of monotypes. Instead of the black printer's ink with which he was familiar he used oil paint thinned with turpentine. Jeanniot later recalled his methods:

'Once he was provided with all that he needed he started work without a moment's delay, not allowing himself to be distracted.

With his strong but well-shaped fingers he grasped hold of each object, each tool of his genius, wielding it with surprising dexterity so that little by little there appeared on the metal surface a valley, a sky, white houses, fruit trees with black branches, birches and oaks, ruts of water after the recent shower, orange-tinted clouds scudding across a turbulent sky above the red and green earth.

All the pieces fell into place harmoniously, colours mingling, and the handle of the brush traced pale shapes in the fresh colour. These pretty things were born with apparent ease, as though he had the model before him.

Bartholomé recognized the places their white horse had passed through at a brisk trot.

After half an hour, no more, came Degas's voice:

"And now, if you are all agreeable, let us pull this proof. Is the paper damp? Where's the sponge? You know soft-sized paper is the best!"

"Calm down, I've got some strong Chinese."

"He's got Chinese? Let's see it then . . ."

I put a magnificent roll down on the end of the table. When everything was ready, the plate placed on the press and the paper laid on the plate, Degas said:

"What a terrifying moment! Go ahead! Start turning!"

It was an old press with a heavy wheel in the shape of a cross. Once the proof was obtained it was hung up to dry. We used to do three or four every morning.

Then he asked for pastels to finish his monotypes, and it was now, even more than in the proof-making, that I admired his taste, his imagination, and the vividness of his recollections. He recalled the variety of the shapes, the structure of the land, the unexpected counterpoint or contrast: it was delightful. . . .'[41]

In many ways the landscape pictures begun at Diénay are a forceful reminder of the differences between his art and that of the Impressionists: he insisted that art requires artifice and believed that the artist's task is to lend, as he put it quoting Delacroix, 'enchantment to truth', as well as to reveal his deeper feelings about the country, feelings which to judge by some of his remarks amount to fear, and which might today be labelled agoraphobia. Standing before one of Jeanniot's landscapes, Degas commented: 'What you have tried to convey is the air outdoors, the air we breathe, the open air. Well! A painting is above all a product of the artist's imagination, it should never be a copy . . .'[42] and then he added a remark that he often repeated, 'The air you see in paintings by the Masters is not the air you can breathe.' Perhaps because of his city upbringing, or perhaps because of some inner fear, his countryside was not solid, like the cones and cylinders revealed by Cézanne, but vaporous, a mingling of air and water. Although he admired and collected the work of Corot, his vision of nature is closer to Turner and more directly influenced by Whistler, about whom he

OVERLEAF, LEFT:
188. *Woman washing herself*, 1892. Pastel on paper, $24\frac{3}{4} \times 18\frac{3}{4}$ in (63 × 48 cm). London, courtesy of Lefèvre Gallery Ltd

OVERLEAF, RIGHT:
189. *Four dancers*, c.1902. Pastel on paper, $25\frac{1}{4} \times 16\frac{1}{2}$ in (64 × 42 cm). London, courtesy of Lefèvre Gallery Ltd

had written two decades earlier in 1873: 'That fellow Whistler really has something in the sea and water pieces he showed me.'[43] The landscapes done at Diénay, like the Whistlerian landscapes he did at Boulogne in 1869, are also vague and watery with dissolving forms, shifting surfaces and swirling air.

Degas was evidently pleased with the results of his experiments at Diénay, and in 1893 he showed a group of landscapes at Durand-Ruel's gallery, his first and only one-man show. There were twenty-one, some done at Diénay and some at a later date. The announcement of his intended exhibition surprised many of his friends, including the Halévys, who were unaware that Degas had painted any landscapes. They asked him how they were done. 'They are the fruit of my travels this summer,' Degas replied. 'I would stand at the door of the coach and as the train went along I could see things vaguely. That gave me the idea of doing some landscapes.' 'What kind are they? Vague things? Reflections of your soul?' asked Ludovic Halévy, reminding Degas of the diarist Henri-Frédéric Amiel's phrase, 'A landscape is a reflection of the soul'. 'A reflection of my eyesight,' Degas replied characteristically. 'We painters do not use such pretentious language.'[44]

The Durand-Ruel exhibition was a success. It was admired by a number of artists, including Pissarro who commented that 'this confounded Degas' stupefied people even with his landscapes. These pictures (plates 185 and 190), which remain among his least-known works, continue to attract artists (among them the English painter Howard Hodgkin, whose own landscapes are recreations of life done from memory in the studio); they deserve Françoise

190. *Autumn landscape*, 1890–3. Pastel over monotype, 12 × 15¾ in (30 × 40 cm). Boston, Museum of Fine Arts (Gift of Denman W. Ross)

191. Self-portrait of Degas with his housekeeper Zoé, photograph. Paris, BN

planned to bring Cavé and Ludovic Halévy, and as an extra inducement he suggested that they make a detour to visit Mont St-Michel. The exact date of departure was not fixed and Degas was afraid that the expedition might not come off; the story was later told by Daniel Halévy:

'For Degas, whom it was difficult to tear away from his studio, this journey was an important matter. He looked forward to it with child-like anticipation. To Cavé, like everything else in the world, it meant nothing. Besides, he rebelled as much against engagements as he did against work; instinctively he rejected being tied down. The day before they were to leave he told Degas gently that he was "prevented" from going. The expedition did not take place. Degas was very angry. "Prevented, what does that mean? You promised; you should come." Cavé listened with a patient smile to the vehement reproaches with which Degas tried to overwhelm him. "That's how it is, Degas. I am prevented from going."

For a long time Degas talked about this broken engagement; and I don't mean for weeks or for months but for years. He talked about it insistently, with that forceful repetitiousness, that wearisome reiteration of which certain intense souls are capable and which was highly developed in him. Degas never tired of a friendship or a hatred, nor of an admiration, a joke or a grievance.'[46]

Degas's plans for visiting Spain in 1889 with the portrait painter Giovanni Boldini proved more successful. The two met in Bayonne and proceeded to the Prado in Madrid where Degas stood, overwhelmed by the Velásquez paintings. 'Nothing, no, nothing can give the right idea of Velásquez,' he wrote to Bartholomé.'[47] Degas then went on to Tangier where he made an observation which is the very essence of Degas and shows his lasting esteem for the artistic heroes of his youth: 'One loves in nature those people who have not been unworthy to appreciate it. I tell you this because Delacroix passed here.'[48] It was with the same feelings of homage that Degas in 1897 went to Montauban, Ingres's home town, where a museum contained his papers and many of his works.

Degas's absences from Paris often inspired him to new artistic efforts and to new means of expression. He certainly benefited from the journey to New Orleans; his long stays at Ménil-Hubert led to the masterpieces of 1870 and the ambitious sculptures of 1884, and the visit to Diénay, as already mentioned, led to the landscape monotypes. When he was recovering from a severe attack of bronchitis at Le Mont-Dore in 1895, Degas once again found a new artistic medium – photography.

His interest in photography was lifelong. As a young man he had used carte-de-visite photographs

Cachin's comment that the coloured monotypes done at Diénay represent the quintessence of all that Degas aimed for and so often achieved – 'a kind of basic fidelity rendered magical by the artist's visual intelligence.'[45]

In his fifties Degas seems to have been infected with an urge to travel. Sometimes these trips were for medical reasons, like those to Cauterets in the Pyrenees to take a cure for his liver complaints, or to Le Mont-Dore in the Auvergne to recover from attacks of bronchitis. Others were for family reasons: for example, in 1886, in an attempt to straighten out his inheritance he went to Naples, in 1890 to Geneva to see his brother Achille who was not well, and in 1893 to Interlaken where his brother-in-law Edmondo Morbilli was ill. Sometimes he went for the fun of it and when Mme Howland, a friend of the artist Fromentin and of the Halévy circle, announced her departure for America (she was married to an American) Degas volunteered to accompany her to Le Havre to catch her boat. As companions he

as a help for portraits and he had adapted some of the poses used by the first portrait photographers for his own portraits. At the Cafés Guerbois and Nouvelle-Athènes he had had the opportunity of meeting perhaps the greatest portrait photographer of the age, and he was doubtless aware of the skills in lighting and composing that Nadar brought to what appeared to be a mechanical process. Degas's own skill of capturing individuals and groups like the portrait of *Désiré Dihau and the Members of the Orchestra* and the *Portraits in an Office* had earned him a reputation for a photographic memory, and in the 1890s, referring back to these earlier pictures, his niece Jeanne Fèvre used to talk of *l'oeil Kodak*,[49] his Kodak eye.

Before the arrival of the first Kodak in 1888,

194. Photograph of Degas with his niece at a window. Paris, BN

cameras were bulky and expensive and photography was limited to professionals and enthusiastic amateurs. The invention of lenses, however, capable of shutter-speeds of 1/50th of a second and faster, made out-door snap-shot photography possible. Degas bought a Kodak in the early 1890s; he was delighted with it and offered to send one to his sister Marguerite in Buenos-Aires. To while away the time at Le Mont-Dore he began to take landscape photographs, sending the negatives to Paris to be developed and enclosing some twenty specific requests to crop one on one side, to take special care to preserve the tonal range of another and so on. He also asked for enlargements of his photographs to be sent to him rolled round a stick, and it may be that he intended to colour them, like the monotypes he had done at Diénay.[50]

Degas seems to have taken some of his photographs at Le Mont-Dore at night. 'A group of people collected near me,' he reported. 'I heard the murmur of their voices. They probably thought I was crazy.'[51] His reasons for these strange experiments are typical of the man and the artist: 'Daylight is too easy. What I want is difficult – the atmosphere of lamps or moonlight.'[52] No moonlight landscapes appear to have survived, but his photographs taken in lamplight have, and these pictures possess, as his niece pointed out, some of the qualities of a Rembrandt – 'composition, lighting, everything recalls the manner of the Dutch artist.'[53] Some show Degas and his housekeeper Zoé (plate 206) in his house on the rue Victor-Massé, with their black shadows and strong chiaroscuro; others were taken at the Halévys' house and at Berthe Morisot's, perhaps the finest being the photograph of Mallarmé and Renoir standing next to a mirror in which Degas is reflected hunched over his camera (plate 193). Daniel Halévy has given a delightful account of a photographic session which took place on 29 December 1895. The dinner-party consisted of Halévy's uncle Jules Taschereau-Niaudets, his aunt and her two daughters:

'After dinner [Degas] went to his studio with Uncle Jules to fetch his camera. They returned together and from then on the "pleasure" part of the evening was over.

Degas raised his voice, became dictatorial, gave orders that a lamp be brought into the little salon and that anyone who wasn't going to pose should leave. The "duty" part of the evening began. We had to obey Degas's fierce will, his artist's ferocity. At the moment all his friends speak of him with terror. If you invite him for the evening you know what to expect: two hours of military obedience.

In spite of my orders to leave, I slid into a corner and silent in the dark I watched Degas. He had seated Uncle Jules, Mathilde, and Henriette on the little sofa in front of the piano. He went back and forth in front of them running from one side of the room to the other with an expression of infinite happiness. He moved lamps, changed the reflectors, tried to light the legs by putting a lamp on the floor – to light Uncle Jules's legs, those famous legs, the slenderest, most supple legs in Paris which Degas always mentions ecstatically.

"Taschereau," he said, "hold onto that leg with your right arm, and pull it in there, there. Then look at that young person beside you. More affectionately – still more – come – come! You can smile so nicely when you want to. And you, Mademoiselle Henriette, bend your head – more – still more. Really bend it. Rest it on your neighbor's shoulder." And when she didn't follow his orders to suit

195. Degas's niece Odette, photographed by him c.1895

196. *Dancer looking at the sole of her right foot*. Bronze, ht. 19½ in (49.5 cm). London, Tate Gallery

OPPOSITE:
197. *Woman seated
in an armchair.*
Bronze, ht. 12½ in
(31.5 cm). Private
Collection

*him he caught her by the nape of the neck and posed her as
he wished. He seized hold of Mathilde and turned her face
towards her uncle. Then he stepped back and exlaimed
happily, "That does it."*

*The pose was held for two minutes – and then repeated.
We shall see the photographs tonight or tomorrow morning, I think. He will display them here looking happy –
and really at moments like that he is happy.*

*At half-past eleven everybody left; Degas surrounded
by three laughing girls carried his camera, as proud as a
child carrying a gun.*'[54]

Most of Degas's photographs that have come to
light are of friends and relatives and, as Pickvance has
noted,[55] many of them reflect the compositional
effects he first explored in his oils. The pictures of
his nieces (plate 195) bring to mind those of the young

Hortense. Henri Lerolle observed that 'he composed
his photographs exactly like his pictures; he didn't
place you in some extravagant manner but in fore-
shortened studies not always comprehensible at first
glance; often half the person would be outside the
plate, as in some canvases.'[56] Photography, like his
sculpture, became an extension of his painting,
another outlet for ideas already expressed elsewhere
in his work. While some painters of this period looked
on photography as a danger to their livelihood, Degas
regarded the medium as friend rather than foe.

The development of his sculpture in the last
quarter of his life follows in many respects what had
taken place in his paintings and pastels. There is a
similar shift from the individual to the universal,
from highly detailed works, like the *Little Dancer of*

198. Double exposure of several portraits, including Degas, by himself. New York, Metropolitan Museum (Gift of Mrs Henry T. Curtiss, 1964)

Fourteen, to figures made of lumps of wax, without eyes, noses or any distinguishing features. Just as his pastels became more spontaneous and expressive, so too did the sculptures; the surface of his pieces became looser and freer, with the twists and blobs of wax remaining visible. In the sculpture, as in the paintings, there was a growing awareness of movement, starting from the relatively static positions of the first works and continuing with figures either at full stretch, as in the case of the horses (plate 182), or in the case of the dancers, poised between movements, balancing on one leg in an arabesque or coiled like a watch-spring as in *The Spanish Dancer* (plate 200). It was the ability to capture movement in sculpture that impressed Renoir, who remarked: 'That is Degas's greatness: movement in the French style.'[57] Finally, having conquered movement in his dancers

and horses, Degas moved on to the more statuesque and massive figures of bathers. *The Tub* (plate 199), which breaks free from the convention of the pedestal, has been called 'An unique work which is among the most original not only of his own pieces but of all nineteenth-century sculpture',[58] and is a complement to his pastels of the late 1880s and 1890s.

As his eyesight dimmed, Degas began to rely more on sculpture as his means of expression. With his thumb and fingers he could feel the shape of his wax figures, but when he used pencil or charcoal and sketch-pad, he found it increasingly difficult to see what he had done. When Durand-Ruel called on him in the last years of his life, he was as likely to find him modelling in wax as painting. Despite his previous unfortunate experiences, when two of his works fell

199. *The tub.* Bronze, ht. 18½ in (47 cm). London, courtesy Sotheby Parke Bernet

200. *Spanish dancer.*
Bronze, ht. 17 in
(43 cm). William
Beadleston Inc

apart because of faulty construction and neglect, Degas continued to pay little regard to the safety or permanence of his figures. Durand-Ruel tells us:

'Degas must have made an enormous number of clay or wax figures but he never took care of them – he never had them put in bronze – they always fell to pieces after a few years, and for that reason it is only the later ones that now exist. When I made the inventory of Degas's possessions, I found about 150 pieces scattered over his three floors in every possible place. Most of them were in pieces, some almost reduced to dust. We put aside all those that we thought might be seen, which was about a hundred, and we made an inventory of them. Out of these, thirty are about valueless; thirty badly broken up and very sketchy; the remaining thirty are quite fine.'[59]

Degas's search for different ways of expressing himself took many unexpected directions. One evening in about 1890 he recited a sonnet which he had composed and dedicated to the Hispano-French poet José-Maria de Hérédia, who wrote nothing but sonnets and was then somewhat of a cult figure in Paris. 'To me, to our little group of friends,' wrote Daniel Halévy, 'Degas's first sonnet came as a surprise.'[60] Valéry, a professional poet, expressed less surprise about the fact that Degas had turned poet – 'That there was in any case a potential writer in him was made sufficiently clear by his *mots*, and by his rather frequent habit of quotation from Racine and Saint-Simon'[61] – than about the fact that he had chosen to express himself in the particularly difficult form of the sonnet. 'Was he tempted by what he heard of the labours and the endless time required to make a good sonnet?' asked Valéry. 'He valued a thing only by what it cost him: work for its own sake was the spur.'[62]

Degas did indeed find sonnet writing full of difficulties. 'What a business!' he once lamented to Stéphane Mallarmé, whom he had known since the 1870s. 'My whole day gone on a blasted sonnet, without getting an inch further . . . And all the same, it isn't ideas I'm short of . . . I'm full of them . . . I've got too many . . .' 'But, Degas,' answered Mallarmé, with his customary gentle profundity, 'you can't make a poem with ideas . . . You make it with words.'[63]

Between Degas and Mallarmé there existed a puzzling lack of communication. They were well-disposed towards each other and must have met frequently at Berthe Morisot's salon, but although Mallarmé understood and appreciated the painter's work (as can be seen by his review of the second Impressionist exhibition mentioned in the previous chapter), Degas does not appear to have appreciated or understood Mallarmé's poetry. Yet in composing his sonnets, he turned to the poet for advice; in a

letter to Berthe Morisot Mallarmé expressed his opinion of Degas's merits as a poet: 'His own poetry is taking up his attention, for – and this will be the notable event this winter – he is on his fourth sonnet. In reality, he is no longer of this world; one is perturbed by his obsession with a new art in which he is really quite proficient.'[64]

Degas wrote about twenty sonnets and his letters and journals contain drafts of other verse. His poetry, like his sculpture, deals with ideas and themes found in his paintings. There are poems about dancers and thoroughbreds, and they are dedicated to the people whom he admired, one to Hérédia, another to Mary Cassatt and another to the singer Rose Caron, the 'divine Mme Caron', whose performance in Ernest Reyer's opera *Sigurd* moved Degas profoundly: 'How well she is able to raise her thin and divine arms, holding them aloft for a long time, without affectation, for a long time and then lowering them gently.'[65] The sonnet addressed to her was warmly received by the Halévy family and the last few lines left them silent:

A Madame Rose Caron.
Ces bras nobles et longs, lentement en fureur,
Lentement en humaine et cruelle tendresse,
Flèches que décochait une âme de déesse
Et qui s'allaient fausser à la terre d'erreur;

Diadème dorant cette rose pâleur
De la reine muette à son peuple en liesse;
Terrasse où descendait une femme en détresse,
Amoureuse, volée, honteuse de douleur;

Après avoir jeté sa menace parée,
Cette voix, qui venait, divine de durée,
Prendre Sigurd, ainsi que son destin voulait!

Tout ce beau va me suivre encore un bout de vie;
Si mes yeux se perdaient, que me durât l'ouïe,
Au son je pourrais voir le geste qu'elle fait.★

★ These noble, long arms, slowly in passion, Slow in a human and cruel tenderness, Arrows sprung from a goddess's soul, False landing in the ground of error; Diadem gilding this pink pallor Of the mute queen with her people in chains; Terrace where a woman in distress descended, In love, ravished, shame-faced with sorrow; After throwing off her ornamented menace, This voice, of divine eternity, Which had just seized Sigurd, just as her destiny predicted! All this beauty will follow me throughout my life; If my eyes failed, might my hearing last, The sound would conjure up the gesture that she makes.

(iii)

After 1894, the year he became sixty, Degas's letters lose their wit and sparkle and contain more complaints about his health and eyesight: he was now a bitter withdrawn bad-tempered man, out of sympathy with his times. In part this change of character was brought on by the realization that he would soon go blind, in part by kidney troubles and attacks of bronchitis; but he was also affected by the deaths of many of his friends and closest relatives. It was at this time, too, that the Dreyfus affair developed.

Throughout his sixties and seventies death was never far from his mind. His brother Achille died in 1893,[66] and following in quick succession were Paul Valpinçon and his brother-in-law Edmondo Morbilli in 1894, Berthe Morisot and his sister Marguerite, and his old companion from his student days in Italy, Evariste de Valernes, in 1896.

Degas was always punctilious about attending funerals. Halévy remembers him as an old man travelling half-way across France to attend the funeral of a friend. Although not a regular churchgoer – he once

engaged a model to come and pose for him on Christmas Day – the funeral service moved him: having attended a mass for the dead, he once remarked to Halévy, 'That Catholic liturgy, that great wheel which turns.'[67]

Funerals struck him as being an appropriate subject for the poet and painter. He sent a poem to Bartholomé in 1890, linking a funeral with a marriage, with the comment: 'What a subject! Inexhaustible.'[68] In a notebook in use between 1877 and 1883 he had jotted down thoughts of making a series of aquatints on the theme of mourning, intended as a study of different blacks, the blacks of the veils worn by mourning women, the blacks of their gloves and the blacks of the funeral companies' carriages which reminded him of Venetian gondolas. Degas also felt that sculpture was a suitable medium to express profound suffering, and he followed with interest Bartholomé's plans for a monument to place over his wife's grave. Bartholomé's most famous work was *Le Monument aux Morts* of 1895, erected at the cemetery of Père-Lachaise, about which an American critic wrote: 'It would be impossible to conceive of a

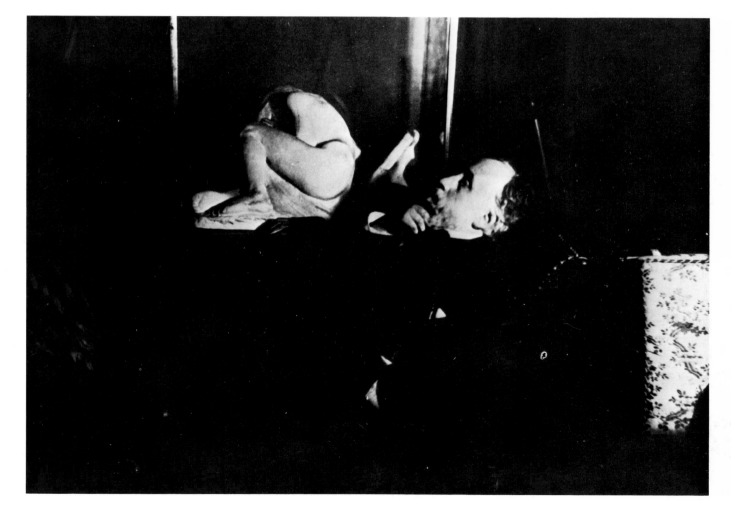

201. Degas with sculpture (Bartholomé?), photograph by his brother René. Paris BN

stronger exhibition of the horror of death. It should be put away in a charnel house and not exhibited in a Christian cemetery. The groups of mourners are so strong as to be revolting.'[69]

Ill, lonely, and nearly blind, he sometimes contemplated suicide, but his Catholic upbringing and his terror of death prevented him. To one of his last models, Pauline, he would sometimes speak of death in a deep mysterious voice, confessing to the fear that it inspired in him.[70] Valéry remembers him suddenly stopping all conversation by saying, 'Death is all I think of'.[71] But, despite his infirmities, he clung obstinately to life; and it has even been suggested that the bus rides which he took in his old age and the long solitary walks were in part inspired by an ancient belief that death could be kept at bay by constant motion.[72]

Degas's letters give glimpses of his inner torments. 'I am sad though gay, or the contrary,' he wrote to Ludovic Halévy in 1897,[73] and to Bartholomé he confessed: 'My sight is getting decidedly worse and I am having some rather black thoughts about it.'[74] In November 1897, after an attack of bronchitis, he wrote to Halévy's wife Louise explaining his absences from their Thursday evenings: 'It is a regimen to which I am now condemned and which prevents me from being seen. Adhesions of pleura to the lungs, that is my weakness and I cannot go out into the street . . .' and he added, 'How relationships change, how worthless one becomes, how one is no longer as one used to be!'[75]

Degas's relationship with the Halévy family came under increasing strain as a result of the Dreyfus affair. In 1894 an obscure army staff captain, Alfred Dreyfus, who came from a Jewish family, was arrested on suspicion of giving information to the Germans. The Prussian defeat of France in the war of 1870 had left a legacy of distrust of Germany and a desire for revenge. To counter the new German empire's intelligence service the French government set up its own department responsible for military security. Dreyfus was a victim of the spy fever which gripped both countries and he was arrested largely because he was Jewish, rather than because of any clear evidence against him. For a time the army kept his arrest quiet, while investigations were made, but the news reached the antisemitic *La Libre Parole* (Degas's favourite newspaper), which printed the headline, 'High Treason. Arrest of the Jewish Officer A. Dreyfus.'[76] Once the news had broken, the army felt compelled to bring Dreyfus to trial and to see that he was convicted. Much of the evidence was manufactured, the rest was circumstantial, but he was nonetheless courtmartialled. Even such a cynic as Edmond de Goncourt (who had right-wing sym-

pathies) remained unconvinced of Dreyfus's guilt. When told of the reactions of a group of little boys who from the trees surrounding the courtyard of the Ecole Militaire had watched Dreyfus's reduction to the ranks, he remarked, 'The judgements of journalists were the judgements of little boys up in the trees, and in a case like this it is really very difficult to establish the innocence or guilt of the accused from an examination of his bearing.'[77]

Degas, like so many Frenchmen, was soon swept up in the havoc caused by the Dreyfus case and subsequent attempts at a retrial. The affair divided families, broke up friendships and split the nation: the Dreyfusards, who were convinced of his innocence, included many writers, artists, liberal politicians, socialists, families of Jewish origins, as well as those opposed to the military and the clergy; the anti-Dreyfusards consisted of the army and its supporters, right-wing politicians, Catholics and antisemites. Faced with these alternatives, Degas followed his natural instinct to side with the army and to adopt an anti-Dreyfusard stance. He had always been a patriot, he was fascinated by the army, and he disliked the Republic and its liberal politicians. Since he was suspicious of writers and intellectuals (the term 'intellectual' was coined by Georges Clemenceau to describe the literary supporters of Dreyfus who signed a manifesto calling for his release), as well as highly excitable and argumentative, the affair took hold of his imagination; as he told Alexis Rouart in September 1898, he found that he was unable to speak of it 'without crying with anger'.[78] Despite the value he placed on friendship, the affair drove him to break with some of his oldest friends, including Ludovic Halévy.

The Halévy family, father and sons, were convinced of Dreyfus's innocence. Daniel's brother Elie was a student at one of the centres of the campaign for a retrial, the Ecole Normale, whose librarian was Lucien Herr, a friend of Dreyfus's lawyer and who had access to information about the army's attempts to keep Dreyfus from being retried. Long before Zola's famous article *J'Accuse* appeared in *L'Aurore* on 13 January 1898, the Halévy family was aware of the army's duplicity; and although an attempt was made to keep the subject from coming up when Degas was present at dinner, it was in vain. Degas was either belligerent, making antisemitic remarks which put his host on edge, or he remained pointedly silent, looking up at the ceiling in an effort to cut himself off from the company which surrounded him. After one such evening, probably in November 1897, he wrote to Louise Halévy to say that he could no longer come to their house.

Degas never saw Ludovic Halévy alive again. But in 1908, having heard of his friend's death, he arrived at the Halévy house and asked to see the body. He was taken to a room where it was laid out and he commanded that the curtains be opened to allow more light into the room. He leaned over the body, looked closely at the face and said, 'This is indeed the Halévy whom we have always known, with the additional grandeur that death gives. This must be kept – recorded.'[79] An artist living nearby was summoned to make a sketch, Degas's eyes being too weak for him to undertake the task.

His break with Halévy and the antisemitic views expressed in his old age are hard to understand but should be put in the context of his times. Degas became antisemitic in the hysterical tide of suspicion of Jews that swept France in the late 1880s and 1890s. When he was born, it has been estimated that there were only 40,000 Jews living in France, the great majority in Alsace, and there was very little racial tension.[80] Pressures on Jews in Eastern Europe and Russia had forced many to emigrate and by 1881 the Jewish population in Paris alone had risen to about 40,000. These newcomers were poor, spoke little French and clung together in isolated communities. They were not welcomed by the old-established French-Jewish families, who, since Napoleon's code had granted them legal equality, had been assimilated into French society. Charles Haas's career was in many respects the ideal to which many of the established French Jews aspired. Born two years before Degas in 1832, of humble origin, he gained acceptance by virtue of his wit, elegance, good taste and success with women. In the 1860s he became a member of the Cercle de la rue Royale, the fashionable men's club painted by Tissot, and after the siege of Paris, in which he conducted himself with great courage and distinction, he was admitted to an even more exclusive club, the Jockey Club, the only other Jew to have entered this bastion of the French aristocracy (the first being a Rothschild). Degas was not close to Haas, but had a grudging respect for him: on one occasion he remarked how simple and delightful he was, but another time he was more critical: 'That Haas, how utterly contrived he is.'[81]

The success of many French Jews did, however, breed resentment, and in the bitter years following the war of 1870 a number of writers began to vent their feelings by attacking the Jewish community, chief among them being Henri Rochefort, the son of a ruined aristocrat, who made a fortune by his articles in *Le Figaro* and in his own newspaper *La Laterne*. He enjoyed baiting everyone – Jews, the Republic, liberals, art collectors – but his saving grace was his

202. *Statue of a schoolgirl*. Bronze, ht. 10¾ in (27 cm). Detroit, Institute of Arts (Gift of Dr and Mrs George Kamperman)

203. *Dancer at rest with hands behind her back and right leg forward.* Bronze, ht. 17 in (43 cm). London, Tate Gallery

204. Photograph of Degas taken by his brother René. Paris, BN

wit. His articles delighted his readers, but twice he behaved so outrageously that he was banished from France, the second time being in 1885. The journalist Edouard Drumont succeeded him, a rabid antisemite, who made up in vehemence for what he lacked in wit. His tirade against the Jews, *La France Juive,* published in 1886, became a best-seller, with 100,000 copies sold in its first year. The book contained a mass of falsehoods and most Jews ignored it, but it and his newspaper *La Libre Parole,* which he founded in about 1892, helped forge the isolated pockets of anti-semitism in France into a cohesive movement. Degas's housekeeper Zoé used to read *La Libre Parole* to the artist during meals and it was undoubtedly Drumont's biased views and slanted facts that pushed Degas into an anti-Dreyfusard stance.

As one century drew to a close and another began, Degas found himself increasingly out on a limb. The modern world with its egalitarian ideas and its technical advances made him either angry or scornful. 'How infamous it is to speak of equality,' he used to say to Pauline, 'when there are the rich and the poor. In days gone by each one stayed in his own place and dressed according to his condition in life;

today the most obscure grocer's boy must read his newspaper and dress like a gentleman. What an infamous century'.[82] He distrusted artists who sought success; 'In my day one did not arrive,' was one of his famous sayings.[83] Mass education seemed to him to bring unhappiness and resentment. Despite his many pictures of bathers, he did not approve of modern theories about hygiene; he also regarded the bicycle as 'comic', the aeroplane as 'small' and the telephone as 'ridiculous'. When Forain gave him a demonstration, he pretended to take an interest. 'How do you know when to pick it up?' he asked. 'It has a bell which rings,' Forain replied. 'Then what?' 'You run and answer it before it stops ringing.' 'Just like a servant,' was his caustic comment.[84] As he grew older, he grew crankier: he dismissed one model because she was a Protestant with the explanation that 'the Protestants and Jews are hand-in-glove in the Dreyfus affair.'[85] He disliked dogs and he loathed flowers. One evening, dining with the Forains, he seized a bouquet which a young cousin of the hostess had placed on the table, carried it at arm's length and dropped it at the end of the garden. It was the smell rather than the colour that displeased him.[86] He once mentioned to Pauline that he much preferred the smell of burnt toast, and he took a piece of bread, brought into the studio to clean a drawing, and threw it on the fire.[87] The room soon filled with black smoke and he smiled with pleasure. When Vollard asked him to dinner, he accepted: 'But listen. Will you have a special dish without butter prepared for me? Mind you, no flowers on the table, and you must have dinner at half-past seven sharp. I know you won't have your cat around and please don't allow anybody to bring a dog. And if there are to be any women, I hope they won't come reeking of perfume. How horrible all those odours are when there are so many things that really smell good, like toast – or even manure! Ah, and very few lights. My eyes, you know, my poor eyes!'[88] He was not an easy guest.

Over the last ten years or so he worked mainly by instinct. He compensated for his failing eyesight by using larger sheets of paper and broad sticks of char-

coal and pastel applied vigorously to the paper. He frequently corrected his drawing by using tracing paper and drawing another version on top, or he would lay a fresh sheet of paper on top of a charcoal drawing and use the counter-proof to start a new work. He drew and redrew the same composition, before selecting a version which he would then set about finishing, adding colour. The faces in these drawings can hardly be made out: they are often eyeless and mouthless, almost repellent. Anger and frustration can be read into the lines, but despite their awkwardness, they are often very moving and emotionally compelling.

Although Degas could no longer attend the ballet with the same enjoyment, around 1895 he glimpsed the possibility of one last new theme. A troupe of Russian folk-dancers in colourful costumes performed in Paris, giving him an idea for a series of pastels (plate 192). These vivid pictures are his final tribute to an art that had obsessed him for forty-odd

205. Self-portrait, photograph by Degas. Paris, BN

206. Degas and his housekeeper Zoé, photographed by himself. New York, Metropolitan Museum (Gift of Mrs Henry T. Curtiss, 1964)

years. The troupe was probably the one which performed at the Folies-Bergère in 1895 and not, as suggested by Lillian Browse,[89] the Diaghilev company which arrived in Paris in 1909. By now the capital of the ballet had moved from Paris to St Petersburg, and it is an irony (which Degas might have appreciated) that the greatest painter of the ballet was too young to witness the great glories of the French Romantic ballet and too old to catch more than a glimpse of the power and the vitality of the twentieth-century Russian dancers.

In 1912 Degas's house on the rue Victor-Massé was torn down to make room for a new development, and he was forced to move to an apartment at 6 boulevard de Clichy. It proved the final blow to any attempt at painting and drawing. When Daniel Halévy met him after an auction in December 1912, Degas explained: 'You see, my legs are good. I walk well. But since I moved, I no longer work. It's odd. I haven't put anything in order. Everything is there, leaning against the walls. I don't care. I let everything go. It's amazing how indifferent you get in old age.'[90] Having abandoned work, his mind began to atrophy: he repeated his stories and *mots* over and over again, his mind dwelt in the past and he began to lose contact with the outside world. If he saw anybody, it was Forain or Bartholomé. Sometimes he would

make a public appearance at an event which reminded him of the past, as, for example, at the Ingres exhibition in May 1911 or at the auction of Henri Rouart's collection in 1912, following his old friend's death. It was at this auction that *Dancers Practising at the Bar* (Metropolitan) was sold to Mrs Havemeyer for 478,000 francs ($95,700), then a record sum for a painter of the Impressionist circle. When asked how he felt about one of his pictures fetching such an enormous sum, Degas gave the now famous reply: 'I feel like a racehorse which has just won a race and gets fed the same bag of oats.'[91]

During his last years it was often difficult for friends to judge how much Degas could see. At least until 1914 he was able to continue to walk the Paris streets, and even later when he was laid up in bed, there were moments when he could see. Daniel Halévy remembers calling on him in 1916 and seeing the aged painter all of a sudden seize the arm of a niece who was attempting to straighten his pillow, 'with more strength than one would believe possible. He placed her right arm in the light which shone from the window. He looked at it with passionate concentration . . . I had been thinking that his strength was exhausted, but here he was, still working.'[92]

During the last four or five years of his life Degas was looked after by Jeanne Fèvre, the unmarried

207. Photograph of
Degas in his old age
at Auteuil, 1915, by
Bartholomé

daughter of his sister Marguerite. For this kindness Degas had Mary Cassatt to thank. Miss Cassatt had found Degas's niece working in a hospital in Nice and had persuaded her to return to Paris to look after her uncle. Mlle Fèvre hesitated, afraid that she might not be welcome, but Mary Cassatt argued that once she was settled in with her uncle he would not be able to part with her. Mary Cassatt also put her in touch with a lawyer who arranged for her and her sisters to be included in Degas's will.

On 27 September 1917 Degas died at the age of eighty-three. Among those attending the funeral were Forain, Bartholomé, Rafaëlli, Vollard, Alexis Rouart, Daniel Halévy, and, despite their many differences over painting and politics, Claude Monet. Mary Cassatt was also present and in a letter dated 2 October 1917 she described the service: 'We buried him on Saturday, in beautiful sunshine, a little crowd of friends and admirers, all very quiet and peaceful in the midst of this dreadful upheaval of which he was barely conscious. You can well understand what a satisfaction it was for me to know that he had been well cared for and even tenderly nursed by his niece in his last days.'[93]

Although Degas was well known to be hostile to the state, Bartholomé had arranged for a representative of the President to attend. Degas also left instructions that there should be no funeral oration, but he told Forain that, if forced to say a few words, he should say simply, 'He loved drawing very much and so do I,' and then return home.[94]

Degas's general hostility to government, matched by his dislike for the administration of the Louvre and the Luxembourg museums and combined with the indifference of great age, made him reluctant to make any plans for the preservation either of the contents of his studio or his impressive collection of Old Masters and works by nineteenth-century artists – Ingres, Delacroix and Daumier – acquired with such passion towards the end of his life. His will left everything to his natural heirs, his brother René and the four surviving children of his sister Marguerite, and subsequently the contents of his studio were sold in four great sales lasting twelve days from 6 May 1918, and his collection of works by other artists in two sales lasting four days from 26 March 1918. The sales raised over twelve million francs and rescued his heirs from poverty. René inherited over four million francs, and on his death in 1921 there was a dispute between his children by his marriage to Estelle Musson and those by his second marriage to Mrs Léonce Olivier, lasting ten years.

The publicity generated by the sale of his studio and by the lawsuits that followed his brother's death would have horrified Degas. In some respects the understanding of his art suffered in that many abandoned and unfinished sketches (which seen in the context of his studio make sense, but seen individually seem crude and awkward) were allowed to circulate. The dispersal of Degas's studio and his collection was a great loss to French museums, but in a broader sense it allowed his work to find new resting places, mostly in America, and to a lesser extent in England and Scotland. His works can also be seen in public collections throughout Europe as well as in South America and Australia. In the end an artist of Degas's stature, whose family and origins were never limited to France alone, belongs to the world.

Notes

Chapter 1

1. Ambroise Vollard, *Degas, An Intimate Portrait*, trans. by Randolph T. Weaver, New York, 1927.
2. Daniel Halévy, *My Friend Degas*, trans. and ed. with notes by Mina Curtiss, Wesleyan University and London, 1964/66. The original French title is *Degas Parle*, Paris, 1960.
3. Ernest Rouart, 'Degas', *Le Point*, Feb. 1937, p. 7.
4. Letter to Evariste de Valernes, Paris, 26 Oct. 1890. Marcel Guérin, ed., *Degas Letters*, trans. by Marguerite Kay, Oxford, 1947, no. 170.
5. Theodore Reff, *The Notebooks of Edgar Degas* (a catalogue of the thirty-eight notebooks in the Bibliothèque Nationale and other collections), 2 vols., Oxford, 1976.
6. Reff, *Notebooks*, op.cit., no. 6, p. 83.
7. Paul Valéry, *Degas Manet Morisot*, trans. by David Paul, New York, 1960.
8. See E. J. Hobsbawm, *The Age of Capital, 1848–1875*, London, 1975, ch. 15.
9. Halévy, op.cit.
10. See Phoebe Pool, 'Some Early Friends of Edgar Degas', *Apollo*, May 1964.
11. Valéry, op.cit.
12. See Jean Sutherland Boggs, 'Edgar Degas and Naples', *Burlington Magazine*, June 1963.
13. Riccardo Raimondi, *Degas e la Sua Famiglia in Napoli, 1793–1817*, Naples, 1958, quoted by Boggs, see above.
14. Valéry, op.cit.
15. *Guerrero de Balde Archives*, Archivo Notarile, Naples, quoted by Boggs, op.cit.
16. Valéry, op.cit.
17. Valéry, op.cit.
18. Valéry, op.cit.
19. P. A. Lemoisne, *Degas et Son Oeuvre*, 4 vols., Paris, 1946–49.
20. Jeanne Fèvre, *Mon Oncle Degas*, ed. P. Borel, Geneva, 1949.
21. Theodore Reff, *Notebooks*, op.cit.
22. Theodore Reff, 'Degas's Copies of Older Art', *Burlington Magazine*, June 1963. The notebook in question is no. 18.
23. Jean Sutherland Boggs, *Portraits by Degas*, University of California Press, Berkeley and Los Angeles, 1962.
24. Reff, *Notebooks*, op.cit., no. 6, p. 83.
25. Reff, *Notebooks*, op.cit., no. 6, p. 21.
26. Joseph C. Sloane, *French Painting between the Past and the Present, Artists, Critics, and Traditions, from 1848 to 1870*, Princeton, New Jersey, 1951.
27. Sloane, op.cit.
28. Sloane, op.cit.
29. The Salon was an annual, sometimes a biennial, exhibition held in Paris of paintings, drawings and sculpture. Under the *ancien régime* it was organized by the artists of the Academies, but after 1791 a jury system was established by the state, consisting partly of the artists themselves and partly of the government's own ministers. Under successive regimes there were changes in the composition of the jury, but every year there were complaints of unfairness and corruption. After the Revolution of 1789 a system of government prizes and medals was instituted, the most coveted being the gold medal of honour. Since the jury was largely selected from previous years' prize-winners, the same artists tended to preside each year, and as a result many exhibitors found themselves rejected year after year. During the reign of Napoleon III the art world in France began to divide into three categories: the Academics, who taught at the Ecole des Beaux-Arts, often looked down on the salon artists and despised the commercial and popular success courted by the exhibitors; the Salon exhibitors and the winners of prizes and medals, who dominated the jury; and the artists rejected by the Salon (Manet, Cézanne and the Impressionists being now the most famous examples), who formed the *avant-garde* of the second half of the nineteenth century. For a useful summary of the organization of the Salon and the effect it had on artists' lives see Jacques Lethève, *Daily Life of French Artists in the Nineteenth Century*, trans. by Hilary E. Paddon, New York and London, 1972.
30. Théophile Gautier, 'De l'Art Moderne', *L'Artiste*, vol. X (1853), p. 135, quoted in Sloane, op.cit.
31. Amaury-Duval, *L'Atelier d'Ingres*, Paris, 1924, p. 211, quoted by John Rewald, *The History of Impressionism*, New York, 4th rev. ed., 1973.
32. Ingres, *Ecrits sur l'Art*, preface by Raymond Cogniat, Paris, 1947, p. 35, quoted in Sloane, op.cit.
33. Halévy, op.cit.
34. Etienne Moreau-Nélaton, 'Deux heures avec Monsieur Degas, 26 Decembre 1907', first published in *L'Amour de l'Art*, July 1951, reprinted in Lemoisne, vol. 1, p. 257, note 218.
35. See above.
36. There are versions of this story in Valéry, op.cit.; P. Lafond, *Degas*, Paris, 1919; P. Jamot, *Degas*, Paris, 1924; Halévy, op.cit.; and Sickert's tribute to Degas in the *Burlington Magazine*, 1917.
37. Moreau-Nélaton, op.cit.
38. Moreau-Nélaton, op.cit.
39. Lemoisne, op.cit., vol. 1.
40. See Theodore Reff, *Degas: The Artist's Mind*, New York, 1976, ch. II.
41. Léonce Bénédite, *Théodore Chassériau, Sa Vie et Son Oeuvre*, 2 vols., Paris, 1931, pp. 137–8, quoted by Sloane, op.cit.
42. See Halévy, op.cit.
43. The *Prix de Rome* was an annual competition for painters, sculptors, engravers, architects and composers providing scholarships for prize-winners to study at the French Academy at the Villa Medici in Rome. In theory it was open to everyone, but in practice the competitors were drawn from the cream of the students at the Ecole des Beaux-Arts. For painters it was a nerve-racking competition requiring great stamina. Candidates were given a set theme and asked to produce a detailed sketch within thirty-six hours. The competitors then had two months to finish the work, but they were not allowed to depart from the main outline of their original sketch. For an account of the ordeal see Jacques Lethève, op.cit., and Albert Boime, *The Academy and French Painting in the Nineteenth Century*, London, 1970.
44. Letter from Louis Moreau to his son, 22 April 1858, Archives, Musée Gustave Moreau, Paris.
45. Lemoisne, op.cit., vol. I.
46. Letter from Georges Bizet to Moreau, 29 May 1858, quoted in Pierre-Louis Mathieu, *Gustave Moreau, Sa Vie, Son Oeuvre*, Fribourg, 1977, trans. by James Emmons, Oxford, 1977, ch. II.
47. Lemoisne, op.cit., vol. I.
48. Mathieu, op.cit.

49. Letter from Moreau to his parents, 12 Feb. 1858, quoted in Mathieu, op.cit.

50. Theodore Reff, 'Some Unpublished Letters of Degas', *Art Bulletin*, March 1968.

51. Letter from Antoine Königswarter to Moreau, 30 Aug. 1859, quoted in Mathieu, op.cit. Königswarter was the son of a banker well acquainted with Degas's father. He later became a banker himself and looked after Moreau's investments.

52. Phoebe Pool, 'Degas and Moreau', *Burlington Magazine*, June 1963.

53. Valéry, op.cit., also quoted in Lemoisne, op.cit., vol. I.

54. Valéry, op.cit.

55. Reff, *Notebooks*, op.cit., no. 11, p. 65.

56. Reff, *Notebooks*, op.cit., no. 11, p. 86.

57. Reff, *Notebooks*, op.cit., no. 11, pp. 94, 95.

58. Lemoisne, op.cit., vol. I.

59. Lemoisne, op.cit., vol. I.

60. Lemoisne, op.cit., vol. I, letter 11 Nov. 1858.

61. Lemoisne, op.cit., vol. I.

62. Lemoisne, op.cit., vol. I.

63. Lemoisne, op.cit., vol. I.

64. Reff, *Notebooks*, op.cit.

65. Reff, 'Some Unpublished Letters of Degas', op.cit.

66. Letter of 18 May 1859, quoted in Mathieu, op.cit.

67. Reff, *Degas: The Artist's Mind*, op.cit., ch. III.

68. Boggs, *Portraits by Degas*, op.cit.

69. Raimondi, op.cit., p. 246, quoted in Boggs, op.cit.

70. Letter from Achille de Gas, 14 May 1859, in the collection of the late Jean Nepveu-Degas, quoted by Reff, *Degas: The Artist's Mind*, op.cit., ch. III.

71. Lemoisne, op.cit., vol. I.

72. Degas exhibited *The Young Spartans* in the fifth Impressionist exhibition (1879), to which he had intended to send the *Little Dancer of Fourteen*; but the sculpture was not ready in time.

73. George Moore, *Impressions and Opinions*, London and New York, 1891.

74. Letter from Degas to Michel Musson, 24 June 1863, quoted in James B. Byrnes, 'Edgar Degas, His Paintings of New Orleanians Here and Abroad', from the catalogue of the exhibition at the Isaac Delgardo Museum, New Orleans, May 1965. At this point Degas did not know that she would suffer from the further tragedy of going blind.

Chapter 2

1. It is no. 2406 in the Salon catalogue of 1865 and the medium is stated as pastel. The medium used is now thought to be oil paint thinned with turpentine (*essence*) on paper laid down on canvas. See the catalogue to the Degas exhibition held June–Sept. 1969, *Degas, Oeuvres du Musée du Louvre*.

2. Quoted by Maria and Godfrey Blunden, *Impressionists and Impressionism*, Rizzoli International Publications, New York, 1976.

3. Emile Zola, *Edouard Manet, Etude Biographique et Critique*, Paris, 1867, reprinted in *Mes Haines, Oeuvres Complètes*, Paris, 1928.

4. The Marshal's speech was reported in the *Moniteur du Soir*, 15 Aug. 1865, and reprinted in the Salon catalogue of 1866.

5. Théophile Thoré, 'Le Salon de 1866', reprinted in the *Salons de W. Bürger*, Paris, 1870, vol. II, p. 276.

6. Zola, see note 3 above. For an account of Zola's pamphlet on Manet and his emergence as an art critic see F. W. J. Hemmings, *The Life and Times of Emile Zola*, London, 1977, ch. 7.

7. In 1863 there were so many protests from artists whose work had been rejected by the Salon jury for that year that Napoleon III authorized a separate exhibition, a Salon des Refusés. A number of artists decided to withdraw rather than to show with the *refusés*, but others, including Manet and Whistler, kept their work in the exhibition. The year 1863 marks a turning point in the history of French art in the nineteenth century, a moment when the old and the new guard clashed in the open. For an account of the exhibition see Ian Dunlop, *The Shock of the New*, London, 1972, ch. 1.

8. Berthe Morisot, *Recollections of Degas*, quoted in Paul Valéry, *Degas Manet Morisot*, trans. by David Paul, New York, 1960, part I.

9. Valéry, op.cit.

10. Degas's letter to the *Paris Journal* is reprinted in Theodore Reff, 'Some Unpublished Letters of Degas', *Art Bulletin*, March 1968. Further unpublished letters were included in the *Art Bulletin*, Sept. 1969.

11. George Moore, *Confessions of a Young Man*, London, 1888.

12. See Théodore Duret, *Edouard Manet et son Oeuvre*, Paris, 1902, and T. Duret, *Histoire des Peintres Impressionnistes*, Paris, 1906. See also Edmond Duranty, *Le Pays des Arts*, Paris, 1881.

13. See Antonin Proust, *Edouard Manet, Souvenirs*, Paris, 1925 (based on an article first published in *La Revue Blanche*, 1897).

14. George Moore, *Impressions and Opinions*, London and New York, 1891.

15. E. Moreau-Nélaton, *Manet Raconté par Lui-Même*, 2 vols., Paris, 1926, vol. II, p. 95.

16. Georges Jeanniot, 'Souvenirs sur Degas', *La Revue Universelle*, 15 Oct., 1 Nov. 1933.

17. Ambroise Vollard, *Renoir, an Intimate Record*, trans. by Randolph T. Weaver and Harold L. Van Doren, New York, 1925.

18. Ambroise Vollard, *Degas, an Intimate Portrait*, trans. by Randolph T. Weaver, New York, 1927.

19. See John Rewald, *The History of Impressionism*, ed., New York, 1973, p. 476.

20. Valéry, op.cit.

21. Letter from James Tissot to Degas, Venice, 18 Sept. (1860?), reprinted in P. A. Lemoisne, *Degas et Son Oeuvre*, 4 vols., Paris, 1946, vol. I, note 45, p. 230.

22. See above.

23. Theodore Reff, *Degas: The Artist's Mind*, New York, 1976, ch. III.

24. See above.

25. Tissot's commentary on Degas's *Interior* is reproduced in Reff, *Degas: The Artist's Mind*, op.cit., p. 226.

26. William Rothenstein, *Men and Memories, A History of the Arts, 1872–1922*, 3 vols., London and New York, 1931–8.

27. Paul Poujaud, letter to Marcel Guérin, 11 July 1936, included in Marcel Guérin, ed., *Degas Letters*, trans. by Marguerite Kay, Oxford, 1947.

28. A shared admiration for Courbet and Dutch and Spanish painting of the seventeenth century provided the basis for a friendship between Whistler, Henri Fantin-Latour and Alphonse Legros, who met in Paris in 1858 and who established a 'society of three'. See Allen Staley, 'Whistler and his World', included in the catalogue of the exhibition, *From Realism to Symbolism, Whistler and His World*, Wildenstein (New York) and Philadelphia Museum of Art, 1971.

29. See William A. Coles, *Alfred Stevens*, University of Michigan Museum of Art, 1977, catalogue entry for no. 5, *Tous les Bonheurs*, 1861.

30. *Degas Letters*, op.cit., letter to Tissot, no. 6.

31. Letter from Pissarro to his son, 10 Nov. 1883. For an account of Menzel's reception in Paris and his opinions of the Impressionists see Ulrich Finke, *German Painting from Romanticism to Expressionism*, Colorado and London, 1974.

32. For an extremely interesting discussion of Degas's relationships with the writers of his period see Reff, *Degas: The Artist's Mind*, op.cit., ch. IV.

33. Daniel Halévy, *My Friend Degas*, trans. and ed. with notes by Mina Curtiss, Wesleyan University and London, 1964/66.

34. E. and J. de Goncourt, *Manette Salomon*, Paris, 1866, ch. CVI, quoted by Rewald, op.cit.

35. *Goncourt Journals*, 13 Feb. 1874, quoted from *Pages from the Goncourt Journal*, ed. and trans. with intro. by Robert Baldick, Oxford, 1962.

36. See Reff, *Degas: The Artist's Mind*, op.cit., ch. IV.

37. See above, ch. V.

38. See Leonard Tancock, Introduction to *Thérèse Raquin*, Penguin,

1962. See also Hemmings, op.cit., who suggests that Zola deliberately arranged to have his book attacked in order to stir up publicity and stimulate sales.

39. See Linda Nochlin, *Realism*, Penguin, 1971; and *Realism and Tradition in Art, 1848-1900, Sources and Documents*, Englewood Cliffs, New Jersey, 1966.

40. Edmond Duranty, 'Sur la Physionomie', *La Revue Libérale*, 2, 1867.

41. Reff, *Notebooks*, op.cit., no. 23, p. 44.

42. Zola, see note 3.

43. This was the age of Auguste Comte and Positivism, when science was regarded with optimism.

44. See Linda Nochlin, *Realism*, op.cit., p. 43.

45. Jeanne Fèvre, *Mon Oncle Degas*, ed. P. Borel, Geneva, 1949.

46. Quoted by Théodore Zeldin, *France 1848-1945*, 2 vols., Oxford, 1973, vol. II, p. 806.

47. See Aaron Scharf, *Art and Photography*, London, 1968 and 1974.

48. See Mark Roskill, *Van Gogh, Gauguin and the Impressionist Circle*, London, 1969, ch. 2. See also F. Scheyer, 'Far Eastern Art and French Impressionism', *Art Quarterly*, 1943.

49. *Goncourt Journals*, Oct. 1863, quoted from *Paris and the Arts, 1851-1896*, from the *Goncourt Journal*, ed. and trans. by George J. Becker and Edith Philips, Cornell University, 1971.

50. Scharf, op.cit.

51. There are some grounds for believing that the painting started as a still life of flowers and that Degas later added the figure of Mme Hertel. See the catalogue entry by Charles S. Moffett, *Impressionism, A Centenary Exhibition*, Metropolitan Museum of Art, Dec. 1974-Feb. 1975, No. 10.

52. *The Correspondence of Berthe Morisot*, comp. and ed. by Denis Rouart, trans. by Betty W. Hubbard, London, 1957, p. 27. The letter was written by Berthe Morisot to her sister Edma, 15 March 1896.

53. *The Correspondence of Berthe Morisot*, op.cit., 2 May 1869.

54. Reff, *Notebooks*, op.cit., no. 21, p. 17. Notebook in use 1865-8.

55. *Oeuvres Mêlées de Saint-Evremont*, ed. C. Giraud, 3 vols., Paris, 1865, I, p. 89, quoted by Degas, see Reff, *Notebooks*, No. 21, p. 36.

56. See Benedict Nicholson, 'Degas as a Human Being', *Burlington Magazine*, June 1963. Nicholson compares some of Degas's remarks about women with Proust's Baron Charlus's conversation with Odette de Crécy.

57. Vollard, *Degas, an Intimate Portrait*, op.cit.

58. Proust, *Edouard Manet*, op.cit. Daniel Halévy read to Degas Proust's memoirs when they first appeared in *La Revue Blanche* in 1897; they soon put Degas into a bad temper: 'Oh! the critics. They won't leave you in peace. What a fate. To be handed over to writers', see Halévy, op.cit. p. 111.

59. Moore, *Impressions and Opinions*, op.cit.

60. Halévy, op.cit.

61. The title of the lithograph is *The Orchestra during the Performance of a Tragedy* (1852).

62. J-A Watteau, *Mezzetino with a guitar* (c. 1719), private collection (Vaduz).

63. Reff, *Notebooks*, op.cit., no. 23, p. 46.

64. Reff, *Notebooks*, op.cit., no. 23, p. 45.

65. Reff, *Degas: The Artist's Mind*, op.cit., ch. V.

66. The envelope is in the Bibliothèque Nationale, Nouv. Acq. Fr. 24839, fol. 596, trans. and quoted by Reff, see above.

67. Charles Sterling, Margarette M. Salinger, *French Paintings*, a catalogue of the collection of the Metropolitan Museum of Art, vol. III. See the entry for *Sulking (Bouderie)*.

68. Reff, *Degas: The Artist's Mind*, op.cit., ch. III.

69. Reff, *Notebooks*, op.cit., no. 18, p. 163.

70. Wildenstein (New York), *Degas's Racing World*, March-April 1968, introduction by Ronald Pickvance.

71. See Zeldin, op.cit., vol. II, ch. 13.

72. See Jean Lennet, *Les Loteries d'Etat en France aux 18e et 19e Siècles*, Paris, 1963.

73. See Pickvance's introduction to *Degas's Racing World*, op.cit.

74. François Thiébault-Sisson, 'Claude Monet, An Interview', *Le Temps*, 27 Nov. 1900.

75. Letter to Tissot, New Orleans, 19 Nov. 1872, *Degas Letters*, op.cit., no. 3.

76. Halévy, op.cit.

Chapter 3

1. E. Moreau-Nélaton, *Manet Raconté par Lui-Même*, Paris, 1926, vol. I, p. 126.

2. *Man about Paris, The Confessions of Arsène Houssaye*, trans. and ed. by Henry Knepler, London, 1972, p. 309.

3. For an explanation of Tissot's conduct see Henry Zerner, *James Jacques Joseph Tissot*, a retrospective exhibition, Rhode Island School of Design, Providence, 1968.

4. *Pages from the Goncourt Journal*, ed., trans. and intr. by Robert Baldick, Oxford, 1962, entry for 31 May 1871.

5. Letter to Tissot, Paris, 30 Sept. 1871, *Degas Letters*, ed. by Marcel Guérin, trans. by Marguerite Kay, Oxford, 1947, no. 1.

6. Walter Sickert, *Burlington Magazine*, 1923.

7. Ibid.

8. Letter to Henri Rouart, New Orleans, 5 Dec. 1872, *Degas Letters*, op.cit., no. 5.

9. *The Correspondence of Berthe Morisot*, comp. and ed. by Denis Rouart, trans. by Betty W. Hubbard, London, 1957.

10. Ronald Pickvance, *Degas's Dancers, 1872-76, Burlington Magazine*, June 1963.

11. Sidney Collin's review appeared in the *Pall Mall Gazette*, 28 Nov. 1872, quoted by Pickvance, op.cit.

12. Letter to Henri Rouart, New Orleans, 5 Dec. 1872, *Degas Letters*, op.cit., no. 5.

13. Letter to Lorenze Frölich (Danish painter and designer who lived in Paris 1851-72), *Degas Letters*, op.cit., no. 4. Letter from New Orleans, 27 Nov. 1872.

14. Letter from René to Estelle, quoted by Daniel Wildenstein, *Degas 1834-1917*, introduction to catalogue of Degas loan exhibition at Wildenstein & Co., New York, 1960.

15. Letter to Tissot, Paris, 1973, *Degas Letters*, op.cit., no. 7.

16. *The Echo*, 22 April 1876, quoted by Pickvance, op.cit.

17. D. G. Rossetti, *The Academy*, 29 April 1876, quoted by Pickvance, op.cit.

18. Letter to Tissot, New Orleans, 19 Nov. 1872, *Degas Letters*, op.cit., no. 3.

19. Letter to Frölich, New Orleans, 27 Nov. 1872, *Degas Letters*, op.cit., no. 4.

20. Letter to Tissot, New Orleans, 19 Nov. 1872, *Degas Letters*, op.cit., no. 3.

21. Letter to Désiré Dihau, New Orleans, 18 Nov. 1872, *Degas Letters*, op.cit., no. 2.

22. For an account of the Musson family, see John Rewald, 'Degas and His Family in New Orleans', *Gazette des Beaux-Arts*, August 1946, and James B. Byrnes, *Degas, His Paintings of New Orleanians Here and Abroad*, Isaac Delgado Museum of Art, New Orleans, 1965. Rewald's article is reprinted in the same exhibition catalogue.

23. See letter to Frölich, New Orleans, 27 Nov. 1872, *Degas Letters*, op.cit., no. 4.

24. Letter to Désiré Dihau, New Orleans, 18 Nov. 1872, *Degas Letters*, op.cit., no. 2.

25. There has been some dispute about the identity of the woman in the Delgado Museum picture. Rewald's article, op.cit., based on information provided by Mr Gaston Musson, tentatively identifies the sitter as Mme Challaire. Byrnes, op.cit., demonstrates that Mme Challaire was probably not the sitter and he opts for Estelle, René's wife, citing evidence that René, in organizing the contents of Degas's studio for sale, identified the woman as his former wife. P. A. Lemoisne, *Degas et Son Oeuvre*, Paris, 1946, also identifies the sitter as Estelle. There is, however, a problem in that the woman does not look like the generally accepted portrait of Estelle in the National Gallery, Washington (Lemoisne pl. 313), and it seems odd

that Degas should have painted a blind woman, even one as adept as Estelle, arranging flowers.

26. Letter to Frölich, New Orleans, 27 Nov. 1872, *Degas Letters*, op.cit., no. 4.
27. Letter to Henri Rouart, New Orleans, 5 Dec. 1872, *Degas Letters*, op.cit., no. 5.
28. Letter to Tissot, New Orleans, 19 Nov. 1872, *Degas Letters*, op.cit., no. 3.
29. Letter to Frölich, New Orleans, 27 Nov. 1872, *Degas Letters*, op.cit., no. 4.
30. Letter to Henri Rouart, New Orleans, 5 Dec. 1872, *Degas Letters*, op.cit., no. 5.
31. Letter to Tissot, New Orleans, 18 Feb. 1873, *Degas Letters*, op.cit., no. 6.
32. Rewald, op.cit.
33. Emile Zola, 'Deux Expositions d'Art au Mois de Mai', *Messager de l'Europe*, St Petersburg, June 1876, reprinted in Emile Zola, *Salons*, ed. by F. W. J. Hemmings and R. J. Niess, Geneva-Paris, 1959 (pp. 171-196).
34. Letter to Tissot, New Orleans, 18 Feb. 1873, *Degas Letters*, op.cit., no. 6.
35. Ibid.
36. Letter to Tissot, New Orleans, 19 Nov. 1872, *Degas Letters*, op.cit., no. 3.
37. See Théodore Duret, *Manet*, Paris, 1919, p. 104.
38. *Pages from the Goncourt Journal*, op.cit., entry for Friday 13 Feb. 1874.
39. Pickvance, op.cit.
40. *Three Dancers* was formerly in the collection of Henri Rouart and is no. 324 in P. A. Lemoisne, op.cit.
41. Paul Valéry, *Degas Manet Morisot*, trans. by David Paul, New York, 1960, part I.
42. Lemoisne, op.cit., vol. II, no. 317.
43. See E. J. Hobsbawm, *The Age of Capital, 1848-1875*, London, 1975.
44. Letter to Michel Musson, 31 Aug. 1876, quoted by Rewald, op.cit.
45. George Moore, *Impressions and Opinions*, London and New York, 1891.
46. Louisine W. Havemeyer, *Sixteen to Sixty, Memoirs of a Collector*, New York, 1930.
47. The story appears in Lemoisne, op.cit., and Valéry, op.cit., and elsewhere.
48. *Reminiscences by M. Ernest Rouart*, quoted by Valéry, op.cit.
49. Letter to Tissot, 1874, *Degas Letters*, op.cit., no. 12.
50. See John Rewald, *The History of Impressionism*, New York, 4th rev. ed., 1973, ch. IX (information provided by Oscar Reutersward, Stockholm).
51. J. de Nittis, *Notes et Souvenirs*, Paris, 1895, pp. 187-8.
52. Letter to Tissot, 1874, *Degas Letters*, op.cit., no. 12.
53. The identity of Monet's picture has been the subject of some confusion. See Rewald, *The History of Impressionism*, op.cit., ch. IX, note 23, p. 339. Louis Leroy's article appeared in *Charivari*, 25 April 1874.
54. Rewald, *The History of Impressionism*, op.cit.
55. Jules Castagnary, 'Exposition du Boulevard des Capucines – Les Impressionnistes', *Le Siècle*, 29 April 1874.

Chapter 4

1. George Moore, *Confessions of a Young Man*, London, 1888.
2. Gustave Caillebotte to Camille Pissarro, 24 Jan. 1881, published by John Rewald, *The History of Impressionism*, The Museum of Modern Art, New York, 4th ed., 1973.
3. See Georges Rivière's description of Degas in 1876 in *M. Degas, Bourgeois de Paris*, Paris, 1935.
4. Daniel Halévy, *Pays Parisiens*, Paris, 1932. See also Daniel Halévy, *My Friend Degas*, trans. and ed. with notes by Mina Curtiss, Wesleyan University and London, 1964/66.
5. Marcel Proust, *Remembrance of Things Past*, trans. by C. K. Scott-Moncrieff, Vol. IV, Within a Budding Grove, Pt 2, p. 176. For an account of Proust's Elstir see I. H. E. Dunlop, 'Proust and Painting', *Marcel Proust, 1871-1922* (Peter Quennell, ed.), London, 1971.
6. Caillebotte to Pissarro, see note 2.
7. Ambroise Vollard, *Degas, an Intimate Portrait*, trans. by Randolph T. Weaver, New York, 1927.
8. Halévy, *My Friend Degas*, op.cit.
9. See William Rubin, 'Shadows, Pantomimes and the Art of the Fin de Siècle', *Magazine of Art*, March 1953.
10. Paul Lafond, *Degas*, Paris, 1918-19.
11. Walter Sickert, 'Degas', *Burlington Magazine*, Nov. 1917.
12. Halévy, *My Friend Degas*, op.cit.
13. Theodore Reff, *The Notebooks of Edgar Degas*, 2 vols., Oxford, 1976, no. 30, p. 202.
14. Reff, *Notebooks*, op.cit., no. 30, p. 205.
15. Georges Rivière, op.cit.
16. Vollard, op.cit.
17. Reff, *Notebooks*, op.cit., no. 30, p. 29.
18. Edmond Duranty, *La Nouvelle Peinture: A Propos du Groupe d'Artistes qui Expose dans les Galeries Durand-Ruel*, Paris, 1876, trans. by Linda Nochlin, and included in the Sources and Documents series, *Impressionism and Post-Impressionism, 1874-1904*, Englewood Cliffs, 1966.
19. Letter to Henri Rouart (1886), *Degas Letters*, ed. Marcel Guérin, trans. by Marguerite Kay, Oxford, 1947, no. 100.
20. Letter to Paul-Albert Bartholomé (Naples), 17 Jan. 1886, *Degas Letters*, op.cit., no. 99.
21. George Moore, *Impressions and Opinions*, London, 1891.
22. Letter to Albert Hecht, *Degas Letters*, op.cit., no. 43. Hecht was a banker, collector and friend of Manet. Degas painted him sitting in the orchestra stalls looking through opera glasses in *The Ballet of Robert Le Diable* (1872), Metropolitan Museum of Art, New York.
23. Theodore Reff, *Degas and Dance*, introduction to exhibition catalogue, *Edgar Degas*, Acquavella Galleries, New York, 1978.
24. P. A. Lemoisne, *Degas et Son Oeuvre*, Paris, 1946-9, vol. 1.
25. Halévy, *My Friend Degas*, op.cit.
26. Lillian Browse, *Degas Dancers*, London, 1949.
27. Letter to Ludovic Halévy, Nov. 1883, *Degas Letters*, op.cit., no. 55.
28. See Théodore Zeldin, *France, 1848-1945*, 2 vols., Oxford, 1973, vol. I, ch. 11.
29. Abbé Timon-David, *Traité de la Confession des Enfants et des Jeunes Gens*, Paris, 1865 and 1924, quoted by Zeldin, op.cit.
30. Victor Frisch and Joseph T. Shipley, *Auguste Rodin*, New York, 1939, quoted by Charles W. Millard, *The Sculpture of Edgar Degas*, Princeton University Press, 1976.
31. Vollard, op.cit.
32. Charles Baudelaire, *The Painter of Modern Life*, 1863.
33. Halévy, *My Friend Degas*, op.cit.
34. George Holden, introduction to Zola's *Nana*, Penguin, 1972.
35. Zeldin, op.cit., vol. II, ch. 13.
36. James D. McCabe jr., *Paris by Sunlight and Gaslight*, Boston, 1870, quoted by Eugenia Parry Janis, *Degas Monotypes*, Harvard College, 1968.
37. Letter to Henri Lerolle, 4 Dec. 1883, *Degas Letters*, op.cit., no. 57.
38. Paul Valéry, *Degas Manet Morisot*, trans. by David Paul, New York, 1960, part I.
39. Valéry, op.cit.
40. Mary Pittaluga and Enrico Piceni, *De Nittis*, Milan, 1963, quoted by Janis, op.cit.
41. Duranty, op.cit.
42. Letter to *The Artist*, April 1935, quoted in Douglas Cooper, *The Courtauld Collection*, University of London, 1954.
43. The quotations in this paragraph come from Douglas Cooper's introduction to his catalogue, op.cit.
44. Armand Silvestre, *Au Pays du Souvenir*, Paris, 1892, ch. XIII, quoted by John Rewald, *The History of Impressionism*, op.cit.
45. Duranty, op.cit.
46. J-K Huysmans, *L'Exposition des Indépendants en 1880*, trans. and quoted by Jean Sutherland Boggs, *Portraits by Degas*, University of

California, 1962.

47. Martelli gave his lecture on the Impressionists at the Circolo Filologico di Livorno, 1879 (published as a pamphlet in Pisa in 1880). It is translated in Nochlin's *Impressionism and Post-Impressionism*, op.cit.

48. Achille Segard, *Mary Cassatt, Un Peintre des Enfants et des Mères*, Paris, 1913.

49. Letter to Mrs Havemeyer, *Pennsylvania Museum Bulletin*, vol. 22, quoted by Julia M. H. Carson, *Mary Cassatt*, New York, 1966.

50. Segard, op.cit.

51. Christian Brinton, *A Glance in Retrospect*, introduction to the Mary Cassatt Exhibition, Haverford College, 1939.

52. Walter Sickert, *Burlington Magazine*, Nov. 1917.

53. Letter to Mrs Potter Palmer, 1 Dec. 1892, Carson, op.cit.

54. Forbes Watson, *Mary Cassatt*, New York, Whitney Museum of Art, 1932.

55. For a discussion of the relationship between Degas and Cassatt see Nancy Hale, *Mary Cassatt*, New York, 1975 and Carson, op.cit.

56. Lionello Venturi, *Les Archives de l'Impressionisme*, Paris and New York, 1939, trans. by Boggs, *Portraits by Degas*, op.cit.

57. Undated letter to Mme Dietz-Monin, *Degas Letters*, op.cit., no. 37.

58. Valéry, op.cit.

59. See Bernard Dunstan, 'The Pastel Techniques of Edgar Degas', *American Artist*, Sept. 1972. The secret formula may have been white shellac dissolved in pure methyl alcohol. See also Reff, *Degas: The Artist's Mind*, New York, 1976, ch. VII.

60. Letter to Henri Rouart, Paris, 26 Oct. *Degas Letters*, op.cit., no. 40a.

61. Douglas Cooper, *Pastels by Degas*, New York, 1953.

62. Alfred Werner, *Degas Pastels*, London and New York, 1969.

63. Denis Rouart, *Degas à la Recherche de sa Technique*, Paris, 1945. Excerpts (trans. by Bernard Dunstan) are quoted in Werner, op.cit.

64. Denis Rouart, see above.

65. Letter to Camille Pissarro, *Degas Letters*, op.cit., no. 34. I have followed the translation by Jane Brenton in Jean Adhémar and Françoise Cachin, *Degas, The Complete Etchings, Lithographs, and Monotypes*, London, 1974.

66. Reff, *Notebooks*, op.cit., no. 26, p. 54.

67. Letter to Bracquemond, c. 1879, *Degas Letters*, op.cit., no. 30.

68. An electric crayon is made of carbon; carbon filaments were used in the manufacture of light bulbs in the nineteenth century; hence the term. Janis, op.cit.

69. *The Ballet Master*, no. 1 in Janis, op.cit., and no. 1 in Adhémar and Cachin, op.cit.

70. Janis, op.cit.

71. Letter to Faure, 1876, *Degas Letters*, op.cit., no. 18.

72. The photographs of Mérante dancing are reproduced in Aaron Scharf, *Art and Photography*, Penguin, 1968, rev. ed. 1974.

73. Reff, *Notebooks*, op.cit., no. 31, p. 81.

74. The Oct. issue of this journal contained an article by E. J. Marey, 'Moteurs Animés, Experiences de Physiologie Graphique', which Degas may also have read.

75. Georges Demeny, quoted by Scharf, op.cit. See ch. 9 which gives a fascinating account of the reaction of French artists to Muybridge's discoveries.

76. Valéry, op.cit.

77. François Thiébault-Sisson, 'Degas Sculpteur', *Le Temps*, 23 May 1921.

78. Some of these drawings are reproduced in *Drawings by Degas*, essay and catalogue by Jean Sutherland Boggs, City Art Museum of Saint Louis, 1966, nos. 102–104.

79. The full title of this great work is *Animal Locomotion, an Electro-Photographic Investigation of Consecutive Phases of Animal Movements*, published by the University of Pennsylvania. It contained 781 plates and cost $600, a large sum by the standards of the day. Degas's name is not included in the list of subscribers, although a number of French artists did support this expensive venture, including Meissonier, Gérôme, Bouguereau, Detaille, Puvis de Chavannes and Rodin. It would be interesting to know to which copy Degas had access. Some of the photographic plates were available separately, see Scharf, op.cit.

80. Sickert, op.cit.

81. Millard, op.cit.

82. Paul Gsell, *On Art and Artists*, London, 1958, quoted by Scharf, op.cit.

83. Valéry, op.cit.

84. John Rewald, *Degas, Works in Sculpture, a Complete Catalogue*, New York, 1944, rev. ed. 1957. Rewald suggests an earlier starting date; Millard, op.cit., argues for a date in the early 1870s.

85. Millard, op.cit., suggests that Degas originally intended to exhibit the nude version, but this work was surely conceived as a study for the larger clothed figure, and it seems likely that Degas wanted to mark his début as a sculptor with a more complex and complete work.

86. J-K Huysmans, 'L'Exposition des Indépendants en 1881', *L'Art moderne*, Paris, 1908, reprinted in app. of Millard, op.cit.

87. Nina de Villars, 'Exposition des Artistes Indépendants', *Le Courrier du Soir*, 23 April 1881, reprinted in app. of Millard, op.cit.

88. Jacques-Emile Blanche, *Propos de Peintre: de David à Degas*, Paris, 1919.

89. Jean Renoir, *Renoir*, Paris, 1962.

90. Paul Mantz, 'Exposition des Oeuvres des Artistes Indépendants', *Le Temps*, 23 April 1881, reprinted in app. of Millard, op.cit.

91. Villars, op.cit.

92. Reff, *Degas: The Artist's Mind*, op.cit., ch. VI.

93. Letter to Henri Rouart, Paris, 26 Oct., *Degas Letters*, op. cit., no. 40A.

94. See Valéry, op.cit.

95. Illustrated in Millard, op.cit.

96. Elie de Mont, 'L'Exposition du Boulevard des Capucines', *La Civilisation*, 21 April 1881, reprinted in app. of Millard, op.cit.

97. Villars, op.cit.

98. See letter to Lucy Degas, the artist's cousin, quoted by Riccardo Raimondi, *Degas e La Sua Famiglia in Napoli*, Naples, 1958. For further discussion of *The Apple Pickers* see Reff, *Degas: The Artist's Mind*, op.cit., and Millard, op.cit.

99. Vollard, op.cit.

100. Letter to Henri Rouart, 22 Aug. 1884, *Degas Letters*, op. cit., no. 66.

101. The drawings of Hortense are reproduced in Boggs, *Drawings by Degas*, op.cit.

102. Letter to Ludovic Halévy, *Degas Letters*, op.cit., no. 73.

103. Letter to Ludovic Halévy, 1884, *Degas Letters*, op.cit., no. 69.

104. For an account of the destruction of the bust of Hortense see S. Barazzetti, 'Degas et Ses Amis Valpinçon', *Beaux-Arts*, no. 190, 21 Aug. 1936, and 28 Aug. 1936.

105. Letter to Henri Lerolle, 21 Aug. 1884, *Degas Letters*, op. cit., no. 63.

106. Caillebotte to Pissarro, 24 Jan. 1881, see note 2.

107. E. Taboureux, 'Claude Monet', *La Vie Moderne*, 12 June 1880, quoted by Rewald, *The History of Impressionism*, op.cit.

108. George Moore, *Impressions and Opinions*, op.cit.

109. Emile Zola, 'Le Naturalisme au Salon', *Le Voltaire*, 18–22 June 1880, quoted by Rewald, *The History of Impressionism*, op.cit.

110. Emile Zola, 'Deux Expositions d'Art au Mois de Mai', *Messager de l'Europe*, St Petersburg, June 1976, reprinted in Emile Zola, *Salons*, ed. by F. W. J. Hemmings and R. J. Niess, Paris-Geneva, 1959.

111. Moore, *Impressions and Opinions*, op.cit.

112. Halévy, op.cit.

113. Stéphane Mallarmé, 'The Impressionists and Edouard Manet', *Art Monthly Review*, 1876, quoted by Rewald, *The History of Impressionism*, op.cit.

114. Wolf attacked Degas in his review of the second Impressionist exhibition, *Le Figaro*, 3 April 1876, criticizing him for of all things his drawing. As Degas's reputation grew, he shifted his point of view and generally praised his work at the expense of his contemporaries.

115. Rewald, *The History of Impressionism*, op.cit.

116. Gauguin to Pissarro, Copenhagen, Spring 1885, quoted by Rewald, *The History of Impressionism*, op.cit.

Chapter 5

1. *The Correspondence of Berthe Morisot*, comp. and ed. by Denis Rouart, trans. by Betty W. Hubbard, London, 1957.
2. Pissarro to his son, March 1886, *Camille Pissarro, Letters to his Son Lucien*, New York, 1943, pp. 73-4, quoted in John Rewald, *The History of Impressionism*, 4th rev. ed., New York, 1973.
3. George Moore, 'Degas: The Painter of Modern Life', *Magazine of Art*, Sept. 1890, reprinted in *Impressions and Opinions*, New York, 1891, and again in the *Burlington Magazine*, XXXII, 1918.
4. Moore's article is discussed by Ronald Pickvance in 'A Newly Discovered Drawing by Degas of George Moore', *Burlington Magazine*, June 1963.
5. J. K. Huysmans, *Certains*, Paris, 1889.
6. Paul Signac, *Le Néo-impressionnisme*, documents, Paris, 1934. See John Rewald, op. cit. for an account of the eighth Impressionist exhibition.
7. George Moore, *Confessions of a Young Man*, London, 1888.
8. Huysmans, op. cit.
9. Moore, *Impressions and Opinions*, op. cit.
10. Félix Fénéon, *Les Impressionnistes en 1886*, reprinted in *Oeuvres*, Paris 1948. Quoted in Jean Adhémar and Françoise Cachin, *Degas, The Complete Etchings, Lithographs and Monotypes*, trans. Jane Brenton, London 1974.
11. *The Correspondence of Berthe Morisot*, op.cit.
12. Ambroise Vollard, *Renoir, an Intimate Record*, trans. by Randolph T. Weaver and Harold L. Van Doren, New York, 1925.
13. Emile Zola, *Nana*, trans. George Holden, Penguin, 1972.
14. Moore, *Impressions and Opinions*, op. cit.
15. Adhémar and Cachin, op.cit.
16. A typical example is Kiyonaga's *Bath House Scene*, reproduced in Theodore Reff, *Degas: A Master among Masters*, The Metropolitan Museum of Art, 1977.
17. Gavarni, *Les Liorettes*, no. 144, in *Catalogue des Tableaux Modernes et Anciens, Collection Edgar Degas*, Estampes Anciennes et Modernes, 5 Nov. 1918.
18. Zola, *Nana*, op. cit.
19. Mary Cassatt, *Morning Toilet*, 1886, $29\frac{1}{2} \times 24\frac{1}{2}$in, National Gallery of Art, Washington, D.C. (Chester Dale Collection).
20. Denis Rouart, *Degas à la Recherche de sa Technique*, Paris, 1945, trans. Bernard Dunstan, quoted by Alfred Werner, *Degas Pastels*, New York, 1969.
21. *Reminiscences by M. Ernest Rouart*, quoted by Paul Valéry, *Degas, Manet, Morisot*, trans. David Paul, New York, 1960.
22. Daniel Halévy, *My Friend Degas*, trans. and ed. with notes by Mina Curtiss, Wesleyan University and London, 1964/66.
23. There were two sales of Degas's collection, *Catalogue des Tableaux Modernes et Anciens, Collection Edgar Degas*, Galeries Georges Petit, 26, 27 Mar. 1918; 15, 16 Nov. 1918, Hôtel Drouot.
24. Halévy, op. cit.
25. See above.
26. Moore, *Impressions and Opinions*, op. cit.
27. Ambroise Vollard, *Degas, an Intimate Portrait*, trans. by Randolph T. Weaver, New York, 1927.
28. See above.
29. M. Joyant, *Henri de Toulouse-Lautrec, 1864-1901, Peintre*, Paris, 1926 (p. 130).
30. Marie Dihau to Professor Paul J. Sachs. See Rewald, op. cit.
31. Pickvance, op. cit. See above, notes 3 and 4.
32. Moore, *Impressions and Opinions*, op. cit.
33. See Douglas Cooper, *The Courtauld Collection*, University of London, 1954.
34. *Dancer Adjusting Her Slipper*, L. 1144, Cleveland Museum of Art, Ohio.
35. *David Hockney by David Hockney*, Nikos Stangos (ed.), London, 1976.
36. Valéry, op. cit.
37. Halévy, op. cit.
38. Valéry, op. cit.
39. Marcel Guérin ed., *Degas Letters*, trans. by Marguerite Kay, Oxford, 1947, letter to Ludovic Halévy, 2 Oct. 1890, Montereau, Hôtel du Grand Monarque, letter no. 147.
40. Georges Jeanniot, 'Souvenirs Sur Degas', *La Revue Universelle*, Oct. and Nov. 1933.
41. Jeanniot, op. cit.
42. Jeanniot, op. cit.
43. Letter to Tissot, 18 Feb. 1873, New Orleans, *Degas Letters*, op. cit., no. 6.
44. Halévy, op. cit.
45. Cachin, op. cit.
46. Daniel Halévy, *Pays Parisiens*, Paris, 1932, quoted by Mina Curtiss, in Halévy, *My Friend Degas*, op. cit.
47. Letter to Bartholomé, Madrid, 8 Sept. 1889, *Degas Letters*, op. cit., no. 125.
48. Letter to Bartholomé, Tangiers, 18 Sept. 1889, *Degas Letters*, op. cit., no. 126.
49. Jeanne Fèvre, *Mon Oncle Degas*, Geneva, 1949.
50. Degas seems to have regarded some of his photographs in the same light as his black and white monotypes, as a first stage for a more elaborate work. A signed drawing belonging to the Redfern Gallery, London, was examined by X-ray and found to have a photographic base. See Aaron Scharf, *Art and Photography*, Penguin, 1968, note 54. Degas's experiments with negatives are discussed in Douglas Crimp, *Positive/Negative: A Note on Degas's Photographs*, *October*, Summer 1978.
51. Halévy, *My Friend Degas*, op. cit.
52. Halévy, *My Friend Degas*, op. cit.
53. Fèvre, op. cit.
54. Halévy, *My Friend Degas*, op. cit.
55. Ronald Pickvance, 'Degas as a Photographer', *Lithopinion*, Spring, 1970.
56. Henri Lerolle to René Gimpel, 7 April 1931. See René Gimpel, *Diary of an Art Dealer*, London, 1966, trans. by John Rosenberg. Quoted by Aaron Scharf, op. cit.
57. Jean Renoir, *Renoir*, Paris, 1962, p. 69.
58. Charles W. Millard, *The Sculptures of Edgar Degas*, Princeton University Press, 1976.
59. Joseph Durand-Ruel, letter to Royal Cortissoz, 7 June 1919, quoted by Millard, op. cit.
60. Halévy, *My Friend Degas*, op. cit.
61. Valéry, op. cit.
62. Valéry, op. cit.
63. Valéry, op. cit.
64. *The Correspondence of Berthe Morisot*, op. cit.
65. Letter to Ludovic Halévy, Sept. 1885, *Degas Letters*, op. cit., no. 94.
66. I have not been able to establish the exact date of Achille Degas's death. In most books on Degas the date is given as 1893 but in *Degas Letters*, op. cit., there is a letter to Désiré Dihau, dated 1895, no. 207, which seems to imply that his brother's death has just taken place: 'You had not forgotten my poor Achille...I am announcing his death to a few friends.'
67. Halévy, *My Friend Degas*, op. cit.
68. Letter to Bartholomé dated 18 Aug. 1890, of which excerpts only appear in *Degas Letters*, no. 135, op. cit. The manuscript with the poem is in the Houghton Library, Harvard, and is quoted by Millard, op. cit.
69. D. Cady Eaton, *A Handbook of Modern French Sculpture*, New York, 1913.
70. 'Recollections of Degas by his Model Pauline', *Mercure de France*, Jan.-Feb. 1916.
71. Valéry, op. cit.
72. See Millard, op. cit.
73. Letter to Ludovic Halévy, Le Mont-Dore, 11 Aug. 1897, *Degas Letters*, op. cit., no. 219.
74. Letter to Bartholomé, Les Bains du Mont-Dore, Aug. 1897, *Degas Letters*, op. cit., no. 218.
75. Letter to Mme Ludovic Halévy, 15 Nov. 1897, *Degas Letters*, op. cit., no. 225.
76. See F. W. J. Hemmings, *The Life and Times of Emile Zola*, London

and New York, 1977, which contains a useful summary of the Dreyfus affair. See also Roderick Kedward, *The Dreyfus Affair*, London, 1965, and Douglas Johnson, *France and the Dreyfus Affair*, London, 1966.

77. Sunday 6 Jan. 1895, *Pages from the Goncourt Journal*, ed. and trans. with intro. by Robert Baldick, Oxford, 1962.

78. Letter to Alexis Rouart, Saint-Valéry-sur-Somme, Sept. 1898, *Degas Letters*, op. cit., no. 98.

79. Halévy, *My Friend Degas*, op. cit.

80. See Théodore Zeldin, *France 1848–1945*, Oxford, 1973.

81. See Mina Curtiss's notes to Halévy, op. cit., and Daniel Halévy, *Pays Parisiens*, op. cit.

82. See note 70.

83. Vollard, *Degas, an Intimate Portrait*, op. cit.

84. The story appears in Jean Renoir, *Renoir*, op. cit., and Halévy, *My Friend Degas*, op. cit. and elsewhere.

85. Vollard, *Degas, an Intimate Portrait*, op. cit.

86. Vollard, *Degas, an Intimate Portrait*, op. cit.

87. See note 70.

88. Vollard, *Degas, an Intimate Portrait*, op. cit.

89. Lillian Browse, *Degas Dancers*, London, 1949.

90. Halévy, *My Friend Degas*, op. cit.

91. This remark appears in several sources. A slightly different version appears in Halévy, *My Friend Degas*, op. cit.

92. Halévy, *My Friend Degas*, op. cit.

93. Quoted by Nancy Hale, *Mary Cassatt*, New York, 1975.

94. Halévy, *My Friend Degas*, op. cit.

Acknowledgements

THE AUTHOR AND JOHN CALMANN AND COOPER LTD would like to thank the various museums and owners of Degas's works for their kind permission to reproduce the works illustrated in this book. The photographs used were obtained from the owners as credited in the captions, apart from those mentioned below.

CLICHÉS MUSÉES NATIONAUX, PARIS: *Nos.* 10, 14, 37, 43, 45, 46, 64, 67, 69, 70, 87, 90, 96, 101, 140, 154.

GIRAUDON, PARIS: *Nos.* 20, 130.

M. ABEL-MENNE, WUPPERTAL: *No.* 27.

BULLOZ, PARIS: *Nos.* 29, 30.

CHAS. P. MILLS, PHILADELPHIA: *Nos.* 66, 106, 159.

ERIC POLLITZER, NEW YORK: *Nos.* 83, 141.

ACQUAVELLA GALLERIES, NEW YORK: *No.* 88.

M. L. PÉRONY, PAU: *No.* 92.

Select bibliography

ADHÉMAR, J., AND F. CACHIN: *Edgar Degas, gravures et monotypes*, Paris 1973

Atelier Edgar Degas, catalogues des tableaux, pastels et dessins par Edgar Degas et provenant de son atelier dont la vente . . . aura lieu à Paris, Galerie Georges Petit, I 6–8 May 1918; II 11–13 Dec. 1918; III 7–9 April 1919; IV 2–4 July 1919

BLANCHE, J.-E.: *Propos de Peintre, de David à Degas*, Paris 1919

BROWSE, LILLIAN: *Degas Dancers*, London 1949

Burlington Magazine, June 1963, important articles by Boggs, Vitali, Pool, Pickvance and Reff

CABANNE, PIERRE: *Edgar Degas*, Paris 1957

Collection Edgar Degas, Paris, Galerie Georges Petit, 26–7 March 1918

Collection Edgar Degas Estampes, Paris, Hôtel Drouot, 6–7 Nov. 1918

COOPER, DOUGLAS: *Pastels by Degas*, New York 1953

FÈVRE, JEANNE: *Mon Oncle Degas*, ed. by Pierre Borel, Geneva 1949

GUÉRIN, MARCEL, (ed.): *Lettres de Degas*, Paris 1945, trans. by Marguerite Kay, Oxford 1947

HALÉVY, DANIEL: *My Friend Degas*, trans. and ed. with notes by Mina Curtiss, Wesleyan University 1964 and London 1966

JANIS, E. P.: *Degas Monotypes*, Cambridge, Mass., 1968

JEANNIOT, G.: 'Souvenirs sur Degas', *La Revue Universelle*, 15 Oct., 1 Nov. 1933

LAFOND, PAUL: *Degas*, 2 vols., Paris 1918, 1919

LEMOISNE, P. A.: *Degas et son oeuvre*, 4 vols., Paris 1946

MILLARD, CHARLES W.: *The Sculpture of Edgar Degas*, Princeton, New Jersey, 1976

MOORE, GEORGE: *Impressions and Opinions*, New York 1891

RAIMONDI, RICCARDO: *Degas e la sua Famiglia in Napoli, 1793–1917*, Naples 1958

REFF, THEODORE: *Degas: The Artist's Mind*, New York 1976

REFF, THEODORE: *The Notebooks of Edgar Degas*, 2 vols., Oxford 1976

REFF, THEODORE: 'Some Unpublished Letters of Degas', *Art Bulletin*, March 1968

REFF, THEODORE: 'More Unpublished Letters of Degas', *Art Bulletin*, Sept. 1969

REWALD, JOHN: *Degas, Works in Sculpture*, New York 1945

REWALD, JOHN: *Degas Sculpture, The Complete Works*, New York 1956

REWALD, JOHN: *The History of Impressionism*, New York, 4th rev. ed., 1973. Contains a useful bibliography

REWALD, JOHN: 'Degas and His Family in New Orleans', *Gazette des Beaux-Arts*, Aug. 1946, reprinted in *Degas, His Family and Friends in New Orleans*, Isaac Delgado Museum, New Orleans 1965

ROUART, DENIS: *Degas à la recherche de sa technique*, Paris 1945

SICKERT, WALTER: 'Degas', *Burlington Magazine*, Nov. 1917

VALÉRY, PAUL: *Degas Danse Dessin*, Paris 1936, trans. by David Paul in *Degas Manet Morisot*, New York 1960

VOLLARD, AMBROISE: *Degas*, Paris 1924

WERNER, ALFRED: *Degas Pastels*, New York 1969

Index

237